ABRAHAM LINCOLN
& WOMEN IN FILM

CONFLICTING WORLDS
New Dimensions of the American Civil War

T. Michael Parrish, Series Editor

ABRAHAM LINCOLN & WOMEN IN FILM

ONE HUNDRED YEARS OF HOLLYWOOD MYTHMAKING

Frank J. Wetta & Martin A. Novelli

Louisiana State University Press

Baton Rouge

Published by Louisiana State University Press
lsupress.org

DESIGNER: Barbara Neely Bourgoyne
TYPEFACES: Calluna, text; Gotham, display

Cover photographs courtesy Library of Congress.

Cataloging-in-Publication Data are available at the Library of Congress.

ISBN 978-0-8071-6972-8 (cloth) | ISBN 978-0-8071-8145-4 (epub) |
ISBN 978-0-8071-8146-1 (pdf)

Thank you for your generous assistance

T. Michael Parrish, George C. Rable, Thomas E. Schott,
and Joseph G. Dawson

CONTENTS

Introduction: Hollywood and the Women in Lincoln's Life 1

1 Framing Lincoln's Angel Mothers: Nancy Hanks and Sarah Bush Johnston 7

2 The Romance of Ann Rutledge in Memory and Film 28

3 Hollywood Interprets the Troubled Courtship of Miss Owens and Mr. Lincoln 58

4 When Abe Met Mary: The Courtship and Marriage of Mary Todd and Abraham Lincoln on Film 67

5 Mrs. Lincoln Goes to Washington: The White House Years 98

6 Redux: *The Last of Mrs. Lincoln* 135

7 Coda: Shirley Temple and Marilyn Monroe in Lincoln's Legacy 143

Conclusion: Fade Out 176

Notes 179

Bibliography 207

Filmography 221

Index 227

ABRAHAM LINCOLN
& WOMEN IN FILM

INTRODUCTION

Hollywood and the Women in Lincoln's Life

Robert Sherwood's *Abe Lincoln in Illinois* (1940). The Scene: 1832. New Salem, Illinois. Interior of Denton Offutt's general store. The shop clerk, Abraham Lincoln, has just "inherited" the bankrupt business from the fast-talking owner, who walks out leaving the little enterprise $1,500 in debt.[1] That afternoon, Mentor Graham, a schoolteacher, arrives to continue with young Abe's grammar lesson.

MENTOR (Louis Jean Heydt): Evening, Abe.

ABE (Raymond Massey): Evening, Mentor.

MENTOR: (*With a book in his hands*): Let's see. Where were we when we left off?

ABE: You said at this lesson we'd review the "moods."

MENTOR: Ah, yes, the moods. (*Mentor closes the grammar book, smiles, and looks at Abe*) Every one of us has many moods. You yourself have more than your share, Abe.

ABE: They express the various aspects.

(*Abe, distracted, is looking out of a window at Ann Rutledge, a young woman of recent acquaintance. She is walking down the street in deep conversation with a young man.*)

MENTOR: Now, name me the five moods . . . Abe?

ABE (*Coming back to the conversation*): Excuse me, Mentor.

MENTOR: I asked you to name me the five moods.

ABE: Oh . . . The . . . uh . . . indicative, the imperative . . . potential, subjunctive, and infinitive.

MENTOR: And what do they signify?

ABE (*Thinking of Ann Rutledge*): The indicative mood is the easy one. That just indicates a thing like "he loved" or "he is loved."

In Sherwood's Pulitzer Prize–winning play of 1938, adapted for the 1940 film, the dialogue is expanded and more revealing of Lincoln's inner man: Mentor explains to Abe that the moods "express the various aspect of your character. So, it is with the English language—and you must try to consider this language as if it were a living person, who may be awkward and stumbling, or pompous or pretentious, or simple and direct." Abe replies that the indicative mood "just indicates a thing—like 'He loves,' 'He is loved.'" He then adds: "or, when you put it into a question, 'Does he love?' or 'Is he loved?'"

This book is about Lincoln the lover—whom he loved and who loved him. It approaches the subject from an oblique angle. It will examine the female characters in Hollywood's story of the intimate life of Abraham Lincoln— the protagonist and his love interests and the connection between biography and film. Drawing principally on the portraits by Lincoln's law partner and controversial biographer William Herndon and the poet and Lincoln biographer Carl Sandburg, moviemakers created a series of films that are critical to understanding Lincoln and those he loved in popular memory.[2]

Sandburg's Lincoln was a perfect match for the "Hollywood technique," as one reviewer of Sandburg noted, "with his approach to storytelling that featured 'shift' and 'cut-back' and 'fade out.'"[3] Like Sandburg, Hollywood screenwriters were, in their approach to biography and history, poets, authors of fairy tales, and singers of folk songs, who thumbed their noses and broke the rules, as Sandberg did, "at the precepts of the historical profession" to produce "imaginary poetry and historical fiction."[4] From the very first film that Lincoln appeared in (*The Martyred Presidents,* 1901), until the present, a period of more than 120 years, Hollywood portrayed Lincoln in a variety of moods and manifestations—child of the log-cabin frontier, lawyer, humorist, politician, emancipator, redeemer of the nation, humanitarian, and sad man of destiny—a cinematic Lincoln made of fact and fiction.

THE BACKSTORY

Lincoln came out of obscurity on the midwestern frontier to become president of the United States, commander in chief of a mighty army, and savior of a nation threatened by a confederacy of rebels. But the legacy of Abraham Lincoln is complicated and his inner life a mystery that reflects a conflicting body of scholarship and popular memory.

Two Abraham Lincolns occupy the scholarly and popular mind: Over the fifteen decades since his murder, Lincoln evolved into both hero and antihero—the Good Lincoln and the Bad Lincoln. The Good Lincoln is the Rail-Splitter, Honest Abe, the Great Emancipator, the Liberator, the Redeemer President, Father Abraham, the Great Humanitarian, the Great Heart, the Hero of the Common Man. The Bad Lincoln,[5] who has yet to appear in the movies, is the demagogue, the dictator, the low jokester, the racist colonizer, the white supremacist, the hangman of Native Americans whose name must be erased from the facade of public schools, the syphilitic who infects his wife, and the "closeted homosexual."

There is an additional, transcendent expression of the Good and Bad Lincoln—the Man of Sorrow or the Man of Sorrows. Lincoln, in the words of those who knew him, or thought they knew him, embraced a melancholy that defined his personality. William Herndon observed that "he was a sad man, a terribly gloomy one—a man of sorrow."[6] In 1908, a temperance lecturer and Prohibition candidate believed he had tapped into the essential Lincoln to explain his sadness. The death of his mother, the loss of Ann Rutledge, the marriage to Mary, the death of two children reveal his enduring torment: "These crushing blows of great grief in the lives of men sometimes bring out the best there is in them, if they are able to overcome and rise above them as Lincoln was able to do. These sorrows kept him close to the common people. They just seemed to have come to this man's life to bring out the best there is in him." And so it came to pass that Abraham Lincoln, like Jesus Christ, "always wore 'sorrow's crown.'"[7] *The Master and His Servant,* a 1913 publication of the United Brethren, also identified parallels in the lives of Jesus Christ and Abraham Linco.. "humble, kind, sorrowful, and loving of their fellow man." Both "we. to fulfill a divine mission."[8] His sufferings left their mark, Sandburg wrote: "The shadows of a burning he had been through were fixed in the depths of his eyes, and he was a changed man keeping to himself the gray mystery of the change."[9] His melancholy, writes Joshua Wolf Shenk, an expert on Lincoln's inner trials, "was obviously a big part of Lincoln's life because it played to the popular understanding of Lincoln as a 'man of sorrows' who faced great internal and external difficulties and endured them, emerging meek, forceful, and grand."[10] Sociologist and poet Kelly Miller referenced this image in his 1913 poem "I See and Am Satisfied." Inspired by the words of the prophet Isaiah foreshadowing the sacrifice of Jesus, Miller observed, "I see Abraham Lincoln, himself a man of sorrows and acquainted with grief, arise to execute the high decree."[11] Confirming this appeal in the *New Yorker* (September 21, 2020), essayist Adam Gopnik states that "Lincoln, the man of sorrows acquainted with grief, is central to understanding the spell he continues to cast on us."

The biographical films (known in the industry as biopics) were the magic wands employed to cast the spell.[12] Hollywood contributed critically to the apotheosis of Abraham Lincoln by bringing Lincoln's women and the Man of Sorrow together on the screen.

Essential to understanding the role of Hollywood in the creation of the myth of Lincoln is understanding how movies reflect the tension between the filmmaker's narrative truth (the Lincoln of Popular Memory) and the scholar's historical truth (the Historian's Lincoln)—the tug between Hollywood's undisciplined imagination and the historian's reconstructed past. Neither scholarship nor popular memory, however, can be assumed to be of one piece. Both popular memory and the historical reconstruction of Lincoln's life are fragmented by the variety of often contrary approaches and interpretations. Of course, Twentieth Century–Fox or Warner Brothers or MGM have had no obligation to teach history or delve into the complexities of Lincoln historiography. The fundamental purpose of their enterprise is to entertain and make money, despite any pretentions to art or historical veracity (when movies claim to be "based on a true story"). Yet, if the final product results in artistic achievement or good history or both, all the better for the reputation of the studio and the enlightenment of the audience.[13]

This book will address the screenwriter's and director's vision, films in the context of Hollywood studio history, the critics' and audiences' responses, and the blurred line between fact and fiction, between biography and mythmaking. It will especially assess how Lincoln's women are at the intersection of biography and film—how films that include them have evolved. And how earlier historical interpretations and films influence recent ones.

THE CAST

With one exception, all the Lincoln films discussed here are, at their core, patriarchal in nature; the women in the scripts exist to explain and enhance the Lincoln myth—giving birth to the nation's savior, nurturing him in his youth, propelling him into politics, prophesizing his destiny, and contributing to his melancholy. The women are essential to understanding the fulfillment of the hero's destiny, but they never upstage the leading man. Screenwriter Alex D. Reid identifies such supporting characters (male or female) as film tropes: the Comic Relief, who lightens the mood or "dramatic load." The Thematic Megaphone is the mentor who dispenses "wise advice" and "helps drive the theme home." The Plot Hinge "delivers exposition" or information that advances the story. The Foil "challenges the protagonist's worldview" yet fights for the same cause though by "different methods." The Love Interest evokes emotion, romance, and passion. But a secondary player may also combine purposes where, for example, the love interest may also serve as both the foil and thematic megaphone: "A secondary character is . . . someone who assists, disrupts, or otherwise complicates the main plot of the story. They can be inconsequential to the plot or they can be the lynchpin that keeps everything together."[14] In this study of Lincoln and women on film, these "secondary characters" are reframed in such a way as to put them more clearly in focus and central to the plot.

In Hollywood's cinematic "Abraham Lincoln," the supporting characters are the mother (Nancy Hanks); the stepmother (Sara Bush Johnston); the tragic lost love (Ann Rutledge); the woman who rejected him (Mary Owens); and the wife and widow (Mary Todd Lincoln). Others in the cast who appear in this study include Elizabeth Keckley, a freewoman of color; and two twentieth-century movie actresses who achieved a certain mythological status of their own—the child megastar Shirley Temple, who gets to sit on Lincoln's lap, and a bodacious glamour queen, Marilyn Monroe, who makes a surprising cameo appearance in the Lincoln legacy.

Hollywood, drawing on a vast testament of near sacred writ about Abraham Lincoln, played a leading role in transforming the life of an ambitious lawyer skilled in the art of political compromise and feint into that of a mythological hero and secular saint. In that context, this study shows how Hollywood projected Lincoln as the sad man of destiny and the role that this circle of women played in the creation of that image.[15] "No one's loved as much as you," his wife, Mary, says to him in Steven Spielberg's *Lincoln* (2012), "no one's been loved so much."

FRAMING LINCOLN'S
ANGEL MOTHERS

Nancy Hanks and Sarah Bush Johnston

Abraham Lincoln has appeared in more than two hundred films. His most unusual role, other than in *Abraham Lincoln: Vampire Hunter* (2012), was the part of Nancy Hanks Lincoln's unborn child in Shirley Temple's 1940 *The Blue Bird*, produced by Twentieth Century–Fox and intended as a reply to MGM's *The Wizard of Oz* (1939). Loosely based on a 1908 play by Belgian Symbolist author Maurice Bernard Maeterlinck, the movie tells the story of two children as they search for the Blue Bird of Happiness. During their fairy-tale adventures, Mytyl and her little brother, Tyltyl, visit the Kingdom of the Future, "a sort of reverse heaven," where children appear in diaphanous togas (blue for boys, pink for girls). Curiously, none are infants. Some are very young; others are approaching adolescence. Here, in a heavenly temple of art deco design, they wait to be born. Clearly, some will acquire greatness; one is a budding scientist tinkering with a light bulb—Thomas Edison? Mytyl and her brother wander through the scene until they meet a disconsolate young boy who, although unidentified, is clearly a pubescent Abraham Lincoln, the future thirteenth president of the United States. The child (labeled "The Studious Boy" in the script) is tall, thin, with black hair. Although the Child of Destiny, he is sad to the point of despondency.

THE STUDIOUS BOY (Gene Reynolds): Hello.

MYTYL (Shirley Temple): Why are you so sad?

THE STUDIOUS BOY: I was just thinking. I'm going to earth very soon now. Almost any day.

MYTYL: Don't you want to go?

THE STUDIOUS BOY: No, I'm afraid not.

MYTYL: You'll like it once you get there.

THE STUDIOUS BOY: There's too much unhappiness. Up here we are all free. But we aren't born free, are we?

MYTYL: Aren't we?

THE STUDIOUS BOY: Some are, perhaps. But so many are born into slavery and greed . . . and injustice and cruelty. And that's what I'm going to fight. I must try to make them see that. People must be the same on Earth as they are up here—free, equal and united.

MYTYL: Then I should think you'd want to go.

THE STUDIOUS BOY: No. They won't listen.

MYTYL: But they will. You must make them listen.

THE STUDIOUS BOY: They'll destroy me.

The conversation ends abruptly when Father Time arrives on a golden ship with silver sails that will take those waiting to be born down to Earth. Predestined, Lincoln (The Studious Boy) will sacrifice himself for the nation to be free, equal, and united. He is the Boy of Sorrow who will become the Man of Sorrow.

Shirley Temple's parents were not happy with the Lincoln sequence and complained about the scene to Darryl F. Zanuck, then vice president and head of production for Fox. "Another in our unborn pack was young Abraham Lincoln, whose lines in our heavenly womb bore distinctive political overtones," Shirley Temple Black recalled in her autobiography. "Why," her father, George Temple (a conservative banker and America Firster), asked, "disinter the origins of the Civil War? FDR was waving the flag and talking about national honor as a reason to fight alongside Britain, and were it not for our good isolationist Congress, we would already be at war. All this reference to war was inflammatory." Though Zanuck said he was willing to "think it over," the Studious Boy scene remained as written.[1]

In the 1976 American-Soviet remake of *The Blue Bird*, The Studious Boy is missing. The most embarrassing part of this *Blue Bird* may be the same cringeworthy scene that helped to sink the 1940 version: the land of yet-to-be-born children. Among the unborn is a babbling tyke who, we learn, "will found the confederation of the solar planets." This little blond boy, somebody points out, will "bring pure joy to all mankind . . . with ideas that no one's had yet!" He is manically happy, this future leader of the General Confederation of the Nine Solar Planets—"an independent union—harmonious and free." Apparently, a little Jeff Davis has replaced the young Abe Lincoln in the script.

NANCY AND SARAH IN HOLLYWOOD

The Studious Boy of the 1940 version of *The Blue Bird* had every reason to be apprehensive about coming to Earth. The real Nancy Hanks Lincoln[2] bore three children: Sarah, the eldest, died shortly after her marriage from complications of childbirth.[3] Thomas Jr. died a few days after his birth.[4] Abraham survived to middle age only to die at the hands of an assassin. Surely, Nancy was apprehensive as well. For women in the nineteenth century, pregnancy and childbirth were frequently traumatic experiences. On average women had seven children, but often even more pregnancies. Many did not go full term or ended in the early death of the baby. Often mothers died or, as a consequence of childbirth, lived out their lives in chronically poor health. Not surprisingly, pregnancy was a time of dreadful anticipation: "nine-months' gestation could mean nine months to prepare for death. A possible death sentence came with every pregnancy."[5] Even if the mother lived, the baby often did not.[6] If The Studious Boy is to save the Union, he must first survive the perilous journey from the Kingdom of the Future to his birth on the Kentucky frontier.

Two films announce the birth of the nation's savior: D. W. Griffith's *Abraham Lincoln* (1930), the master filmmaker's first talking motion picture, and James Agee's *Mr. Lincoln* (1952), the very first television miniseries.[7] Griffith's life of Lincoln begins with a birthing scene announced as the camera tracks across a barren forest. The wind whistles, a dog howls; it is a dark and stormy dawn. Lincoln's father is chopping wood outside the log cabin. The midwife appears at the door: Tom (William L. Thorne): "How's

Nancy standin' it?" Midwife: (Lucille La Verne): "She's a prayin'." The baby is "homely as a mud fence." A neighbor boy (uncredited in the film), an implied cousin, visiting with his mother, judges that the child will "never amount to nothin'." Then he asks Nancy (Helen Freeman) what she will name him. The camera pans to her face. It clear that this has been a difficult birth.

Exhausted, Nancy looks up from her bed and very, very slowly, pronounces each syllable, "A . . . bra . . . ham." (In the Tim Burton–produced *Abraham Lincoln: Vampire Hunter,* Little Abraham, in the script by Seth Grahame-Smith, remembers this of Nancy: "Mama once told me that I hadn't cried when I was born. That I'd simply opened my eyes, looked at her smiling face, and smiled back.")

As Agee imagined it, Lincoln's birth is near identical in tone and image to Griffith's account, but here Thomas (Crahan Denton) is next to Nancy (Marian Seldes), holding her hand. The midwife, Aunt Peggy (Doris Rich), coaches Nancy as she cries out loudly during the hard pain of labor. As Agee constructs the scene:

> NARRATOR (Martin Gable): And the beginning? No one alive in
> this world could remember the beginning. But the stars have long
> memories. One hard night in February, eighteen hundred and nine,
> they looked down on a little cabin in a fold of the Kentucky hills;
> and they saw how it all began: a very humble and obscure event; as
> ordinary as death.
>
> CUT TO: CLOSE CUT: (*past the opaque rawhide window; past the shut
> door of ax-hewn planks with rawhide latchstring; and along black clay-
> chinked logs to an extreme close shot of a broken chink which lets through
> weak, shaky light*)
>
> MIDWIFE: (*almost crooning; also straining with sympathy*) Bear down,
> honey, bear down, bear down, me lady . . . (*With a sudden terrifying
> intensity*) Bring him now![8]

As the midwife exits, she looks back and says, "Youngin', you sure picked yourself a bitter morning." Tom returns to sit by Nancy. She is tired but apparently now free of pain. He is happy as well as kind to her. She asks, "What did I promise you, Tom?" "A son," he answers. She tells him he is a good man. He says he will make breakfast. "I'm much obliged," she replies in a deep country accent.

For Griffith and Agee, the nativity of Abraham Lincoln is prophetic as well as melodramatic. The cold, bitter morning in both movies foreshadows Lincoln's fate. The setting is Sinking Spring Farm, not Bethlehem. Lincoln is born in a log cabin, not a stable. His father is Thomas, not Joseph. His mother is Nancy, not Mary . . . and she is not a virgin. Although there is no mention of the Star of Bethlehem or shepherds, the "ancient stars" in their courses look down on the little cabin.

What is the role of Nancy Hanks Lincoln? Writing in April 2021 for the *Wall Street Journal,* Catholic bishop Robert Barron says, in a reflection on the meaning of Easter: "I have always been drawn to the tombs of famous people. . . . When on retreat at St. Meinrad Monastery in southern Indiana, I would often take a morning to visit the nearby Lincoln Boyhood Memorial, on the grounds of which is the simple grave of Nancy Hanks. . . . I always found it deeply moving to see the resting place of this backwoods woman, who died uncelebrated at the age of 35, covered in pennies adorned with the image of her famous son."[9] She is the mother of the nation's redeemer.

How has Hollywood defined her and her relationship with her son Abraham? Griffith's film includes Nancy only in the birthing scene. Agee's Lincoln story evolves in five television episodes: "The End and the Beginning," "Nancy Hanks," "Growing Up," "New Salem," and "Ann Rutledge." Nancy Hanks Lincoln appears in the first and second installments. At the end of the first episode, she gives birth to the child. The second episode focuses more on Nancy, her son, and what Agee sees as the poor but idyllic life of backwoods pioneers. The narrator speaks in a deep, measured tone. Filmmakers call such omniscient dialogue the "Voice of God": This is the Lincoln home: Abe and sister Sarah sleep in the loft, Tom and Nancy on a bed made of "poles and rope." The cabin is plain but cozy. The reality was different: little comfort and even less privacy. Lincoln biographer Michael Burlingame calls it a "dismal abode" of 18 by 20 feet. Crude furniture—a slab table, stools, and a bedstead.[10] It was not cozy. It was a cramped, crowded space. At one time, eight people lived in a similar hovel—Thomas and his second wife, Sarah Bush Johnston, as well as Sarah Lincoln, Abraham Lincoln, Elizabeth Johnston, John D. Johnston, Matilda Johnston, and cousin Dennis Hanks, who came to live with them at the Pigeon Creek Farm in Indiana.

"A woman gets up early on a farm," the narrator explains in Agee's story.

"It's her job to get each day underway." For little Lincoln, "she is apt to be the first thing a child sees and keeps looking at the longest." He "constantly watched his mother and tagged after her"—observing "the person he loved most in the world going through the grave, unconscious, immemorial rituals of a woman taking care of her family." Those immemorial rituals involved much hard work for women such as Nancy. As historian Margaret Walsh observes, "Rarely was a farm a 'going concern' without female participation." Wives "controlled the home, cooking, cleaning, washing, making or repairing clothes." Other duties, she notes, involved the kitchen garden, an orchard, and the family cows and chickens. They would, as needed, till the land as well. They might even bring in a bit of cash selling butter and eggs.[11] During Lincoln's childhood in the early nineteenth century, the work on and management of the pioneer family farm was an economic and socially necessary partnership. Man and wife were "mutually dependent." Tom and Nancy would be partners not only in everyday farm work but in raising the children as well.

Despite Agee's loving portrait of Nancy and despite his description of Abe's close observation of her, rearing childen on the nineteenth-century frontier was hardly bucolic. This was a hard and often brutal life.[12]

Yet, Agee, influenced by Carl Sandburg, created an idealized relationship between Nancy and Abe from a compound of myth and reality. Agee had an agenda. According to film scholar William Hughes, Agee's portrait of Nancy in an Arcadian frontier had more to do with a mid-twentieth-century nostalgia for a simpler age than with the realities of the mid-nineteenth century. "The message James Agee embedded in 'Nancy Hanks,'" Hughes states, "was no different than that of a popular book for teen-aged girls of the 1950s, which informed its youthful readers that a wife and mother 'knows that as a woman she will be doing a great deal more for others than for herself.'" No doubt, many women and girls ignored or resisted their prescribed role, but Agee's "'Nancy Hanks' seemed to speak with the authority of history. The effect of placing this familiar version of domestic relations in historical dress created an impression that these arrangements are timeless or universal. The families watching this episode in their new suburban homes might well have concluded that contemporary gender roles were the way they had always been and would continue to be."[13]

Where in Agee is the truth about the unrewarding life of Thomas Lincoln and his two wives? Where is the sharp edge of real pioneer life? *Mr.*

Lincoln's austere sets and costumes convey some sense of it. The bleak black-and-white photography adds to the ambience (there was no color television as yet). But the sentimental romanticism about Lincoln's two mothers conveyed by the plot, tone, narration, and dialogue is more Cold War liberalism and moral earnestness than historical reality. *Mr. Lincoln* conveys a message more reflective of the mid-twentieth century than the mid-nineteenth. Agee (novelist, movie critic, screenwriter, journalist, and poet) was a 1950s New Deal liberal—sympathetic toward the poor and oppressed, inclined toward radical observations but not to radical solutions. Here are the simple folk. They are the precursors of those Depression-era impoverished sharecroppers that Agee wrote about in *Let Us Now Praise Famous Men* (1941).[14] Agee's Lincoln emerges from the people—we the people.

No scene in the episode captures the romance of Agee's Nancy Hanks more than when the family sits together in front of the cabin after a day's hard work. Abe watches closely as Nancy leans back and sings "The Skye Boat Song," a lullaby about Bonnie Prince Charlie, the Stuart pretender to the throne of England, the anticipated savior of the Scots:

Speed bonnie boat like a bird on the wing
Onward the sailors cry.
Carry the lad that's born to be king

Over the sea to Skye.[15]

It is a beautifully imagined scene.

The evidence is conflicting over Nancy's legacy to her son, though it is clear that Lincoln inherited her predilection toward depression, and her early death traumatized the child of nine. In the script, Tom's hardness and Nancy's tenderness tug at the boy. Agee created tension between the two over the child's education. Here Tom confronts his wife. He has discovered that she had sent Abe and his sister to the village school despite his opposition.

TOM: Nancy, where are the youngins?

NANCY: School.

TOM: I told you about that. Told you what I would do. Sent them off behind my back.

NANCY: Yes, Tom.

TOM: You know I got nothin' against learnin', Nancy. You know that. How's a boy goin' to learn how to work lollygaggin' around a school house every time I need him. Gal too, matter of that. Every time I want him and the gal too. . . . Answer me!

NANCY: These things mean more than work.

TOM: You're just stuck up because you can read a word or two.

NANCY: Don't mean just readin', writin'.

TOM: What does? What does? Answer me that!

NANCY: I mean real learnin'.

TOM: I don't see what you mean.

Indeed, Tom Lincoln was frustrated when the boy showed more interest in books than in splitting rails, but he did pay for a bit of schooling for young Abe. People had conflicting memories about Tom Lincoln's skills, economic success, and reputation. No controversy, however, attends the fact that Lincoln drifted away from his father, refusing to visit him even as he lay dying. The fact that Lincoln eventually rose so far above his father's station in life explains, in some measure, the disconnect between the two men. He was, on the other hand, affirmative about his relationship with his two mothers. Of Nancy, Lincoln said, reputedly, "All I am or hope to be I owe to my angel mother." A favorite quotation around Mother's Day, it is also the opening intertitle in the Lincoln film by director A. J. Edwards, *The Better Angels* (2014).[16] Writing in 1922 for the Kentucky Historical Society, Lincoln enthusiast Thomas McGregor neatly summed up the popular image of Good Mother Nancy: She was "gentle, almost mystical." His blessed mother, Nancy, and his father, Tom, "walked with God and true to His merciful guiding hand, their boy was thus shaped and the instrument fashioned to preserve and save this Union, once and forever."[17]

The popular encomiums to Nancy do not reflect Lincoln's own ambivalent feelings about her lowly origins, although he expressed his love for her. Tom's genealogy is well recorded; we know much less about Nancy's origins. Significantly, the poverty of his parents and his mother's obscure, perhaps disreputable ancestry clearly embarrassed him. Tom and Nancy were, according to Lincoln himself, "of undistinguished families."[18] Nancy's mother, Lucy, had a sluttish reputation; a grand jury in Mercer County, Kentucky, charged her with fornication.[19] Gossipy neighbors even whispered about Tom's courting of Nancy since the couple reportedly once stayed together overnight on a trip to a revival meeting. Lincoln certainly believed that Nancy was born out of wedlock and neglected by her mother.

Whatever his anxieties about Nancy's ancestry, Lincoln credited her with possessing extraordinary intelligence; she was, he asserted, a "genius." Additionally, although he never formally joined a church, he claimed his churchgoing mother's faith as the source of his moral values: "I remember her prayers and they have always followed me."[20] She read the Bible to her children and taught them the rudiments of their ABCs.[21] Semiliterate, she could read but almost certainly not write. Despite her limited skills, Nancy had a better education than most of her neighbors.[22] She introduced her boy to Noah Webster's *American Spelling Book* (1809). Children called it the "Blue-Backed Speller" from the color of its binding. Lincoln's familiarity with the King James Bible was also a major influence on the cadence and rhythm of his later writings. If this love of reading came from his mother, from Tom he inherited his talents as a storyteller. This was his father's one true gift to his son.

According to Herndon,[23] Lincoln asked one day in a remarkably intimate reference to Nancy's parentage, "Did you ever notice that bastards are generally smarter, shrewder, and more intelligent than others?" Herndon emphasized the point: "When Lincoln spoke to me . . . he [referred] to his mother's *mind,* nothing else."[24] Michael Burlingame interprets this to mean that Lincoln was referring to traits he received from Nancy's father, rumored to have been a well-born, rich Virginia planter. This was no "sentimental paean to Nancy Hanks."[25] Historian and Mary Lincoln biographer Catherine Clinton confirms that "bastardy and secrecy were embedded within [Lincoln's] family and played a role in shaping his psyche."[26]

There is a prosaic variation on Lincoln's "angel mother" tribute. He actually said, "All that I am or hope to ever be I get from by mother—God bless her."[27] Which mother? Lincoln biographer David Donald argues that whenever Lincoln referred to Nancy as an "angel," he used it only to distinguish her from his still living stepmother, Sarah.[28] Whatever he had in mind, he became obsessed with the family story as he tried to orient his own ambitions.

Sarah Lincoln had more impact on Lincoln's development than did his birth mother. When Sarah, "a pious, gentle, intelligent, and well-liked woman," according to an early popular biography of Lincoln,[29] moved in with Tom, she washed the children, dressed them appropriately by the standards of backwoods society, created a loving home, and continued to support his education. She, not Nancy, set him free from the trap of Tom's inertness. Nancy achieved far less.

In any case, Lincoln, unlike James Agee, had no illusions about the pastoral beauty of farm life. He bitterly hated farming and left that life as soon as he reached age twenty-one and emancipation from his father's control. He expressed no remorse about leaving Sarah behind as well. Lincoln took no pride in his origins. Reading was his emotional and intellectual liberation from the dirt, the backbreaking labor, the boredom, and the commonality of death around him. Lincoln had few good memories of farm life on the frontier and what he saw as its stifling culture. He "did not speak or write a great deal about his early years on family farms," historian James Tackach writes, "perhaps because he came to be embarrassed by that segment of his life or because such a life lacked any distinctive or noteworthy elements."[30] There was no little irony in the Rail-Splitter image his supporters promoted during the 1860 presidential campaign, since Lincoln "had taken no political advantages of his hardscrabble beginnings, which he had spent nearly three decades trying to escape."[31]

No photograph or painting of Nancy exists, and the descriptions of her vary widely. "A heavy built Squatty woman," according to one source but a remarkable six feet tall by another. (Tom was probably five foot ten.) No contemporary called her beautiful. Nancy certainly could not have been as attractive as Marian Seldes, the statuesque actress who plays her in *Mr. Lincoln.* Her son inherited Nancy's physical features as well as her persona, if some recollections of her are accurate. Tall with a high forehead, angular and lean, with long arms, his mother had large ears, nose, and mouth, with "a big head on a long, stringy neck." She, like her son, even exhibited "a sad appearance" or "melancholy" approaching depression.[32]

In *Mr. Lincoln,* as the family prepares to move to Indiana for what Tom hopes will be better economic opportunities, Nancy takes a last look at the Kentucky cabin. That life, foreshadowing her death, was "the best she would ever know."

Nancy Hanks's cruel end from the "milk sickness" (caused by drinking cow's milk defiled by the deadly white snakeroot plant) follows immediately upon Tom's angry outburst about the children's education. He notices that Nancy is ill and burning with fever. He is solicitous, musing that a doctor or "witch" can help, but he knows of none. Resigned to her fate, Nancy says it is useless. No doctor or witch, no medicine or magic charm could ease the pain or cure the disease.

The episode does not describe her death. The last we see of Nancy, she slumps down at the door of the cabin. Her agonizing last days in the little room crowded with family members would have been a traumatic passing, not a romantic Hollywood death. Her putrid breath would have suffused the cabin with its odor.[33] The poison also brought on severe constipation and intestinal pain, tremors, constant vomiting of acrid, dark matter to accompany descent into a fatal coma. She died on that bed of poles and ropes— thirty-four years old.[34] Death on the frontier was a constant reality. Some 20 percent of children at the time lost a parent before they were fifteen.[35] The passing of Nancy Hanks takes a bizarre turn in the story of Lincoln among the vampires. In the film, a vampire, "Jack Bart" (a slaveholder) poisons Nancy. Shortly before her excruciatingly painful death, she calls to little Abraham:

NANCY: (*weakly*) Come and lie next to me.

YOUNG ABRAHAM: (*sweet and tender*) I have been writing, Mama: "Days as swift as an Indian arrow flying like a shooting star. The present day is here, and then slides away in haste, that we can never say is ours, but only say is passed." (*Nancy passes*) Mother? Mother?

William Herndon described the death of Nancy Hanks this way: "Amid the miserable surroundings of a home in the wilderness Nancy Hanks passed across the dark river. Though of lowly birth, the victim of poverty and hard usage, she takes a place in history as the mother of a son who liberated a race of men. At her side stands another Mother whose son performed a similar service for all mankind eighteen hundred years before."[36] Nancy is the Blessed Mother of the Nation's Redeemer.

In Agee's *Mr. Lincoln,* as in reality, young Abe helped his father fashion the coffin. Nancy Hanks Lincoln's death merits a simple eulogy by the film's narrator: "Nancy Hanks was born in 1783 and died in 1818." She left behind a well-meaning widower but one helpless with children. Tom immediately sets out to find a new wife. He goes back to Kentucky to locate Sarah Bush (now the widow Sarah Bush Johnston), a woman he had once courted. He had proposed to her years ago, but she turned him down. Tom Lincoln's courtship of Sarah (called "Sally" here) in the film has a real sense of authenticity to it:

> SALLY (Blanche Cholet): Tom Lincoln, I seen ya riding down the road. I swore it was you.
>
> TOM (Crahan Denton): Sally Bush! (*He abruptly addresses her*)
>
> SALLY: Sally Bush *Johnston!* (*She reminds him forcefully*)
>
> TOM: Sally Bush you are a widow woman and I am a widow man. We both got youngins (*She has three children*). I courted you once, I'm courtin' you again. Will you have me?

She says she has debts; he agrees to pay them. The scene is closely, if not precisely, based on what the two may have actually said to each other. Here is the proposal as Sarah remembered: "Well *Miss* Johnston, I have no wife & you have no husband[.] I came *a* purpose to marry you[.] I knowed you from a gal & you *knowed* me from a boy—I have no time to loose and if you are willing, let it be done Straight off."[37] A bit stunned at his directness, she agrees to the proposal if he pays off her creditors. He kept his word to the tune of three dollars. And so they married. Later, as they prepare to go to Indiana, Tom is loading a wagon with Sarah's possessions—a bureau, table, spinning wheel, chairs, a chest of drawers, forks and spoons, china plates, and two beds.[38] This is a woman of substance, by frontier standards. All of this is true to history.

In the film, Tom complains about bringing a useless fancy chest of drawers all the way back to Indiana. You could sell it, he tells her, and buy five cows. She replies forcefully that she is worth a lot more than five cows, which sounds like something she would have said. As she turns to go back into the house, Tom grouses, "Dad burn women!" It is clear in *Mr. Lincoln,* as in reality, that this particular marriage is a union of equals, despite the perceived conventions of the time. According to Catherine Clinton, "Many accounts mentioned Nancy Lincoln's submission to her husband; she did not cross him. By contrast, Lincoln's stepmother made demands on her husband."[39] When they arrive at the Lincoln farm, Sarah, shocked at the sight of ragged Abe and his sister, immediately begins the rescue of Nancy's children from Tom's neglect. She soon wins her stepson's affection.

Later, young Abe seeks out a minister to provide Nancy with a proper graveside service. The combined family of Lincolns and Johnstons gathers together to sing the haunting hymn "A Fountain Filled with Blood." It is one of the most affecting scenes in Agee's hagiography. The circuit-riding minister lauds Nancy as a faithful wife and mother. (She was.) The camera pans across the family and then focuses on Sarah's face as she draws Abe to her side:

> There is a fountain filled with blood,
> Drawn from Immanuel's veins,
> And sinners plunged beneath that flood
> Lose all their guilty stains:
> Lose all their guilty stains,
> And sinners plunged beneath that flood
> Lose all their guilty stains.

Nothing but a rough wooden plank with her initials, N. L., cut into it marked Nancy's grave. In real life, some months following her death, a group of twenty family and neighbors gathered at the site. David Elkin, a hard-drinking, illiterate preacher, led the memorial service.[40] Years later, Lincoln expressed an intent to provide his "angel mother" Nancy with a proper headstone. He never got around to it. He visited Sarah in her old age but never invited her or any of his family to the White House. From time to time he reluctantly sent money to help Tom Lincoln and his stepbrother, John Johnston. He considered both of them deadbeats. In real life, as well in the films of Griffith and Agee, Lincoln moved onward and upward to a better life. Both Nancy and Sarah dearly loved little Abe and nurtured his talents. He, in turn, held fond memories of them but no desire to return to the world they represented or to have Sarah close.

Robert Sherwood's *Abe Lincoln in Illinois* (1940) imagined the moment when Abe (Raymond Massey) leaves home. The scene is set in 1831. Abe, Tom (Charles Middleton), and Sarah (Elizabeth Risdon) are in the cabin. A hard rain falls outside. By the fire Abe is reading Shakespeare. Abe's laziness annoys Tom, but Sarah understands and gives Abe a wink. "Maybe someday, if he gets an education," she says, "he will write poetry." Then two cousins come through the door with a proposition: they can make twenty dollars each transporting hogs from Springfield to New Orleans. This is Abe's chance to escape the farm.

SARAH: So, you goin' Abe?

ABE: I guess I better do it, Maw. I know I can trust the old man to your care.

SARAH: I couldn't have loved you more than if you were my own son.

ABE: I'll always be thank'in you Maw for your kindness to me.

SARAH: Wherever you go, whatever you do, remember what the Good Lord says: "The world passeth, but he that doeth the will of God abideth forever."

ABE: I'll remember Maw. Good bye.

SARAH: Good bye, dear Abe.

No doubt the real Sarah loved the boy, and he returned that affection. A unique bond existed. "His mind & mine—what little I had[—]seemed to run together[—]move in the same channel," she said years later.[41] *The Better Angels* and *Abe Lincoln in Illinois* may unduly romanticize the relationship between Abe and Sarah, but both honestly reflect their mutual affection. Nevertheless, what memories he had of Kentucky and Indiana he kept close, except for one brief reflection: In 1844, he returned to Little Pigeon Creek, Indiana, where the family lived until moving to Illinois in 1830. The visit some twenty years after he left the community inspired Lincoln to write an autobiographical poem, "My Childhood Home I See Again." Poetry held a special place in Lincoln's mind. Emily Dickinson called such thoughts "The Dark Parade." The date is not clear, but he may have completed the poem on February 25, 1846. By this time in his life, Lincoln had become a successful lawyer, a bourgeois gentleman. Here are two excerpts:

My childhood-home I see again,
And gladden with the view;
And still as mem'ries crowd my brain,
There's sadness in it too.

O memory! thou mid-way world
'Twixt Earth and Paradise,
Where things decayed, and loved ones lost
In dreamy shadows rise.
And freed from all that's gross or vile.

∎

How changed, as time has sped!
Young childhood grown, strong manhood grey,
And half of all are dead.
I hear the lone survivors tell
How nought from death could save,
Till every sound appears a knell,
And every spot a grave.
I range the fields with pensive tread,
And pace the hollow rooms;
And feel (companions of the dead)
I'm living in the tombs.

Half his childhood friends are dead. He speaks of graves and tombs. An analysis of the poem by historian James Tackach concludes that the environment of the "old farm fields . . . remained, in some way, a fundamental part of him, despite his attempt to distance himself from them physically and emotionally."[42]

In the episode entitled "Crossing the River" from the television series *Sandburg's Lincoln* (1974–76), Abe (Hal Holbrook) plans a visit to his step-mother, Sarah (Beulah Bondi) in Coles County, Illinois, shortly after his election to the presidency. He will give himself a break from all the office seekers plaguing him, and he asks his son Robert to go with him. He can change his fancy northeastern Harvard fashions for simple butternut jeans and get close to the people (if not the frontier life itself). Robert refuses. "I don't know those people," he says. The West is just a wilderness to Robert—wild and overgrown. He wants no part of it. So, Lincoln goes alone back to the past.

He arrives at Sarah's cabin in a buggy. He calls out to her, and she meets him at the door. He calls her "Aunt Saree." As they talk in the cabin, he realizes that she is almost blind. She notices that he has changed: "Don't get fine and uppity with me, Abraham," she gently scolds him for losing his country accent. "I'm no one but the boy you made," he replies. She disagrees. No, "that was Nancy that made ya." It was indeed Nancy who birthed him, Abe replied, but it was she, Sarah, who "made me live, that made me human." She tells him that the spirit was always inside him—"Boy, it was in ya, there," pointing to her heart. In the next scene they visit Tom's grave. "Did you weep when he died?" she asks. Clearly this is painful for Abraham. "Some hard rub'ns there," she observes of the father-son relationship.

She also recollects Tom's proposal to her and how he told her he owned a prosperous farm in Indiana—"a kind lie," she says. She then recalls that once she asked her husband which wife he liked the better—her or Nancy. Tom replied with a joke: that this reminded him of the man who owned two horses. One kicked and the other bit. He did not know which was worse. They both laugh. If Abe inherited anything from his estranged father, it was his talent for humor; Lincoln too would frequently begin a joke or a story with the opening: "Now that reminds me . . ." Sarah arranges some dried flowers on the grave. The initials T. L. mark his resting place. Lincoln kneels and seems to be praying. As he departs, Sarah says, "Don't forget me, son," That would be "impossible," he replies. But that is the last he will see of her. The past is truly behind him now. He is changed forever; Sarah notices it. He leaves her with a photograph of himself.

Sarah was seventy-three when Lincoln actually visited her. It was an emotional reunion, she later recalled. Weeping, she declared: "I did not want Abe to run for Presdt., did not want him elected—was afraid somehow or other . . . that Something would happen [to] him . . . and I would see him no more." He responded: "No, no Mama. Trust in the Lord and all will be well. We will see each other again."[43] "She was all of a mother to him," is how Sandburg imagines the visit. "He was her boy more than any born to her. He gave her a photograph of her boy, a hungry picture of him standing and wanting, and wanting. He stroked her face a last time, kissed good-bye, and went away."[44] "There was practically nothing in his surroundings in Kentucky, or at Gentryville, Ind., where he lived after his mother's death, to touch the imagination of a young boy," Lincoln scholar Frederick Trevor Hill concludes. This environment provided no "fair chance" in life. It was an "animal-like existence."[45]

Abraham's two mothers reappeared in an Amazon streaming movie, *The Better Angels* (2014). Directed by A. J. Edwards, a protégé of acclaimed filmmaker Terrence Malick, it tells the story of the Lincoln family and of Lincoln from age eight to twelve.[46] After consulting with Malick about the scope of the film, Edwards narrowed its focus: "There was real wisdom in finding a target for the heart of the story, and that was how his two mothers guided him. This was the essential component that he [Malick] and I developed from the start."[47] The Sundance Film Festival provides this synopsis: "Set in the harsh wilderness of Indiana, this is the story of Abraham Lincoln's early youth. It tells of the hardships that shaped him, the tragedy that marked him forever, and the two women who guided him to immortality."[48]

The character of Dennis Hanks (Lincoln's cousin as voiced by Cameron Mitchell Williams), who lived with the Lincoln family, narrates. The dialogue is really incidental; people say things that seem to float out into the air. This is no traditional biopic; this is a film about mood and image. *The Better Angels* is a striking, quite beautiful film (it has to be to have any impact at all); the black-and-white cinematography by Matthew J Lloyd (director of photography, Marvel Comic's *Spider-Man: Far from Home,* 2019) is in keeping with the extraordinary visual images characteristic of Malick's films. Like Malick's creations, this movie is less about narrative than about atmosphere and an "imagined frontier." This is particularly true of those starting with *Days of Heaven* (1978), a love story set against the expanse of the Texas Panhandle in 1916 that won the Academy Award for Best Cinematography, and *The Thin Red Line* (1998). Afterward, Malick moved to Paris and disappeared from filmmaking for several years to write screenplays.

The Thin Red Line, based on the World War II novel by James Jones, is no traditional war movie. It is primarily a reflection on nature and grace amid the horrors of combat in the Pacific. Critic Roger Ebert accurately described Malick's films as having a unifying theme that "human lives diminish beneath the overwhelming majesty of the world."[49] Malick's work, after *The Thin Red Line,* validates Ebert's insight, especially *The New World* (2005), nominated for the Oscar's Best Cinematography, and *The Tree of Life* (2008), which also received a nomination for Best Cinematography. The tone of his filmmaking resembles the writings of Walt Whitman, Herman Melville, and Hart Crane. His movies are about "the isolated individual's desire for transcendence amidst established social institutions, the grandeur and untouched beauty of nature, the competing claims of instinct and reason, and the lure of the open road."[50]

The Malick-Edwards treatment of Lincoln's boyhood in *The Better Angels* focuses on the years 1817–19. The young Lincoln and those around him, including his mother, stepmother, father, and a sister (only one sister appears in the film; there were actually two, one a stepsister), exist in an environment tied to the natural world—the land, water, forests, and even the stars. The landscape shapes their behavior. The young Abraham, who barely speaks until a few lines near the end of the film, seems to be becoming aware of this world. Yet, he seeks not to tame it—his mother's death convinces him of that impossibility—but to comprehend it. His obsession is with reading despite his father's opposition. His mother and later his stepmother are encouraging. The schoolmaster declares that "he will not stay in these woods forever" and even offers to tutor him during off-sessions. "He will make his mark" by the time he is thirty. (Jesus began his public ministry at the age of thirty.)

This young Lincoln notices things outside books and the schoolroom that will also "teach" him. At one point, his father sends him—alone—on a three-day walk to work in a tannery. On his journey, a group of Black men in chains silently pass by. Lincoln's reaction to this is unclear, as he returns home not yet ready to leave the woods to confront the world that he will transform. Near the end of the film, he tells his father, "I want to be as strong as you." His father, seeming to finally recognize that his son will take a different route in life, replies, "You'll be twice the man I am." Tom hands him an axe, symbolic of the famous rail-splitter imagery.[51] It is an odd angle for the film to take, since it does not explain this sudden change in the relationship between father and son. And this surely does not reflect Tom's real opinion of Abraham. In fact, he was closer to his stepson, Johnny Johnston (Sarah Bush Johnston's boy), than to his own child.

The demands of Kentucky and Indiana frontier life soften when the film focuses closely on the relationship between young Abe and his mothers. The women frolic with the child in bucolic meadows. Nancy dances around a maypole; Sarah joins in with neighbors to the tune of fiddle music celebrating the new church Tom built for the little congregation. As Primitive Baptists, though, there was no way these people would have rejoiced by dancing around a maypole . . . let alone outside a church.[52] Tom is tough and crude but at heart a decent man; Nancy and Sarah are protective—defending Abe when his father disciplines him. Actress Brit Marling, who plays Nancy, is quoted as saying that in today's Hollywood "we are starting to see the female gaze."[53] The German-born Diane Kruger plays Sarah. Named "The Sexiest International Import in 2012," she was cast as Helen in the Brad Pitt film *Troy* (2004). Film critic Todd McCarthy writes that in *Better Angels* Tom's second wife, Sarah, is "of surpassing beauty." Diane Kruger is the product of "idealized Hollywood" casting. Yet, a "photograph of the real Sarah suggests a resemblance to a character no one would want to meet in the woods in a Grimm's fairy tale."[54] This is unkind: the one photograph of the real Sarah was taken in her old age. In any event, neither actress—too fragile in shape, too dreamy in mood, too Hollywood in appearance—comes off as a mid-nineteenth-century pioneer woman. As sociologist Jackie Hogan judges, the two mothers "are implausibly flawless . . . in their wifely and maternal devotion." Their calico costumes "do little to disguise their Hollywood perfection."[55]

The Lincoln household seems a better fit for the Summer of Love of 1967 than the hardscrabble environment of the Lincoln, Hanks, and Sparrow clan. Hogan notes how the film depicts a world where the boy "spends his days chopping wood and plowing fields under the critical eye of a stern father, and exploring the wonders of nature with a loving, angelic mother." When Nancy dies, Abe endures with "stoic grief." Soon the new but "equally angelic mother," Sarah, entices Abe into another equally warm and supporting relationship.[56] Hogan, for her part, finds the message in the film not only disturbing but disconnected from historical reality. It is as if the filmmaker conceived of a place where little Abe, removed from the corruptions of the greater society, was home-schooled in an idealized frontier in preparation for his mission. The Studious Boy is at one with nature. In *Better Angels,* this is a fantasy frontier when the common people live in harmony with the environment. The land is yet unspoiled. Little Lincoln's mothers dance with nature; Tom seeks to tame it.

The narrator introduces Nancy: "She couldn't read or write none. Had to make her mark, instead. She was a believer. Now you can mark your place in your book. She knew so much of what she believed was yonder. Always yonder. Every day came scrubbing, washing. . . . There was so little time to sing or think about the glory. Her mind and his seemed to run together." Edwards based Hanks's description of Lincoln's mother on Carl Sandburg's impressionistic image of Nancy Hanks in his biography of Lincoln. Sandburg's Nancy also "believed in God, in the Bible, in mankind, in the past and future, in babies, people, animals, flowers, fishes, in foundations and roofs, in time and eternities outside of time she was a believer, keeping in silence behind her gray eyes more beliefs that she spoke. She knew . . . so much of what she believed was yonder—always yonder."[57] Later, we meet Sarah: "She was a widow. She had been fendin' for herself for a while now." Neither woman is identified by name. Nancy "undoubtedly did her best to kindle a spark of ambition in her son, but she was an uneducated, delicate, and even sickly house drudge."[58] Sarah was illiterate. Both women marked an *X* in place of signatures.

Better Angels is a meditation on life; it is not a true biographical film either in its confusing episodic approach or its disregard for essential information. And that view of the Indiana countryside? The movie was filmed in New York State, a far different environment. But there is a scene in *The Better Angels* that surely rings true. Sarah pages through some books with Abe. She presents them to him as treasured gifts. The film shows the title page of John Bunyan's *Pilgrim's Progress.* The book opened an "exciting new world" for him.[59]

Like Griffith, like Agee, Edwards focuses on the beatific world in which the boy is formed and prepared for greatness—a portrait of the Savior of the Union before he enters the years of his public life. *Variety* critic Peter Debruge approved: "This mesmerizing period piece, which nobly seeks to grasp the spiritual nature of young Abraham Lincoln's formative years, splits its attention between heaven and earth, brushing its fingertips over the tall Indiana grasses one moment, then swirling its gaze upward to consider sunlight streaming through the thick forest the next."[60] Historian William E. Bartelt, an authority on Lincoln's boyhood, observes that, despite the problems with historical accuracy, "This artistic film accomplished the goal . . . of depicting young Abraham Lincoln's relationships with his mother and stepmother."[61] But film critic Glenn Kenny responded that those looking for a "meat and potatoes" account of the life of young Abe Lincoln would be disappointed. The film, although "pictorially beautiful and emotionally evocative," is an exercise in "inchoate Transcendental philosophy," typical of the Malick approach to filmmaking. Its "minimalist dialogue contains questions such as 'Where is your spirit?'"[62]

Tom teaches Abe how to split rails, plow a field, scythe weeds, and compete in wrestling; in line with the dictates of the cult of domesticity, Nancy and Sarah recognize that they are responsible for the boy's moral development. Abe became his mothers' son. In an interview Edwards was clear about the meaning of his film when he compared it to *Ben Hur* (1959). In that film, "You have a story that's about Christ but you never name Christ. You just feel him. . . . You get it through Miklos Rozsa's score. That's where Christ is most present in the film."[63] (When interviewed about his role as the emerging hero in John Ford's *Young Mr. Lincoln* [1939], Henry Fonda recalled, "I felt as if I were interpreting Christ himself on film.")[64]

The Better Angels begins with images of a windswept Lincoln Memorial devoid of any human presence. The narrator says that he visited Sarah's place at Easter 1865 to bring news of the assassination: "I had to go out to the farm to tell her. She was living . . . there alone." Sarah responded to the visit: 'I knowed they'd kill him. I'd been waiting for it." The Studious Boy had predicted such a fate.

2

THE ROMANCE OF
ANN RUTLEDGE
IN MEMORY AND FILM

In the spring of 1928, the *Atlantic Monthly* received a letter from one Wilma Frances Minor of San Diego, California, a newspaper columnist, short story writer, novelist, biographer, actress, movie stunt double, and vaudeville entertainer. She was also a Hollywood screenwriter for American Standard and Mirror Films, an early studio. Her movie projects included "The Song of Courage," "The Desert Rat," and "Meeting Mother."[1] She presented a fascinating proposal. Miss Minor claimed to possess a previously unknown collection of Lincoln memorabilia, including letters exchanged between Lincoln and Ann Rutledge, a young woman the future president met when he lived in New Salem, Illinois, for six years in the 1830s. Would the *Atlantic* be interested in publishing the collection in book form? If so, might such a book be eligible for the magazine's five-thousand-dollar nonfiction biennial award (about eighty thousand dollars in 2021)?[2]

The story intrigued the magazine's aristocratic owner and editor, Ellery Sedgwick. This was a truly unique find—a sensational literary coup. Established in 1857 in Boston, the *Atlantic* became the most prominent literary and cultural periodical in America, publishing articles by Julia Ward Howe, Harriet Beecher Stowe, Mark Twain, and Ernest Hemingway, among others. The Rutledge narrative, if verified, would provide one of the few insights into Lincoln's early personal life. But there was a problem. The foundation of the story, based on disputed evidence, was suspect.[3] And Lincoln, a prolific letter writer, made no mention of the affair in any of his own writings. Someone needed to check out the proposal.

Sedgwick and Minor exchanged a series of telegrams and letters in which they discussed a variety of matters including the development of a movie script. (It would be one of the new "talkies.") Minor came to meet with the editor in person. Sedgwick then presented samples for verification to Reverend William Eleazar Barton, a Lincoln scholar.[4] Fascinated by the revelations and infatuated with the attractive Miss Minor (she was married but kept it secret), Barton was equivocal but encouraging. Sedgwick also sent samples to Worthington Chauncey Ford, a former president of the American Historical Association, who had edited Albert J. Beveridge's biography of the Lincoln, until then the most complete account of Lincoln's early life up to 1858.[5] Ford had no doubt the items were phony. The editor then contacted Ida Tarbell, the famous muckraking journalist and Lincoln biographer.[6] "My faith is strong that you have an amazing set of true Lincoln documents," she judged, calling them "extraordinary."[7] (Later she wrote, reflecting a popular consensus: "I have always been a believer in this romance." I have "believed it was the only time romance touched Abraham Lincoln.")[8] Sedgwick also called on Carl Sandburg to render an opinion. "These new Lincoln letters," he judged, "seem entirely authentic— and preciously and wonderfully co-ordinate and chime with all else known of Lincoln." Despite the uncertain provenance of the letters, Sedgwick charged ahead and published the story in a three-part series in the winter of 1928–29—"The Setting–New Salem," "The Courtship," and "The Tragedy"— under the general title "Lincoln the Lover."[9] He announced the series in a full-page ad: "No longer need the biographer spend years of research, or the romancer dream of the idyll as it might have been. Here, for the first time, revealed in Lincoln's own words, the tender love he bore for his 'Dearly Valued Ann.'"[10]

The passages were dramatic, revealing, and priceless (though Minor settled for $1,500 at the start). Here were windows onto Lincoln's inner life during his early years. In the spring of 1835, for example, when his purported sweetheart became ill, she wrote to Abe, "Pleas do not cum to-nite I am ailing with a cole, Ma sez I must take a swet rite after supper." Suspiciously, the letter changes tone from the nearly illiterate beginning to this poetic closing thought: "Think of me as I think of you for I am thine forever and ever." In reply, Lincoln expressed his concern for Ann's health, regret for his poor fortune in life, and his doubts about the hereafter. "It greatly pains me to hear from Nancy [Ann's sister] regarding your condition," Abe wrote. "I have been saying over and over to myself surely my traditional bad luck cannot reach me again through my beloved. I do long to confirm the confidence you have in heaven [she once gave him, as recorded in the Minor collection, a treasured Bible as a token of her affection]—but should anything serious occur to you I fear my faith would be eternally broken."[11] It was his last message to her; she died on the August 25, 1835. It was a romantic tale for the ages. It was too good to be true . . . and it was. The papers proved to be a hoax.

Paul M. Angle, a Lincoln scholar and executive secretary of the Lincoln Centennial Association in 1925, had no doubt that the letters were fakes.[12] Oliver R. Barrett, "the greatest of the modern Lincoln collectors," concurred.[13] Both authorities were adamant: the letters were forgeries and poor ones at that. When a handwriting expert also exposed the fraud, the game was up. When she first approached Sedgwick, Minor said that "the letters, diaries, and keepsakes of Abe and Ann" had been "held sacredly in the family archives for many years" and then willed to her mother, Mrs. Cora DeBoyer.[14] Now Wilma, in desperation, explained that the letters were true but came from an unusual source. Her mother was, she revealed, a fortune teller and clairvoyant. She recorded the letters herself after receiving messages from the beyond. As Minor explained: "It has been given to us for a divine purpose. On another plane those people [Abe and Ann] must exist." Mama was not sure she could contact them, but she would give it a try. So, "she went into a trance and the guide said he had asked the people [Lincoln, Ann, etc.] and they said they would give me the story."[15]

Of course, this convinced no one. It was a huge embarrassment for the editor and his magazine. But the affair proved to be a landmark in Lincoln scholarship. The hoax marked the beginning of an offensive by professional historians against the Lincoln popularizers that would transform Lincoln literature. Talk of a lawsuit against Minor faded as all involved shunned publicity. There is a footnote to the story: The chances are good that the author of the Lincoln-Rutledge correspondence was in fact William Francis Mannix. He was a journalist and "colossal hoaxer" best known for his forgery entitled *The Memoirs of Li-Hung Chang* (1913), the reputed recollections of a late nineteenth-century Chinese mandarin. Mannix may have been at one time a paramour of Cora's, although he had died before Wilma concocted the scheme. Scholar Madelyn Kay Duhon concludes that "Mannix's exploits and the Lincoln-Rutledge letter hoax are on par in terms of boldness, cunning, and puckish humor."[16]

Wilma's plan to publish a book, win a prize, and write a movie script fell through. No major motion picture based on the Minor letters ever appeared. But a film about Abraham Lincoln's love life would still appeal to movie audiences. Wilma Minor, in fact, was not the first person to see the cinematic possibilities. Filmmakers had already produced two Abe and Ann silent films in 1914 and 1924. Later, the Lincoln-Rutledge affair also appeared in four popular productions made during Hollywood's classic age and the advent of the television era.

But first, who was Ann Rutledge? What is known about her relationship with young Abraham Lincoln? What is its significance? The part of Ann Rutledge in Lincoln's life swings back and forth from modest friendship to eternal soul-centered devotion. The Abe-Ann "love affair" is the stuff of sentimental nineteenth-century fiction in all its vivid romanticism. Here is a tragedy worthy of an Emily Brontë novel.

■ ■ ■

Anna Mays Rutledge was born on January 7, 1813, in Kentucky. Most references refer to her as "Ann," but it is sometimes rendered "Anne." Her sister said they always called her "Annie."[17] Ann was one of ten children born to James and Mary Ann Rutledge, who moved to Illinois, where James became one of the founders of a village, New Salem, in 1829. There he opened a tavern and boardinghouse. Lincoln lived on and off with the Rutledge family in 1834–35. That part of the story is well documented. Much of the backstory to the romance is speculation, though scholarly opinion now points to a real connection between Abe and Ann. Nevertheless, the evidence is hardly rock solid, and scholars dispute the depth of the relationship.

Those who remembered Ann said that she was pretty, though perhaps not as Hollywood pretty or beautiful as the actresses who portrayed her on film—Ruth Clifford, Una Merkel, Pauline Moore, Mary Howard, Joanne Woodward, and Grace Kelly.[18] If Ann Rutledge resembled Grace Kelly, she would have been a woman of staggering beauty.

In any case, descriptions of Ann vary: Brown hair. Perhaps a redhead. Or was she a blond? Heavyset. Plump. Round in form. Five foot three. 150

pounds. No, she was slim. Good teeth. John McNamar (aka John McNeil), a suitor, recalled that "Miss Ann was a gentle Amiable Maiden without any of the airs of your city Belles, but winsone and Com[e]ly withal a blond in completion with golden hair, red cherry libs & a bonny Blue eye." Another witness remembered that "Miss R was a good looking, smart, lively girl . . . with a moderate education, and without any of the so-called accomplishments." And this from William Greene (aka "Slickly Bill"), whose memory was vivid if not entirely reliable: "This young lady was a woman of Exquisite beauty, but her intellect was quick—Sharp—deep & philosophic as well as brilliant. She had a gentle & kind heart as an ang[e]l—full of love—kind[n]ess—sympathy."[19]

Whatever the case, Lincoln found Ann attractive enough. She and Abe studied grammar together and enjoyed each other's company. One contemporary source reported that she had plans to attend college, the Jacksonville Female Academy, at a time when higher education was rare for anyone and especially for a woman. Complications ensued. She was already engaged to John McNamar, a person of some wealth and a friend of Lincoln. He had a mysterious past. He had come West, bought land in the New Salem area, and then returned to the East to deal with certain ill-defined family matters. He had been gone for almost three years and had stopped writing letters. In the meantime, Lincoln began to court Ann. Some claim that Lincoln proposed to Ann, but they needed to clear up the relationship with McNamar first so they could be properly engaged. (McNamar would later deny that Lincoln ever courted Ann.) A proposal depended on ability to support a wife and children. It is unlikely that Lincoln was really prepared to marry Ann at this time. The same problem emerged when he courted Mary Todd. No one could remember what Ann had to say, though one New Salem resident thought that Ann felt obligated to McNamar and would have married him if he had returned. This is when tragedy struck: Ann died of "brain fever."

Though her death was most likely due to typhoid, or perhaps malaria, encephalitis, or even meningitis, the so-called brain fever was a popular Victorian literary plot device. Emma Bovary, when rejected by her lover, Rodolphe, went into a decline due to brain fever. In *Wuthering Heights,* Cathy Linton is torn between two lovers, Heathcliff and Edgar. "Subjected to such emotional stress," she, too, developed brain fever, which, in her case, "ultimately contributed to her death."[20] Ann's death resulted from the emotional conflict between her obligation to John and her love for Abe. This is the romantic answer—a gooey layer of sentimentality. Her real death, like that of Nancy Hanks Lincoln, was decidedly unromantic. The season in which she fell ill, the spring and summer of 1835, devastated the denizens of New Salem—hard, continuous rain and then oppressive heat followed by swarms of aggressive mosquitoes. Great blackflies and their cousins, the vicious yellow biting flies, added to the misery.[21] Sandburg, however, painted the events with a patina of romance: "August of that summer came: Corn and grass, fed by rich rains in May and June, stood up stunted of growth, for want of more rain. The red berries on the honeysuckles refused to be glad. The swallows and the martins never came."[22]

Ann lingered for six weeks, amid several bad omens. Eight days before her death a tornado struck, taking down trees and fences. Wolves roamed the landscape.[23] The Rutledge one-room cabin, like the Lincoln hovel at the time of Nancy's cruel death, was crowded with eleven sick and dying people: "The situation [was] made worse, much worse, by nearly everyone being plagued either by extreme diarrhea typical of malaria, or a variant of it, a form of constipation that would suddenly explode into it." No hint of privacy shielded the disgust and the humiliation. Nor would there have been any privacy for a romantic final moment between Abe and Ann as in the movies.[24] Hollywood had to invent an alternate goodbye: Ann calls for Abe in her last agonies. When he arrives, everyone leaves, and the couple spend some time alone together in her final moments.[25]

Apparently, her death distressed Lincoln. Some said his grief was so great that he contemplated suicide and had to be restrained. He mourned her and obsessed about rainwater leaking into her grave. Perhaps Lincoln himself, like Ann, was sick, "worn down to emaciation by his malarial infection and overwork."[26]

Death had dogged him since childhood. He experienced the death of his mother when he was nine and she was thirty-four. The death of his sister Sarah followed the birth of a stillborn child. She was only twenty. Maybe Ann's death was not traumatic for Abe but still painful. But she, too, died young; she was twenty-one or twenty-two. Even in an age when the death of infants, young mothers, family members, friends, and neighbors was common, this would have been hard to endure. Between about 1750 and 1880, 20 to 30 percent of children died before age ten. Relying on a doctor before modern medical training was generally useless; actually, it was often "a positive mistake."[27] Surely, these terrible events affected Lincoln's mind and his reported spells of depression. Not surprisingly, the story has always centered on Abraham Lincoln, not Ann, on his state of mind and the impact her death had on his future.[28]

It was William Herndon who created the popular story of Abe and Ann in a sensational lecture given on November 16, 1866: "A. Lincoln—Miss Ann Rutledge, New Salem—Pioneering, and the Poem Called Immortality—or, 'Oh! Why Should the Spirit of Mortal Be Proud?'" Although the facts were fragmentary, Herndon admitted, his sources convinced him that if Abraham had married Ann, that "sweet, tender, and loving girl, he would have gravitated insensibly into a purely domestic man." Her death profoundly changed his life. He "leaped wildly into the political arena as a refuge from his despair." To his everlasting regret, he married Mary Todd on the rebound.[29] The story came to Herndon from Rutledge family recollections and other New Salem sources. He interviewed some 264 people who had known Lincoln during his formative years. Some eighteen to twenty of the witnesses to the relationship asserted that Lincoln loved Ann, courted her for a time, and mourned her death.

Writing in 1945, Lincoln scholar James G. Randall dismissed Herndon's oral evidence as nothing more than "one person reporting what another person had written him concerning what that person recollected he had inferred from something Ann had casually said to him more than thirty years before."[30] Historian and psychoanalyst Charles B. Strozier, who knows a great deal about the private Lincoln, writes, "since there is no single thread of good evidence on the subject, the episode must be passed over quickly."[31] (Could these stories about Ann be what psychologists call "false memory"?)[32] Michael Burlingame, author of a two-thousand-page biography of Lincoln, came to an entirely different conclusion about the origins of Ann's story and Herndon's sources: "When I examined the records myself, I saw: these aren't the unreliable memoirs of old codgers drooling on their walkers and making up stories."[33]

If the romance lacked solid evidence at the time, it did not stop Carl Sandburg, in a moment of exquisite poetic excess, from rhapsodizing, "He was twenty-six, she was twenty-two; the earth was their footstool; the sky was a sheaf of blue dreams; the rise of blood-gold rim of a full moon in the evening was almost too much to live, see, and remember."[34] This would not be too much for future screenwriters. This was the stuff of classic Hollywood romance.

Of course, Mary Lincoln would have none of it. Her understandable white-hot anger at Herndon's assertions appears in a letter to Lincoln's former campaign manager and later US Supreme Court Associate Justice David Davis. Writing in March 1867, a year after Herndon's infamous lecture, Mary was emphatic: "Every one [sic] has had a little romance in their early days—but as my husband was *truth itself,* and as he always assured me, he had cared for no one but myself . . . I shall assuredly remain firm in my conviction—that *Ann Rutledge* is a myth—for in all his confidential communications, such a romantic name was never breathed."

Neither, she contended, "did his life or joyous laugh, lead one to suppose his heart was in any unfortunate woman's grave—but in the proper place with his loved wife & children." She ended the letter with a threat regarding Herndon and his "vivid imagination. . . . I assure you, it will not be *well with him*—if he makes the least disagreeable or false allusion in the future. *He* will be closely watched." Further, she "would not believe an assertion of Herndon's if he would take a thousand oaths, upon a Bible."[35] But Mary's fury was no match for the compelling love story of Abe and Ann. Caroline Healy Dall, a feminist writer and women's rights activist, was in the audience during Herndon's lecture and became so fascinated with the tale that she, with Herndon's encouragement, promoted it in a series of articles. The affair "could no more be left out of a true life of Lincoln," she wrote, "than Dante's love of Beatrice, or Petrarch's love of Laura . . . could be omitted in the biographies of these poets, and still leave them intelligible. For thirty years after the period it describes, his terrible sorrow continued to move him at times out of himself, and it is the only explanation of many significant facts."[36]

ANN RUTLEDGE IN HOLLYWOOD

For Hollywood, Ann's story, whatever its controversial facts, was too good to let go. In Griffith's *Abraham Lincoln,* in a scene following Ann's burial, Lincoln sits by the fire in desolate mourning. He stares blankly, reciting the first stanza of William Knox's *Mortality* (1824), said, with slight evidence, to be Lincoln's favorite poem:[37]

Oh! why should the spirit of mortal be proud?
Like a swift-fleeting meteor, a fast-flying cloud
A flash of the lightning, a break of the wave
He passeth from life to his rest in the grave.

As the scene ends, Lincoln runs out of the house and throws himself on
Ann's grave amid howling wind and thunder. An intertitle appears with
verses from the poem:

Yea! Hope and despondency, pleasure and pain
Are mingled together in sunshine and rain
And the smile and the tear, and the song and the dirge,
Still follow each other, like surge upon surge.[38]

What explains Lincoln's fascination with the poem? It is well known that
Lincoln suffered from depression. The poem fed the affliction. Essayist
Joshua Wolf Shenk diagnosed the familial sources of this melancholy—it lay
in Lincoln's temperament: "Three elements of Lincoln's history—the deep,
pervasive sadness of his mother, the strange spells of his father, and the
striking presence of mental illness in the family of his uncle and cousins—
suggest the likelihood of a biological predisposition toward depression."[39]

To be fair to Griffith, his sentimental tone, terribly dated in the new
Hollywood of 1930, would not have been alien to Lincoln, whose melancholy and sentimental nature also reflected the zeitgeist of middle-class,
mid-nineteenth-century America. Griffith did not invent Lincoln's intense
reaction to the death of Ann, if the disputed contemporary recollections
can be believed. "The intensity of Lincoln's despair," historian David S.
Reynolds observes, "can be attributed in part to cultural influences. His
extreme reaction to Ann's death may have been a case of life imitating art.
The popularity of mournful songs and poems in the 1830s worsened his
vulnerability to gloom."[40] Perhaps Lincoln knew among the greatest hits
of the era the lyrics to "The Light of Other Days."

The light of other days is faded,
And all their glories passed.
For grief with heavy wing had shaded
The hopes too bright to last;

The world which morning's mantle clouded,
Shines forth with purer rays!
But the heart ne'er feels, in sorrow shrouded,
The light of other days.[41]

Whatever the cause or causes of Lincoln's profound sadness evident in his real life, the two scenes in the film are also typical of the Griffith style—a combination of historical details sauced with Victorian sentimentality and dramatic overload. In this case Griffith tapped into what Joshua Shenk believes explains Lincoln's greatness: "His story endures in large part because he sank deeply into that suffering and came away with increased humility and determination." The Studious Boy became the Sad Man in search of his destiny: "In his strange mix of deference to divine authority and willful exercise of his own meager power, Lincoln achieved transcendent wisdom, the delicate fruit of a lifetime of pain."[42] Lincoln biographer Benjamin P. Thomas says of Ann and Abe: "Regardless of its genuineness it is, and will remain, the best-known incident of Lincoln's New Salem life. It has become part of American folklore [and Hollywood's history], and popular opinion resents any efforts to disprove it. There is an unexpressed, perhaps unconscious feeling that a life with so much sadness, so much tragedy as Lincoln's deserves to be enriched by such romance."[43]

After his descent into desperation, Lincoln rides to Springfield. The tone of Griffith's film brightens when he meets the spirited Mary Todd. Awakened for a time from his depression but still harboring Ann's memory, he is vulnerable to the allure of this charming Kentucky belle. Griffith's account of the courtship of Miss Todd has all the hallmarks of the director's Victorian romanticism, already dated in the emerging Hollywood of the sex-obsessed pre-Code era.

How, then, do Ann and Mary figure into the popular imagination of twentieth-century America? Shenk believes he has an answer. "In the 1920's and 1930's," he writes, "people scarcely distinguished the facts of Lincoln's melancholy from the twin myths of his love for Ann Rutledge and his dreadful marriage to the woman now known as 'Mary Todd Lincoln.'" He continues: "In the Progressive Era, the nation was busy exalting its sixteenth president, and it needed a love interest for the narrative—his widow would not do."[44] Thus, Saint Ann of New Salem filled the role perfectly. The short-lived Rutledge affair left the blanks to be filled in. She died before she could become his wife and his widow and before all the messy history that might have played out in the relationship.

The stories of Abe, Ann, and Mary existed against the background of the emerging new industrial America and all its inherent social and economic issues. These problems, coupled with the dominant historical interpretation that emphasized postwar North-South reconciliation and the legacy of the Brothers' War, led politicians and filmmakers to the Lincoln matrix. Lincoln's personal struggles and the crisis of the Union in the 1850s and 1860s were still fresh. When Teddy Roosevelt evoked Lincoln to legitimize his Progressive principles in his Lincoln Centennial Address of February 12, 1909, he remarked on Lincoln's psychological burden—the unhappiness that he bore: "He grew to know greatness, but never ease, Success came to him, but not pleasure."[45]

D. W. Griffith could not have said it better. Four years later, Roosevelt repeated the theme in his "The Heirs of Abraham Lincoln" speech on February 12, 1913: "We Progressives and we alone are today the representatives of the men of Lincoln's day who upheld the hands of Lincoln and aided him in the great task to which he gave his life, and in doing which he met his death."[46]

Hollywood looked to Carl Sandburg, who, in turn, looked to William Herndon and Ida Tarberll for inspiration about the Ann-Abe love story. Sandburg was one of the nation's most famous poets—a romancer of the Progressive spirit. Later, Franklin Roosevelt adopted Lincoln as a sort of political mascot for New Deal progressivism, connecting the Great Humanitarian to the Democratic social-reform agenda.[47] Sandburg's hugely popular six-volume biography of Lincoln, which FDR endorsed (although it is doubtful he read it), was critical in defining Lincoln's popular image and Ann Rutledge's as well. The first two volumes, *The Prairie Years,* appeared in 1926. The second part, *Abraham Lincoln: The War Years,* won the Pulitzer Prize in 1940. (The volumes became the source for a well-received television miniseries in 1974 staring Hal Holbrook.) Here is how Sandburg imagined the love affair:

After the first evening in which Lincoln had sat next to her and found the bashful words tumbling from his tongue's end really spelled themselves out into sensible talk, her face, as he went away, kept coming back. So often all else would fade out of his mind and there would be only this riddle of a pink-fair face, a mouth and eyes in a frame of light corn-silk hair. He could ask himself what it meant and search his heart for an answer and no answer would come. A trembling took his body and dark waves ran through him sometimes when she spoke so simple a thing as, "The corn is getting high, isn't it?"[48]

"The corn is getting high, indeed!" literary critic Edmund Wilson sniped at Sandburg's midwestern sentimentalism.[49] But Ann proved at first just beyond Lincoln's reach: "It can't happen that a sucker like me can have a gal like that." And here is Sandburg's account of Ann's death: "Ann Rutledge lay fever-burned. Days passed; help arrived and was helpless. Moans came from her for the one man of her thoughts. They sent for him. He rode out from New Salem to the Sand Ridge farm. They let him in; they left the two together and alone a last hour in the log house, with slats of light on her face from an open clapboard door."[50] Sandburg's story of Abe and Ann was historical fiction, or a prose poem, costumed as biography.[51]

Consider this mundane story: An awkward young man meets a sweet young girl. Mutual attraction ensues. They talk a bit about the future and make plans. They consider an engagement, then she dies. He is greatly saddened by her death but then moves on with his life, gets married, and becomes a famous person. So what? Nothing of interest here to build a movie script on. If Sandburg's Abe and Ann story was imperfect as history, it was, nevertheless, perfect for Hollywood. Here is the Hollywood treatment: An awkward young man and a fragile, funny, beautiful, and charming country girl meet cute. They have deep conversations about his future. She sees in him a person of remarkable potential, which she encourages. Then she dies. He never recovers and turns to politics for the fulfillment of his destiny. Meanwhile, plagued by an ill-considered marriage to a nagging, unstable, politically ambitious woman, he mourns his lost love for the rest of his life. Now, this is the stuff of successful movie scripts. As for the movie's location, see the now restored New Salem village, twenty miles from Springfield, Illinois. Almost nothing of the original site remained when historic restoration began in earnest in the 1930s. Like most restored sites, there is little in this New Salem to remind the visitor of the hard, dirty, and violent life in a frontier settlement. But for a location scout, in the classic age of Hollywood, such an idyllic setting would be perfect.

Since the historical record is never complete, it is Hollywood's privilege to fill in the blanks. What was so compelling about Ann and Abe provided more than enough space to frame Lincoln's love life as a conventional Hollywood love story. Even better, it fit the conventions of the Hollywood biopic in which a man of destiny is supported or inspired by a good woman, or, in Lincoln's case, a few good women. All that was needed was a screenplay that expanded on what was known or suspected about the relationship. More important than the veracity of the romance is the question of why this appealed to the American public. What in the story of Ann Rutledge made it so compelling that Hollywood made ten movies that included the affair? How did the movies reflect the public interest in Lincoln in general and the tale of Ann Rutledge in particular?

Although he does not specifically include the Man of Sorrow among his five images of Lincoln, historian Merrill D. Peterson identified: the Savior of the Union, the Great Emancipator, the Archetype American, the Self-Made Man, and the Democratic Champion of the Common Man. Those images evolved in two broad phases. In the 1870s and 1880s, the Lincoln of folklore emerged based on the reminiscences of his contemporaries. Popular biographies, collectors, and the creators of popular culture, drawing on various episodes in Lincoln's life, including the Rutledge story, all helped construct the image of Abraham Lincoln. In the 1920s and 1930s (coinciding with the arrival of movies as mass entertainment), scholars clashed with popularizers over the veracity of Lincoln narrative.[52] Historian Barry Schwartz discovered other specific phases in the evolution of the romance of Abe and Ann as reflected on film and other forms of public expression. During the Progressive and New Deal Eras, "the Ann Rutledge story articulated the common man's fears and moral mood in a time that put the premises of American society to their severest test."[53] It connected strongly to an American public receptive to the image of an Abraham Lincoln who would have understood the hard times and social turmoil brought on by the second industrial revolution, the economic collapse of the 1930s, the worldwide challenges of the Second World War, and the anxieties of the 1950s. Abraham Lincoln, the future Savior of the Union, fell in love with a pretty, sweet, nurturing, unaffected country gal. This was the Lincoln of collective memory. By the 1960s, however, public attitudes had shifted. What place did the quaint story of Abe and Ann's courtship hold in the cultural, social, and moral confusions of postmodern America? Was it still relevant? And who, other than antiquarians and old-fashioned romantics, even cared about Ann Rutledge anymore?

She became irrelevant when the public's attention turned to the legacy of slavery (forget the Brothers' War), racial justice, and women's rights. The memory of Ann Rutledge became a victim of the cultural and sexual revolution. Today "Ann Rutledge's place in his story seems superfluous, if not downright distracting,"[54] This, remarkably, had little if any influence on Hollywood's treatment of Ann. Her image endured on film.

Ann of Blessed Memory, as Lincoln's one true love, first appeared in *Lincoln the Lover* (1914), perhaps the inspiration later for the general title of the *Atlantic* series. It is only ten minutes long with a clever, if improbable, historical structure. Having just given his inaugural address on March 4, 1861, the new president returns to the White House. He sits before a fireplace and thinks back to his days in New Salem. The flashbacks include his first meeting with Ann, the grammar lessons he taught her, and her engagement to a scoundrel by the name of McNamar who abandons Ann. With McNamar gone, Ann and Abe fall in love. They plan to marry, but tragedy strikes—she dies suddenly from a fever. We next see him standing at Ann's grave during a snowstorm. The movie ends as he awakes from his reverie. He is still sitting before the fire—it is 1861 again.[55] Abe remains heartbroken after all these years; he cannot let her memory go. In essence, this brief film captures what became Hollywood's Ann Rutledge trope—a story told time and again about young Lincoln's first and only true love, pasted into script after script—the awkward young Lincoln, the pretty young girl, Lincoln standing at the grave. Now we understand why he is the Man of Sorrow. Ann had to die so that Abraham Lincoln could fulfill his destiny.

When *The Dramatic Life of Abraham Lincoln* appeared in 1924, American poet Carl Sandburg, on the verge of becoming Lincoln's most popular biographer, reviewed the movie in a series of five columns as film critic for the *Chicago Daily News*.[56] The research that the producers, Al and Ray Rockett, put into the project impressed him. They claimed to have consulted five thousand books and, according to Sandburg, "were dissatisfied with the attempts of 90 percent of these to make Lincoln into . . . something far-off and mystical" and "remote from all human activity." They were after "the real and human man."[57] Al Rockett, however, was not always dedicated to serious filmmaking; he also produced the first Three Stooges short, *Soup to Nuts* (1930).

His reviews of *The Dramatic Life* provided Sandburg the opportunity to reveal some of his first reflections on Lincoln and the women in his life—

Sarah Bush Johnston Lincoln, Ann Rutledge, and Mary Lincoln. He noted that Sarah "had a profound practical effect upon the boyhood of the greatest of Americans, yet she had a strange strain of mysticism." He took the opportunity in the column to praise the work of William Herndon, who, he believed, was "anxious that the truth about Lincoln should be told the world at the time when mythmakers were distorting the martyr's memory into something unreal and misty."[58] Ann's story "is told as that story is usually told. Ann seems to be the same old-fashioned movie heroine seen in the movies of old-fashioned times."[59]

Though no copies of the silent film *The Dramatic Life of Abraham Lincoln* survive, it can be reconstructed, in part, through contemporary reviews. Lincoln film scholar Mark S. Reinhart was able to piece together the highlights of the screenplay. The film unfolds in four parts (Kentucky and Indiana; New Salem; Springfield; and the presidential years) that trace Lincoln life from his birth to his death. On the whole, the film was reasonably accurate. But, as Reinhart points out, "the major problem is simply that it is a silent film, and to effectively tell the story of Lincoln's life . . . you need to hear his words as well as see his physical presence."[60] It was the first motion picture for actor George Billings, who played Lincoln and went on to other Lincoln impersonations on film. At the end of his career, he toured the country in a two-man play. Henry Fonda,[61] in his first professional performance, played Lincoln's secretary, John Hay. Ruth Clifford played Ann Rutledge. Afterward she became a member of John Ford's stock company of actors (*Drums along the Mohawk* [1939] and *The Searchers* [1956]). For a time, Clifford did the voices for Minnie Mouse and Daisy Duck in Walt Disney cartoons.

The making of *The Dramatic Life* is surely more interesting than the movie itself. A. M. R. Wright wrote a tie-in biography of Lincoln illustrated with movie stills.[62] The filmmakers were careful, he wrote, in "the handling of the materials in a way to avoid offense and eternal vigilance against that exclusive thing known to film crafters as 'hokum.'" In the pursuit of truth, they tracked down Grace Bedell, then living in New York State, who as a child had written the famous letter encouraging Lincoln to grow a beard. In Long Beach, California, they discovered a certain Mr. Paris Henderson who claimed that he knew Lincoln during his days on the Illinois judicial circuit. They even claimed to have located a retired actress living in Los Angeles who, under the stage name Helen Truman, was in the cast of *Our American Cousin* at Ford's Theater the night Lincoln was assassinated.[63]

Their research into the people in Lincoln's life connected to the growing demand for actors to exhibit more authentic, low-key performances or naturalism on film. These early character studies may not have actually reflected the look and personalities of the real women in Lincoln's life, but they did create the first film images: "Nancy Hanks was characterized by a natural refinement, a calm disposition and braveness of spirit that met blizzards, births, poverty and pioneering undaunted. Her good judgment and fine memory served invaluably in guiding her son on toward things better than cabin life presented."[64] Lincoln's stepmother, Sarah, "was a robust, good-natured, capable soul and 'a good manager' of Tom Lincoln as well as the house."[65] For Lincoln as "the young backwoodsman accustomed only to the stocky country girls and work-coarsened women of his acquaintance, Ann was an unbelievable vision of all that was dainty and fair."[66]

■ ■ ■

D. W. Griffith's career by 1930 was in an advanced state of decay. True, many Hollywood veterans still held him in high esteem, but his pictures no longer made money—the mortal sin of film production. Having taken to excessive drinking, Griffith was a has-been. "Unfortunately," critic Gordon Berg writes, uncharitably, "Griffith had spent most of his creative juices during Hollywood's silent era, those that remained were profoundly pickled, probably swimming in his native Kentucky bourbon."[67] Nevertheless, the head of United Artists/Art Cinema, Joseph Schenck, who produced films starring comic legends Roscoe "Fatty" Arbuckle and Buster Keaton, had faith in him, at least for now. This was to be Griffith's comeback film.[68] It was not, however, a good match. Schenck was ambivalent about talking pictures, and this would be Griffith's first attempt at sound. Additionally, the studio executive became distracted by other projects. In the event, Schenck stuck with Griffith when he came up with the concept of a film based on the life of Abraham Lincoln.[69]

Griffith biographer Richard Schickel notes that Griffith's "admiration for [Lincoln] dated back to boyhood, when he was imbued with the not uncommon post–Civil War southern reverence for the magnanimity and wisdom of the man."[70] It was one of the Lost Cause tropes: Abraham Lincoln, reflecting the idea that the Civil War had been a "Brothers' War," welcomed the heroic former rebels back into the Union on generous and humane terms. His assassination, however, allegedly ushered in the madness of Radical Reconstruction. This fit the theme of the popular idea of national reconciliation perfectly. The love for Dearly Valued Ann reflected the kind, generous, and tragic soul who, through his own experience of loss, understood the loss and suffering of the former Confederates. When Griffith decided to make the biopic of Lincoln, he first turned to Carl Sandburg for a script and received this telegram:

> KEENLY INTERESTED IN SEEING LINCOLN PICTURE DONE WHICH WILL BE A SERIES OF PERSONALITY SKETCHES SETTING FORTH HIS TREMENDOUS RANGE OF TRAGIC AND COMIC. . . . KNOW ALMOST PRECISELY WHAT IS WANTED FOR A HISTORIC ACCURACY WOVEN WITH DRAMATIC INTEREST. . . . ALL PAST PRESENTATIONS HAVE FAKED HOKUM WHILE NEGLECTING ESTABLISHED AND ENTERTAINING DRAMATIC VALUE OF LINCOLN.[71]

Sandburg's romantic imagination was a good fit for the Griffith treatment, but his asking fee of thirty thousand dollars ($430,000 in 2021) went way beyond the film's budget. Griffith relied instead on his own Victorian sentiments and the assistance of another bard, Stephen Vincent Benét, the author of the *John Brown's Body* (1928), an epic poem of the Civil War.[72] There was more than enough dramatic interest, tragedy, and comedy. There was also more than enough faked hokum to create a movie. Benét, however, never had much faith in the picture. And like other novelists (F. Scott Fitzgerald and William Faulkner), he had no real appreciation for screenwriting. Reflecting on an initial draft of the script, he wrote to his wife, Rosemary: "I'm damn sure they won't use it but will try to cheese it up with love interests and Negro comedy characters."[73] Benét was right to be pessimistic. "It's doubtful," Berg judges, that "even Benét's lilting prose could have saved this prosaic, episodic paean" to Lincoln.[74] Schenck, unhappy with the screenplay, fired Benét and assigned one of his associates, John W. Considine Jr., to take over. A veteran producer and script doctor, he pushed Griffith aside.[75] Get some rest, he advised Griffith. Considine then rewrote the love scenes between Abe and Ann, yet retained the full measure of Griffith-Sandburgian sentimentality.[76]

Promoted as *D. W. Griffith's Abraham Lincoln,* despite Considine's work, the completed movie traced Lincoln's life from birth to death. It is still the only available film that does this. For its part, the love story of Abe and Ann begins as a romantic comedy and ends as a tragedy. Walter Huston[77] played Abe, and Una Merkel was Ann. Griffith tested Merkel as Mary Lincoln but then decided to cast her as Ann Rutledge. Because Merkel was essentially a comic actress, some thought her miscast as the object of Lincoln's devotion.[78] Here we first meet the couple. She is reading from a law book; he is splitting rails:

> ANN: In this sense, the term law includes any edict, decree, order, ordinance, statute, resolution, rule, etcetera, etcetera.
>
> ABE: Well, my old daddy taught me how to work, but he never taught me to like it.
>
> ANN: I reckon I better keep on with the lesson.
>
> ABE: I'd rather keep on with something else.
>
> ANN: You made a bad bargain making me the professor.
>
> ABE: Well, he told me about that too. He said: "When you make a bad bargain hug it all the tighter."
>
> ANN: But he didn't mean this kind of bargain.
>
> ABE: Well, don't you like it, Ann, when I hold you tight?
>
> ANN: I guess every girl sorta likes that. . . . Now, Abe, what is the law?
>
> ABE: Well, professor, law is a rule of human conduct.

The conversation is interrupted when a farmer pulls up in a wagon. He had hired Abe to split the rails. Well, Abe, he inquires good-naturedly, will you finish the job? Abe and he joke a bit. Lincoln assures him he will produce all the rails and some extras. Satisfied, the farmer drives off. Ann tries to find a better position on a stack of logs but misses her step, resulting in a pratfall—the comic relief:

> ANN: Now, Abe, your professor needs a seat where there's more law and less temptation. (*As she slips and falls*) Oh! Abe! Ohhh! Ohhhh!
>
> ABE: Are you all right, Ann?
>
> ANN: I think so.

ABE: Are you hurt?

ANN: My legs are still on me.

ABE: Scared me worse than it did you.

ANN: Did it, Abe?

ABE: You know Ann, if anything happened to you, I don't think I
could live.

Ann is the funny sidekick to the young Abe until fifteen minutes into the
film, when he arrives at Ann's bedside; she is dying:

ABE: No, no, Ann dear, you're not going to leave me! I won't let you!

ANN: We must be brave, dear. Don't take me away! Don't take me
away! It's so dark and lonesome going!

ABE: Ann, you mustn't let go!

ANN: If they'd sing, I wouldn't be so afraid.

(*A woman is heard singing in the background*): *"In the sweet by and by,
We shall meet on that beautiful shore"*)

ANN: We will meet there, dear.

ABE: Oh . . . I love you so. I love you so!

Of the Herndon-Sandburg–inspired appearances of Ann Rutledge on film,
three more—two feature films and a television series—are worth considering: John Ford's *Young Mr. Lincoln* (1939), *Abe Lincoln in Illinois* (1940),
based on the Robert E. Sherwood play, and James Agee's *Mr. Lincoln* (1952).
Consider, first, Ford's portrait of young Lincoln. It opens with a stanza from
Rosemary Benét's poem "Nancy Hanks."[79]

If Nancy Hanks
Came back as a ghost,
Seeking news
Of what she loved most,
She'd ask first

"Where's my son?
What's happened to Abe?
What's he done?"

But the focus in the film is not on Nancy or Ann; the Lincoln-Rutledge romance takes up barely ten minutes of screen time. A movie tie-in pamphlet, a *Film Guide to the 20th Century–Fox Picture, A Cosmopolitan Production, Young Mr. Lincoln: A Study Plan Prepared in Hollywood* (1939), provided viewers with the historical background to the affair: "At the time, Ann was a slender, beautiful girl of nineteen with bright blue eyes and a rich crown of auburn hair. Daughter of the local tavern keeper, she was the most dexterous needle worker in the little town of New Salem." Her "untimely death plunged the future President into profound grief, followed by a profound period of melancholy. He cherished her memory until the day he died. . . . It was inevitable that he and the eldest daughter of the Rutledge family should be drawn together, Ann was also a student of nature, ambitious, and superior to any girl Lincoln had ever known."[80]

The love story aside, this is essentially a courtroom drama based loosely on a true murder case that Lincoln argued in 1858, long after the period in which the film is set. The cinematic world of Lincoln's youth is sweetened with the usual Fordian comic scenes, sentimental music, frontier families, and archetypal countryfolk. So, what is the significance of Ann's role? A clue can be found in Ford's westerns. The director was a hard-drinking "man's man," more at ease with his drinking buddies among his repertory company of manly men (John Wayne, Ward Bond, Victor McLaglen, among others) than with actresses. *Young Mr. Lincoln* is as much a frontier film, set as it is in early Illinois, as the seven westerns he filmed in Monument Valley, Utah. Ann is a frontier woman, but "Ford assigns to women," film historian Howard Movshovitz writes, "the 'other' side of life, not the arena where men fight out the issues of law, justice, race and the wilderness."[81] The "other side" is where the women wait for the men to return from the battle. Here is where they provide their men with the quiet time to reflect on the meaning of it all and find counsel and a certain peace.

Ford's Abe and Ann meet on a summer day by the Sangamon river, already acquainted. She teases him about reading *Blackstone's Commentaries* when she finds him lying on the ground with his feet up against a tree. She tells him her father and everyone else in New Salem, including her, thinks he is very smart and very ambitious, even if he will not admit it. He claims he never had more than a year of education, but Ann reminds him he has taught himself poetry and Shakespeare and now the law. She hopes they will go to the same town where they will attend different schools but be together. Abe tells Ann that he loves her red hair, which she claims no one likes. Any expectations that moviegoers may have had about the romance continuing are abruptly terminated as the next scene flashes forward to winter (ice floes choke the river that flows in the background). Ann is dead and buried. There is no death scene. But in the most memorable part of the film, one of the best-imagined scenes in film history, Abe visits her grave as he tries to make up his mind whether to leave New Salem and fulfill his destiny. As the tune "The Dew upon the Blossom" plays in the background, he speaks of his self-doubts and his future while placing flowers on her grave: "Well, Ann, I'm still up a tree. Just can't seem to make up my mind what to do. Maybe I ought to go into the law, take my chances. I admit, I got kinda a taste . . . for somethin' different than this in my mouth. Still, I don't know. I'd feel such a fool . . . settin' myself up as a-knowin' so much. Course, I know what you'd say. I've been hearin' it every day, over and over again. 'Go on, Abe. Make somethin' of yourself. You got friends. Show 'em what you got in ya.'" Film scholar Geoffrey O'Brien says of this scene, "The linked sequences encompassing Lincoln's muted courtship of Ann Rutledge and his visit to her grave are as beautiful as anything in American movies."[82]

So pleased was he with Abe's graveside conversation, Ford replicated the moment ten years later in *She Wore a Yellow Ribbon* (1949). Captain Nathan Brittles (John Wayne) is a cavalry officer in the West at a turning point in his life. Required by army regulations to retire, he comes to water the flowers at his wife's grave and speak to her of his future: "Well, Mary . . . only six more days to go . . . and your old Nathan will be out of the Army. Haven't decided what I'll do yet. Somehow, I just can't picture myself . . . back there on the banks of the Wabash . . . rocking on the front porch. No, I've been thinking . . . I'd maybe push on West. New settlements, California."

In *Young Mr. Lincoln*, Abe decides his future by standing a stick on its end next to the grave, saying if it falls toward him, he will stay; if it falls toward her, he will leave. Of course, the stick falls toward the grave, and he admits, a bit oddly, since he seems to ignore Ann's part in the divination, that he might have tipped the stick just a little. Was he rejecting Ann's hold over him? Or was he following her wishes? It had to be the latter; this had to be so, since Ann's death would let him leave New Salem and fulfill his destiny. Ann's death sets him free. He is relieved of any obligations to the kind of life symbolized by the village. According to critic Derek Malcolm: "The scene, gentle and done with great economy, so that it doesn't seem hopelessly simplistic, expresses a lot about Ford: it was his way of saying that to honour the dead properly you have to fulfil the aspirations they had for you. Time and again the film is organised around such crucial Fordian values."[83] Graham Greene, writing in the *Spectator,* had a similar observation: "His love of Ann Rutledge is touched with unexpected restraint—an inarticulate duologue on a river-bank and a monologue over a grave."[84]

Embedded in the story of the murder trial, the heart of the film, is Lincoln's relationship with an older woman—Mrs. Abigail Clay (Alice Brady), the mother of the two young men (Matt and Adam) accused of the crime. The trial in the movie plays loose with the actual trial of Duff Armstrong that occurred in 1858. This was the famous "moonlight case" in which Lincoln, reportedly, used an almanac to discredit an eyewitness account of a homicide. In the film, this is the new lawyer's first major case. In a critical scene, Abigail and her two daughters are preparing to return home to await the trial when Lincoln shows up. The young Mr. Lincoln admits that he is inexperienced:

> ABE: You know I'm just a' sort of jackleg lawyer . . . without much experience in this business. But as long as you want me, I'll do the best I can. Still, you might feel a lot safer if my partner was here. Or you could get Steve Douglas.

> MRS CLAY: We don't know nothin' about lawyers or that kind of thing.

> ABE: Well, at any rate . . . I'll drop around in the morning and have a little talk with the boys. One of these days I'll take a ride into the country and let you ladies know how things are comin'. You know . . . my mother, Nancy Hanks . . . would be just about your age if she was alive. Got an idea she'd be a whole lot like you too. A whole lot like you. Well, good-bye, ma'am.

In the brief encounter with Abigail, Lincoln is the one who gives back. He is not just her lawyer. Mrs. Clay ("a simple country woman," Lincoln calls her) personifies those women in his life who loved him, nurtured him, protected him, and, most importantly, prepared him for glory. The memories of Nancy and Sarah remain close.

Writing in the *New York Times,* critic Frank Nugent praised the performance of Henry Fonda—"the warmth and kindness, the pleasant modesty, the courage, resolution, tenderness, shrewdness, that Lincoln, even young Mr. Lincoln, must have possessed." But more than that Nugent welcomed the Illinois frontier community that Ford and scriptwriter Lamar Trotti created on film: "The prairie types have been skillfully drawn. One knows, somehow, that they are Lincoln's kind of people, that think as he does, laugh at the same jokes, appreciate the same kind of horseplay." Among minor characters, he noted Alice Brady as the frontier mother. "The result," he wrote, "is not merely a natural and straightforward biography, but a film which indisputably has the right to be called Americana."[85] Over the years, *Young Mr. Lincoln* attracted a body of film literature in America and in France analyzing the movie in the context of John Ford as one of the great auteurs of filmmaking. "Suppose some truant good fairy were to ask me," the famed Russian director Sergei Eisenstein said, "'As I'm not employed just now, perhaps there's some small magic job I could do for you, Sergei Mikhail? Is there some American film that you'd like me to make you the author of— with a wave of my wand?' I would not hesitate to accept the offer, and I would at once name the film that I wish I had made. It would be *Young Mr. Lincoln,* directed by John Ford. What is there in it that makes me love it so? It has a quality . . . that every work of art must have—an astonishing harmony of all its component parts, a really amazing harmony as a whole."[86]

■ ■ ■

Carl Sandburg again provided the template for the Lincoln-Rutledge romance for a film based on Robert Sherwood's successful Broadway play of 1938. Sandburg and Sherwood played as fast and loose with Lincoln's life as had Ford's *Young Mr. Lincoln.* Raymond Massey, who had created Lincoln in the stage version to great acclaim, repeated the role in the film.[87] Massey had a remarkable physical affinity with Lincoln, unlike Henry Fonda, who had to make do with a prosthetic nose. Mary Howard[88] is Ann Rutledge. In this film, the "romance" is developed in greater detail, including a deathbed scene with Abe holding her hand and declaring that "my life belongs to you until the day I die."

Abe and Ann "meet cute" according to the Hollywood trope. As he travels downriver with a group of men taking a boatload of sixty pigs to New Orleans, they pass New Salem. Here the boat runs aground and the pigs escape. Townspeople rush to help. They capture the pigs and return them to the boat. During the chaotic scene, Abe meets Ann. He is rolling on the ground grasping one of the runaway pigs. Ann is giggling. Lincoln looks up:

LINCOLN: My name's Abe Lincoln.

ANN: And mine's Ann Rutledge.

LINCOLN: I . . . I don't know the name of the pig.

It is love at first sight. When Abe leaves New Salem to continue his trip downriver, he looks back intently. Ann is smiling and waving from the riverbank. Later, his employer announces that he liked New Salem so much he will return there and open a general store; he offers Abe a job, and Abe accepts. Abe cannot get Ann out of his thoughts. Upon his return, he immediately comes to her rescue as a group of ruffians enter her father's tavern and demand free whiskey. Ann berates them, but they ridicule her and her father. She asks the townsmen for help, but none will stand up to the bullying leader of the gang. Abe steps in, wins a hard-fought wrestling match, and is hailed by the whole town as the "new champion." As he becomes more attached to Ann, he sees her with her beau "John McNeil." He later learns the man is leaving "for a few months." Before John leaves to go back East, he meets with Ann:

JOHN (Maurice Murphy): You understand don't you, Ann?

ANN (Mary Howard): How long will you be gone, John?

JOHN: Oh, two or three months, that's all.

ANN: I'll miss you every minute of the time. (*At this point John gives her a cameo.*)

JOHN: This was my mother's. My father gave it to her when they became engaged. All you must ever think about . . . all I'll ever think about is that I love you. And you are going to be wonderfully happy.

ANN: John ... Tell me that again. Tell me we're going to be happy.
(*They kiss.*)

Two years pass, and John has not returned. Abe, now the postmaster, gives Ann a letter from John and watches as she reads it and begins to weep. Later, he again sees her weeping in the woods and offers, first, consolation, and then, in a sudden outburst, a declaration of love. She is a "fine girl," and he has loved her for a long time. Ann declares that she cannot love Abe "now," but she may come to love him, for "he can fill any woman's heart."

Abe continues to love Ann from afar, but she is uncertain. During a dance in celebration of Lincoln's campaign for the state legislature, Ann becomes ill and faints. At first, it seems nothing serious, but shortly there-after, she develops "brain fever." Abe rushes to her bedside:

ANN: You've come to me and I wanted you so much. Come close to me. Tell me we will be happy.

ABE: We're going to be happy Ann, I know I got less than nothing to offer you. But whatever I am, whatever I could be, my life belongs to you and it will be until the day I die.

ANN: I love you. Oh, I love you. I knew you'd come back to me. Don't ever go away from me again. We will be happy.

But here the movie challenges the Ann and Abe legend. As Ann dies, she lets slip from her hand the cameo that John McNeil gave her before he left for New York. You see, it is not Abe whom Ann loves, but John. In her delirium, she believes it is John, not Abe, who has come to her bedside. Next, we see Abe sitting mournfully as he waits for the stage that will take him to Springfield, where he has been elected to the state legislature. His supporters rejoice but not Abe. What little happiness he had within him died with Ann.

About 1866, Isaac Cogdal, an old friend of Lincoln from the New Salem and Springfield days, in an interview with William Herndon, recalled a conversation about Ann shortly before Lincoln left for Washington in 1861. Is it true that you loved her and suffered deeply because of Ann's death? Did you, in fact, "run a little wild" because of her death? Cogdal asked. Lincoln replied: "I did really. I ran off the track. . . . I loved the woman dearly and sacredly. She was a handsome girl, would have made a good wife, was natural and quite intellectual, though not highly educated. I did honestly and truly love the girl and think often, often of her now." But Cogdal's story is surely apocryphal. He was one hundred years old when he recovered this memory, and it is completely unverifiable. For certain, Lincoln would not have made such a statement knowing how his famously jealous wife would react. It is extremely unlikely, too, that a man so private about his inner life would reveal himself in response to such an impertinent intrusion.[89] Nevertheless, the old man's reminiscence fits the legend of Ann Rutledge perfectly—too perfectly.

The election of 1860 is like a death sentence. He accepts his political fate with dread. He is the sacrificial victim in the nation's redemption. He is the Man of Sorrow. The sad Studious Boy, now matured, accepts his destiny. He is, like the anticipated Savior in the Hebrew Testament, "a man of sorrows, and acquainted with grief."[90] Sherwood drew his interpretation of the impact of Ann's death from Sandburg as well as from Lincoln biographer Nathaniel Wright Stephenson. In his interpretation of her death, he conflates the impact of the passing of Nancy Hanks and the death of Ann Rutledge: "The sunny Lincoln, the delight of Clary's Grove, had vanished. In his place was the desolated soul—a brother to dragons, in the terrible imagery of Job—a dweller in the dark places of affection. It was his mother reborn in him. It was all the shadowiness of his mother's world; all that frantic reveling in the mysteries of woe to which, hitherto, her son had been an alien."[91] The Abe-Ann "love affair" in film is the stuff of sentimental nineteenth-century fiction in all its wild romanticism.

As popular as the Sherwood version was, James Agee's *Mr. Lincoln* is the most beautiful and moving version of the Lincoln-Rutledge story on film. Broadcast by CBS from mid-November 1952 to February 1953, it is a five-part television series, filmed in Kentucky, Indiana, and Illinois. Agee had been fascinated with Lincoln since college and, when approached to write for the program, accepted quickly. Sandburg's *The Prairie Years* provided his inspiration because he wanted a poetic approach to the subject. Both Agee and Sandburg viewed Lincoln as a "mythical figure."[92] According to Agee's biographer, "in particular, Agee wished to explore the tricky problem of Lincoln's relationship to women." Further, "He had heard of a supposed romance between the president-to-be and a young woman named Ann Rutledge." Despite the historical controversy over the authenticity of the story, "Agee took it at face value."[93]

Royal Dano, in one of the finest film portrayals of the man, is the lanky Abraham Lincoln. Dano made his forty-two-year-long career as a character actor in various roles including "the Tattered Man" in *The Red Badge of Courage* (1951), directed by John Huston. He was also the voice for Walt Disney's audio-animatronic Abraham Lincoln in "Great Moments with Mister Lincoln," first presented as part of the Illinois pavilion during the 1964–65 New York World's Fair. The Lincoln robot later starred in the "Great Moments with Mr. Lincoln" attraction at Disneyland. Finally, the Dano-voiced Lincoln came to rest at the Hall of Presidents at Disney World.

Joanne Woodward,[94] largely unknown in Hollywood at the time, is Ann Rutledge. Abe meets Ann Rutledge when he first comes to New Salem and asks her for directions. Later, while he is a store clerk, she comes and buys two spools of thread. They do not exchange a single word, but they glance meaningfully at each other. Abe loses his first election but wins a second one in 1834. He visits Ann to say goodbye, saying he will miss her when he goes off to Springfield. He then declares that there is a possibility of love. Ann is happy at the news and vows to break her engagement to "John," but Abe's response is ambiguous. Ann declares he should make up his mind.

Months later, having grown close through his letters to her, they sit at ease, joking with one another. Abe says they cannot marry for a while; he is a poor man. Ann indicates she does not care how poor they would be. Love will conquer. Abe responds that marriage would be "his end," that he has a feeling there is something in the world that he must live up to. He talks about his concern for people: their sadness, their heartbreak, their broken lives. (This is the legacy of The Studious Boy. The boy was father to the man.)

In 1835, Abe is struck down by the malaria then ravaging New Salem. He recovers and is asked to try a legal case. Friends tell him that Ann is down with "the fever" as well and wants to see him; he chooses to try the case (which he wins), but during the delay Ann is fading fast. He rushes to her home and enters her bedroom; they stare at each other without a word. In the scene, Abe stands in the doorway. Ann, as beautiful as ever, looks at him with sorrow and fear. He utters no words of comfort or love. We do not see her death; he emerges from the room in shock, says nothing, and staggers off, zombie-like in despair.

Abe slides into depression, telling his friend Jack Armstrong that he has killed three people: his mother, his sister, and Ann. He admits he was scared to marry Ann. He even thought of her death, something he did not want but somehow was "relieved" at the possibility. Now she is gone, and he is immobile with grief. If they had married, Ann would now be several months pregnant with his child.

His friend Bowling Green forces him to recognize that it was cold ambition that kept him from marrying Ann, and now he has to live with it for the rest of his life. He can die like Ann did, or he can start over. This is something he owes to himself, to all of his friends, and especially "to that dead girl." Agee puts his own moral twist on the tale. Remarkably, it is not Ann by her death who leaves Abe, but Abe who leaves Ann. It is Abe's heartbreaking moral imperative. For Lincoln this means despair and pain, but now he is free, truly free, of the burden of Ann Rutledge.

He cannot quite yet see the "big" thing that he will have to do, but with God's help he will find it and be fit for it. Abe rouses himself to go back to his legislative duties. As he rides out of town, he passes a simple wooden grave marker with "A.R." carved into it. It is a curious last scene: Abe rides by Ann's grave and, without looking down, simply tips his hat and rides on to Springfield. There is no graveside conservation with the dead Ann as in *Young Mr. Lincoln* or mournful farewell; his exit is perfunctory. He gives a quick tip of his hat as he passes her grave—that is all.

Because Agee's version of the affair generated a good deal of mail from viewers questioning the veracity of the story, the producers arranged a live television debate between Agee and Columbia University professor Alan Nevins. This imperious professor was a force to be reckoned with. He was in the process of writing what would be his magisterial eight-volume history of the Civil War, *The Ordeal of the Union* (1947–71). Journalist Alistair Cooke, the series host, led the discussion in front of a live audience. He called the bonus episode a "courtroom" of sorts in which the viewers would ultimately decide the truth about Ann and Abe.[95] In the session, Nevins claimed that *Mr. Lincoln,* despite its favorable audience reception, had little to do with the real Abraham Lincoln; this was uninformed popular history. Nevins was condescending; Agee was desolate but would not give in.[96]

NEVINS: He has tampered with the truth. He has taken a myth . . . and presented it to a great American audience as if it were verified truth.

AGEE: (*sick at the time, restless, and gazing upward*): It has been definitely proved that there is no Santa Claus, but of course there is a Santa Claus. There are two kinds of truths.

Yes, Agee admitted, he "was entirely guilty" of mythmaking. But it was myth in service to a deeper truth. He would not be bound to Nevins's narrow, unimaginative historicity. The story of Abe and Ann was not necessarily real, but it was truthful. In preparation for the series, before the encounter with Nevins, Agee wrote notes on his ideas about the romance: "I have always liked the Ann Rutledge legend, and I felt that through it, a good deal could be understood, and suggested, about Lincoln as a young man. . . . I can only hope—and believe—that . . . *if he did* love Ann Rutledge, this is more or less the way things happened." Later, Agee reflected on the issue and how legends contain a truth that will "awaken the heart and the soul."[97] At the end of the episode, as Lincoln rides away, we hear again the musical coda to his early life and the myths about the women who formed him. It is Nancy singing with the faint voice of an angel:

Speed bonnie boat like a bird on the wing
Onward the sailors cry.
Carry the lad that's born to be king

Even beyond what we know and do not know about Nancy Hanks Lincoln and Sarah Bush Johnston Lincoln, there is the enduring ambiguity of Lincoln's relationship with Ann Rutledge (1813–1835). She was either a chance acquaintance of Lincoln's in New Salem, Illinois, between 1833 and 1835 where Lincoln occasionally boarded with her family, or Ann Rutledge was the great, lost love of his life, whose death brought him close to suicide and then to chronic melancholy for the rest of his life. The ghost of "angelic" Ann Rutledge lingers on in Lincoln lore as a contrasting character to the "demonic" Mary Todd.

From Lincoln's former law partner William Herndon to the twentieth-century biographer and myth-maker Carl Sandburg, Ann embodied the prospect for love and happiness in Abe's life. For many others, the "romance" between Ann and Abe is just sentimental feel-good fiction. For the studio dream factories, however, the romance was real enough, and Lincoln's pain at her loss was deep, enduring, and prophetic. If Ann Rutledge had never lived, surely a screenwriter would have invented her. From *Young Mr. Lincoln:*

ABE: You're might pretty Ann.

ANN: Some folks don't like red hair.

ABE: I do.

ANN: Do you, Abe?

ABE: I love red hair.

HOLLYWOOD INTERPRETS THE TROUBLED COURTSHIP OF MISS OWENS AND MR. LINCOLN

In 2019, Sotheby's auction house possessed a letter (dated December 13, 1836) from Abraham Lincoln to Miss Mary S. Owens, a Kentucky belle. The company set the price at between $500,000 and $700,000. The documented provenance proved its authenticity (unlike the love letters in the Wilma Minor collection, it did not come through the intercession of a medium.)[1] It is the first of three letters that Lincoln wrote to Miss Owens during a curious and troubled courtship that lasted on and off for four years. Unlike the Abe Lincoln–Ann Rutledge affair, the Mr. Lincoln–Miss Owens affair is well documented and well known among Lincoln scholars and enthusiasts. But Mary never rivaled Ann Rutledge in Lincoln lore, and she appears in only one Lincoln film, "The Prairie Lawyer," episode 3 (April 1974) in the television miniseries *Sandburg's Lincoln.*

In 1836, one year after the Ann's death, an event that supposedly drove Lincoln to near suicide, Lincoln sought the affections of another woman— Miss Mary S. Owens. His quick rebound from the "tragedy" of Ann's demise led Mark E. Neely, a leading authority on Lincoln, to conclude that the brief interval between Ann's death and the appearance of Mary Owens in the romantic life of Abraham Lincoln "was an important step in deflating the Ann Rutledge myth."[2] Miss Owens herself, in response to an inquiry from William Herndon, stated in 1866: "As regards Miss Rutledge, I cannot tell you any thing [sic], she having *died* previous to my acquaintance with Mr. Lincoln; and I do not recollect of ever hearing him mention her name."[3] Does she protest too much? Surely, in a town as small as New Salem, someone, perhaps Mary's sister, told her about Ann, even if Lincoln never mentioned it. Here is a synopsis by Lincoln scholar Harold Holzer: His "first serious crush was on a chaste New Salem girl named Ann Rutledge, who was safely engaged to another suitor who left town for a trip. Her untimely death sent Lincoln into a deep depression but he later recovered enough to *half-heartedly* pursue a portly but well-to-do woman named Mary Owens who ultimately rejected him for his chronically indifferent behavior."[4]

Should Miss Owens be so easily dismissed? The leading authority on the relationship between Lincoln and Owens, Gerald McMurtry, writes, "For the romantic bent of the human mind, we have devoted columns of print to the pathetic story of Ann Rutledge, of which we know almost nothing, and seldom give more than passing mention to his affair with Mary Owens, of which there is an abundance of evidence."[5] The Owens story deserves more than a sidebar; the courtship of Mary and its portrayal in *Sandburg's Lincoln* offer real insight into the man and, importantly for the purposes here, a better understanding of the women in his life.

Mary Owens may have played only a supporting role, but if Lincoln is the hero of the common people, should not those people get more screen time? Film historian David Thomson says: "We are all supporting players in the lives of great hams who insist on being the center of attention" (*Guardian,* July 1, 2010). Lincoln is rightly always the center of attention. But the women who circle in and out of his life also deserve attention—women who were supporting actors in the drama of Abraham Lincoln.

Of the "portly" Miss Owens, we know this: She was born in Green County, Kentucky. Her father, Nathaniel Owens, was a planter, "a gentleman of considerable means." She was heavyset—five feet five inches tall and weighed between 150 and 180 pounds—"not pretty." Though "matronly," she had "fair skin," "deep blue eyes," and "dark curly hair," Sandburg writes.[6]

She was far less attractive than the lovely Ann of romantic imagination, but something appealing in her character transcended conventional beauty: "Spunky and unconventional," she was "good natured," well-dressed, sharp, and had a quick wit. In the nomenclature of the day, she was "gay and lively." A photograph of her shows her at middle age—a round face encased in a tight Victorian bonnet—her eyes set wide apart. A prominent chin. She is no beauty. Catherine Burns, the actress who plays Mary in the television series, is attractive with blond curls.[7] Burns has wide blue eyes and is pleasingly plump, though she is in no way fat. Her performance conveys Mary's self-confidence and lively spirit.

The real Mary Owens was something of a rebel who chafed at the social restrictions that defined a woman's place in mid-nineteenth-century society. In a sentence that has a remarkably modern ring to it, she stated to a male friend: "I am *transgressing* the circumscribed limits laid down by tyrannical custom, for our sex." She refused any "groveling."[8] Well-educated, Mary expected a good marriage. Her father was a wealthy slaveholder (in 1840, he held twenty-four people in bondage), a lawyer who served as a sheriff, a justice of the peace, and a county judge. In 1816, he sent Mary to the Nazareth Academy, a Catholic school. Later, he opened his own school, the Brush Creek Academy, where Mary herself taught and had access to a substantial library.[9]

When Lincoln courted her, she found him wanting. She met him in New Salem while visiting her sister, Mrs. Bennett Abell. Lincoln and Mary went riding together and attended other functions. She found him more than appealing, but he was frequently inattentive and lacking in gentlemanly qualities. During one outing, she complained, he failed to lead her horse across a creek as the other fellows did for their female companions. She then returned to Kentucky. It was a long-distance relationship. Though Lincoln's letters to Mary Owens went unanswered, the prospects still seemed promising to him.

MARY OWENS IN TELEVISIONLAND

Two scenes in the *Sandburg's Lincoln* episode "Prairie Lawyer" (1974) present a perceptive interpretation of the Lincoln-Owens affair. No record of their private conversations exists, but in brilliant performances, Hal Holbrook as Lincoln and Catherine Burns as Mary capture perfectly the nature of the courtship. Although the film necessarily invents scenes, it conveys feelings well supported by the historical evidence and the conventions of the era. In the first scene, Lincoln meets with Mary in Springfield after her long absence during which she failed to reply to his letters. Lincoln sits uncomfortably on a small, low couch, a floppy brown hat on his knees with his long, skinny legs drawn up near to his chest. Nervously, he looks to the right and left. Mary suddenly appears as a shadow in the doorway. At first, we do not see her face. As she addresses him, he jumps up and drops his hat.

MARY: I'd say your manners have improved.

LINCOLN: Well, I haven't had much occasion to polish them.

MARY: I thought your letters were most delicately phrased.

LINCOLN: But not worth answerin'.

MARY: I'm not good at letters. I believe in eyes. Do you believe in eyes, Mr. Lincoln?

LINCOLN: I read in the play of Richard the Second, ah, ah . . . "Even in the glasses of thine eyes, I see thy grieved heart." If Shakespeare can believe that eyes can communicate then I could not disbelieve. (*Abe stands and walks over to Mary.*) How was that?

MARY (*laughing*): From the man who would help a hog out of mudhole but wouldn't lend his arm to the lady he was with, it's a real improvement.

LINCOLN: (*moves to sit next to Mary*): Did I make any sense?

MARY: You know you did.

LINCOLN: I didn't mean you had a grieved heart.

MARY: I understand. I wouldn't confess it if it were. (*Lincoln takes her hand.*)

LINCOLN: Would you not tell me what your thoughts are?

MARY: What a cold hand.

LINCOLN: My hands are a long way from a fire.

MARY: What thoughts would you like to hear, Mr. Lincoln?

LINCOLN: We have matters pending.

MARY: Your proposal of marriage?

LINCOLN: If you take it serious.

MARY: Did you mean it seriously?

LINCOLN: If you took it that way. I wrote you.

MARY: Yes, I know.

At this point, Lincoln suddenly digresses with dark tales of "ugly things"—murder, lawlessness, and bitter race relations, a story hardly designed to foster romance. The first is about the lynching of Francis McIntosh but without mentioning his name. A mob hauled McIntosh, a mixed-race freeman accused of murdering a policeman in St. Louis in April 1863, from the jail, chained him to a tree, and burned him alive. Lincoln mentions newspaper editor Elijah Lovejoy as well, murdered by mob violence for his abolitionist opinions.[10] The third reference is to a miscarriage of justice involving a young defendant. In real life, Lincoln described the deaths of McIntosh and Lovejoy in a speech to the Springfield Young Men's Lyceum on January 27, 1837. The address championed the need for law and order, even if, as in the case of McIntosh, Lincoln believed the victim to be guilty. The speech marked a seminal event in Lincoln's life since it established his reputation as an effective orator. But here with Mary, Lincoln is curiously oblique. What is the point? Does he really want to marry her? This is no proposal; it is a warning about a life filled with sorrow.

> LINCOLN: If you would be pleased, I would be pleased. It's just I feel I have so little to offer I hesitate to ask anyone to share this countryside. You see I know this roughness is not your normal home way. The race question is bitter here and the politics (*pauses*) why even in St. Louis a free mulatto man was taken by a mob in the street and chained to a tree and burned to death. And in Alton, the white Presbyterian minister came to edit a newspaper, and they threw his press in the river and he was brave and he got himself another press shipped in and they burned that down, shot the man to death. And, and (*hesitates*) . . . it would be no boon to you to live in this place where a young boy who can only sign an "x" in place of his name could be hanged for a crime he probably didn't do. These are my thoughts, Miss Owens. (*pauses*) Maybe. There are ugly things here, not just in the South.

(She is not shocked nor does she comment on these "ugly things." A pause gives Lincoln the opportunity to tell one of his "stories.")

MARY: You're not ugly. I deny that you're ugly.

LINCOLN: Well, that's welcome news. It's only last week when a man offered to shoot me because he said I was uglier than he was and I didn't deserve to live.

MARY: Is this one of your stories, Mr. Lincoln?

LINCOLN: It's gospel truth, ma'am!

MARY: But you're still here!

LINCOLN: Well, I told him to go on and shoot cause if I was uglier than he was I didn't care to go on living. Poor man was dispirited into immobility. *(Mary laughs heartily.)*

MARY: I had forgotten what good company you could be.

The mood lightens; he inquires, in his county patois, if she still plays the "pie-ann-a." And does she still sing? Indeed, she replies, I play the "piano." She sings too:

> A frog went a-courtin' and he did ride, M-hm
> A frog went a-courtin' and he did ride, M-hm
> Sword and pistol by his side, M-hm
> He rode up to Miss Mousie's door, M-hm, M-hm

We next see Lincoln engaged at court in a murder case. In the concluding scene in the episode, Mary returns. She arrives at his law office in Springfield. Her visit is a surprise. There is a certain affection between them, but this is well short of love. Clearly, both are frustrated.

MARY: We had much pleasure in each other's company.

LINCOLN: Are you saying "no"?

MARY: There are many little things: courtesies, refinement, links in the chain of a woman's happiness—my happiness!

LINCOLN: That I don't know about.

MARY: They are not your way. I'm not part of this place. . . . No, I won't marry you, Mr. Lincoln. I wouldn't be happy and you wouldn't be happy with me. I came hoping to be convinced otherwise and while there is affection between us there is not the kind that makes for love of a lifetime.

LINCOLN (*taking her hand*): I am at fault because I don't have the knack of expressing the depth of . . .

MARY: No. Your failure is you lack the skill to hide your deepest feelings and now like the lawyer you are, you don't want to lose your case; you continue to plead although you know in your true heart that you are relieved. (*Mary goes to the door.*) If you come to visit me again, come as a friend. No more talk of marriage. I'd be delighted to see you, Mr. Lincoln.

After she leaves, Lincoln, alone in the parlor, sits down, looks at the floor, and, with disgust at his own failure and awkwardness, shakes his head and says out loud, "Frog went a-courtin' and he did ride."

In a long letter—more than 1,200 words—dated April 1, 1838, to Mrs. Orville Browning, a close friend and confidant, Lincoln recounted the story of the courtship that began in the fall of 1836. Depending on how it is read, the letter provides either a knee-slapping example of the proverbial Lincoln humor or reveals an unflattering streak of cruelty in the writer. Or, there is a third meaning: this was a way for him to explain obliquely his own awkwardness around women. He did not mention Mary Owens by name, but it is clear she is the brunt of the "joke": A lady friend intended to visit her family in Kentucky. When she returned to New Salem, she would bring her sister on the condition that Lincoln would marry her. This is a jolly idea. Let her come. Caution told him that the young lady might be a little too willing. Still, he "was most confoundedly well pleased with the project." The sight of her shocked him: "I knew she was over-size, but she now appeared a fair match for Falstaff; I knew she was called an 'old maid,' and I felt no doubt of the truth of at least half of the appelation [sic]; but now, when I beheld her, I could not for my life avoid thinking of my mother; and this, not from withered features, for her skin was too full of fat, to permit its contracting in to wrinkles"; he continues, "from her want of teeth, weather-beaten appearance in general, and from a kind of notion that ran in my head, that *nothing* could have commenced at the size of infancy, and reached her present bulk in less than thirty five or forty years; and, in short, I was not all pleased with her."

Yet, Lincoln pursued the relationship. He delayed as long as he could, then he proposed marriage. In fact, he proposed several times with no luck. She refused him. Was Lincoln really that serious about marriage? Or were his intentions a matter of honor only—an example of Lincoln's famously "indecisive matrimonial ambitions."[11] After all, he did write the lampoon of the relationship with Mary Owens on April Fool's Day. Was the joke on Mary or himself or both? "I very unexpectedly found myself, mortified almost beyond endurance," he wrote. "I was mortified, it seemed to me, in a hundred different ways. My vanity was deeply wounded." He abandoned the cause. "Others have been made fools of by the girls," he concluded, "but this can never be with truth said of me. I most emphatically, in this instance, made a fool of myself. I have now come to the conclusion never again to think of marrying; and for this reason; I can never be satisfied with anyone who would be block-head enough to have me."[12]

And what of Mary Owens? How did she remember the affair? In 1866, in a letter to William Herndon, she wrote bitterly, "The last message I ever received from him was about a year after we parted. He told my sister to say 'Tell your sister that I think she is a great fool because she did not stay here and marry me.' Characteristic of the man."[13] Regardless, she could not let go of Mr. Lincoln entirely. There is a clue to an enduring affection for Mr. Lincoln: she kept the three letters he wrote to her as small treasures and hid them away in the rafters of her house for safekeeping.

She went on to find a happy marriage to a Mr. Jesse Vineyard, with whom she had five children. And she maintained that vivacious, independent spirit. She would have made a good partner for the young lawyer—a woman, much like Mary Todd, well-educated, outspoken, and attuned to the broader prospects of life. But in Mary Owens's case, she was emotionally stable. A gravestone at the Pleasant Ridge Baptist Church cemetery in Weston, Missouri, reads:

Abraham Lincoln's Other Mary
Here Lies Mary Owens Vineyard
1808–1877
Who Rejected Abraham Lincoln's Proposal of Marriage in 1837[14]

In most versions of "Frog Went a-Courtin,'" Frog and Miss Mousie live happily ever after, but one version concludes:

Now is the end of him and her
Guess there won't be no tadpoles covered with fur.

WHEN ABE MET MARY

The Courtship and Marriage of Mary Todd and Abraham Lincoln on Film

Two Mary Lincolns occupy the popular and scholarly minds—the Bad Mary and the Good Mary. The former exhibits an infamously disagreeable personality. As a young woman she is a spoiled brat, unpopular, given to making sarcastic remarks. Later, she is the nagging, overbearing shrew—a loony harridan with a fiery temper. Explosive by nature, she wears her husband down verbally, physically, and emotionally; one painful outburst after another renders him cheerless and at times crestfallen. She is the cross the Great Man bears, the woman he weds but never loves. If Lincoln was the Man of Sorrow, Mary was his crown of thorns.

Prone to fits of extreme jealously, this Mary is also unfaithful to her husband. She governs her young sons with a harsh Victorian discipline. Pretentious (she speaks French with a comical accent). Rude, condescending, and officious, "Proud Mary" holds tight to personal and political grudges. She whips a reluctant Lincoln forward into public life. Nonetheless, the pair do not pursue the same ambitions. She craves sharing in the power and the glory of high office and advances inappropriate ambitions for herself in the public sphere and is furious at his reluctance to accept his vocation.

She meddles in public business and alienates members of the president's cabinet. More than a mere nuisance to the president and his staff, Mary is in fact a traitorous and conniving person, interfering with federal patronage for her own purposes and to benefit her relatives, leaking military secrets, and harboring rebel sympathizers in the Executive Mansion. She is an opium addict as well as a petty thief who pads expense accounts and defrauds the federal government. Woefully out of her element among the sophisticates of Washington, she publicly embarrasses her husband and scandalizes polite society with her odd and outrageous behavior. She is hysterical over the death of her son Willie, while thousands of mothers whose sons have died in the war bear their grief with quiet dignity. Gullible, she is easy prey to charlatans, flatterers, opportunists, unscrupulous shopkeepers, spirit mediums, and other oily manipulators. This vain woman is at once both pathologically parsimonious and a high-maintenance shopaholic. By 1875, her increasingly delusional behavior forces her loving son Robert to have her committed to a lunatic asylum. This is the trove of her faults and failures. Mary Lincoln, this vexed and troubled woman, is a disaster as a wife, as a mother, and as a First Lady.

The Good Mary is a spirited, coquettish, well-bred Kentucky belle. Progressively educated for the times, she speaks fluent French and is knowledgeable about local, state, national, even international affairs. Her talents overflow the mastery of domestic arts expected of the nineteenth-century woman. A clever conversationalist, she displays a quick intellect that complements Lincoln's exceptional mind. They share a love of books, poetry, and politics. And although their relationship began amid troubling moods of anxiety and indecision that resulted in a breakup of their first engagement, the romantic attraction between the two survived. The Good Mary adores her husband; he in turn adores her. He calls her "Mother" or "Molly." She calls him "Father" or, affectionately, "Mr. Lincoln." Good Mary is a devoted wife. After their marriage, she always refers to herself as Mary Lincoln and never as Mary *Todd* Lincoln.[1] He was, she wrote in 1869, her "lover— husband—father—& all, all to me—Truly my *all*."[2] It was a strong and enduring love: a marriage made not of female subordination but of modern companionship. She is generous and kindhearted. To her children, she is a caring, indulgent, even playful mother. A born politician at heart, she serves as Lincoln's ambitious political partner in an equal relationship. Because she defies the patriarchal expectations of her day, she is a subject of ridicule and suffers accordingly. She shares his Whiggish political persuasion (both she and Abe idolized Henry Clay), promotes his career, and revels in his success. She served him as a source of critical social and political connections and as a fashionable and savvy political hostess during the Illinois years. Later, as America's first "First Lady," her courtly presence graces elegant buffet receptions and popular levees. She ensures that the president is properly attired and invites literary figures to the Executive Mansion. She redecorates the People's House to reflect the dignity of a great nation. Further, she escapes her southern slaveholder family origins by espousing abolitionist sympathies well in advance of her husband's position on the issue.[3] During the presidential years, and for a time afterward, Mary embraces a free Black woman as her closest female confidant and counts Frederick Douglass among her friends. She raises money for a particularly unpopular cause—the relief of escaped enslaved people living in feculent contraband camps.[4] Quietly and without publicity, she attends wounded soldiers and writes letters to their families for them. She is loyal to both her husband and to the Union.

A creature of excitement, Mary Todd exhibits a sharp wit and an "unusual gift for sarcasm."[5] She fascinates men with the haughty "carriage of her head" and is "brilliant, witty, [and] well trained in all the social graces from earliest childhood." Young Mary is "a fascinating, alluring character."[6] A conflicted yet well-intentioned woman, Mary Lincoln of the Washington years and afterward has been much maligned by her enemies. She may not have been easy to live with, but she is much loved by her husband and children. Following the assassination, she fights with great energy and purpose for her right to a proper government pension, for her freedom from her unjust incarceration forced on her by the priggish Robert Lincoln, for a fitting design and location for her husband's tomb, and, ultimately, for her own dignity and reputation.

Who, then, was the real Mary? How does one make sense of the split personality and the multiple interpretations? Where does Bad Mary leave off and Good Mary begin? Did the two live side by side? Did one Mary, from time to time, yield the upper hand to the other? It is a challenge to convey Mary's complexity of character and personality—her "messy humanity."[7] Was she a person of bad character, dishonest and conniving? Did she have a deeply disturbed personality—is there a clinical explanation for her behavior? Making sense of the Lincoln marriage is equally challenging. Was Mary a political asset for Lincoln or the opposite? Was the Lincoln marriage a "domestic hell on earth," or was it the relationship embodied in the words on her Etruscan gold wedding ring—"A. L. to Mary, April 4, 1842, Love is Eternal"? Erika Holst, who has studied the motivations and rituals of courtship during Lincoln's Springfield years, states that "when the chips were down, he married for love. For Mary's part, she plainly declared 'my hand will never be given where my heart is not.'"[8]

The two Marys are contrapuntal and converge at the intersection of history, biography, film, and fiction. Mary is the only woman in Lincoln's intimate life for which enough documentation exists for a full biography. Life-story evidence for his birth mother, his stepmother, and for Ann Rutledge and Mary Owens is fragmentary at best. A plethora of evidence, and no little dispute, exists about Mary Todd Lincoln's public and private behavior and her physical and mental health. Her contrary nature, self-absorption, and self-destructive demons complicate attempts to understand her.

The secular Maryologists (biographers, historians, novelists, playwrights, and filmmakers) divide into bipolar camps, with the Bad Mary critics on one side and the Good Mary apologists on the other.[9] Lincoln biographer Michael Burlingame, chief among the modern Bad Mary critics, eviscerates the woman. Quoting the anti-Mary statements of William Herndon, the so-called "Herndon Informants," and close associates of Lincoln, among many other sources, he affirms that Mary Lincoln was a "perfect devil" who made the marriage "a hell on earth," a psychological graveyard ruled over by a "a hellion—a she-wolf."[10] Following publication of his Lincoln biography, Burlingame claimed he found shocking evidence of her moral and behavioral malfeasance. He also discovered, he claims, the cause of Mary's bilious nature—she suffered from premenstrual syndrome (PMS), a chronic and complex dysfunction resulting in physical pain and emotional stress. Its symptoms include anxiety, depression, mood swings, irritability, headache, and weight gain. Understanding her story, he states, is essential to understanding Lincoln: "If you don't tell that story, if you sweep it under the rug, then you miss an important element of what Lincoln had to deal with during the war. Not only did he have difficult generals, congressmen, senators, cabinet members, newspaper editors, and office seekers to deal with—on top of that, instead of a comforting haven from the outer world, it was even worse at home. It makes the sorrow he had to deal with throughout the war even more poignant." Nevertheless, Burlingame provides a soupçon of sympathy for Mary. "I hasten to add," he concludes, "that Mrs. Lincoln is more to be pitied than censured." Considering all the suffering in her life—the parental rejection and the deaths—"she had a great deal to cope with. I think a lot of her problems were inherited. Mental instability was a feature of many people in her family—brothers, sisters, nephews, nieces, uncles, and cousins,"[11] (To be fair to Mary, however, Lincoln for his part was far from an ideal husband, often away from home and distant in his emotions.)

Burlingame is less forgiving of Mary's biographers, who, he judges, have "written without fear and without research" about Mary Lincoln and "the legend of the happy marriage." These "Maryiolators," as he labels them, include Ruth Painter Randall, Jean Baker, and Catherine Clinton, among other "apologists for Mary Lincoln."[12] In 2021 he launched a second offensive against this school of thought in *An American Marriage: The Untold Story of Abraham Lincoln and Mary Todd.* He is particularly hard on Jean Baker, accusing her of shoddy research corroded by a politicized, feminist agenda.[13]

Burlingame and the other Bad Mary scholars, Baker counters, assume that because they dislike the woman, then Lincoln, too, must have loathed her: "We have too many historians deciding that they don't like Mary Lincoln and with extraordinary vehemence extrapolating their personal judgments into the [Lincoln] marriage.[14] Their ahistorical "judgmental style" fits rather too neatly into the legend of Lincoln's martyrdom.[15] Thus, "denigrating Mary Lincoln enhanced her husband's growing reputation of a man of tolerance and forbearance."[16] Importantly, they fail to understand Mary in context of the expectations for women and marriage in the nineteenth century. "Remember," Baker cautions, "this marriage was bound together by three strong bonds—sex, parenting, and politics. And keep in mind that story, corroborated by several observers, that when Lincoln learned that he had won the Republican nomination and later the Presidency, he hurried home, saying as he turned the corner, 'Mary, Mary we are elected.'"[17] Burlingame and Baker come across as if they are divorce lawyers arguing over whose client should get custody of Tad and Willie.

The case for Mary rests principally on the feminist position that she challenged the patriarchal restraints of the age. She challenged as well the potent image of Lincoln "as a man among men," as cultural historian John Dean states. "Lincoln possessed and has maintained a potent masculine identity," he further argues. "When Lincoln's personal secretary John Nicolay began doing field research in the 1870s for the biography that he and fellow Lincoln secretary John Hay would write, they did not interview a single woman. (And until quite recently Mary Todd Lincoln was seen as a drain on his masculine energies and reputation.) The Lincoln Memorial in

Washington is itself directly inspired by one of the seven wonders of the ancient world: the Temple of Zeus at Olympia."[18]

Mary's defenders point out that she was clever, curious about the larger world, and willful. In mid-nineteenth-century America, however, women like that faced stiff odds. Their proper role in the world, as historian Barbara Welter explains, existed only in their relationship to men. In important ways women were morally superior to men—if they understood their proper place in society. A good and true woman exhibited the virtues of piety, purity, submission, and domesticity. The outside material world of business and politics was the dominion of men; the interior world of the home was the dominion of women. Between 1785 and 1815, books and magazines began emphasizing the proper place of the mother in a family in particular and the proper place of a woman in society in general. A proper woman in America's emerging bourgeois society was religious, dependent, effeminate, passive, and responsive. The home was repurposed as the woman's realm. Here a true woman would find her authority, joy, and influence. The woman plays out her role in life first as a daughter, then as a wife, and then as a mother. This is heroic motherhood, her small yet critical enterprise while her man kept busy with the world's business. Yet, almost immediately upon the appearance of this vision of the woman's place, changes in the American economy and society began to undermine it. The cult of domesticity sought to put or keep a woman in her defined and proper place in a fast-changing world. Not all women conformed to its conventions. On the contrary, unconventional women, such as Mary Todd, confronted and subverted the system.[19]

This is the redeeming counternarrative. The smart, unconventional, unruly, and politically engaged Mary brought no little talent to the gender wars. Stacy Pratt McDermott, one of Mary's advocates, explains that she "understood politics better than many of her male contemporaries." She read widely, participated in political rallies, attended court cases, wrote political commentaries, gave advice, and stated opinions: "She enjoyed that engagement; it fueled her spirit and her mind, and it enriched her relationship with her famous husband."[20] In short, Mary was highly intelligent, sharped-tongued, emotional, passionate, and a perfectly companionable mate for Lincoln.[21]

In attitudes and actions, Mary audaciously affronted the cult of true womanhood, thereby suffering a long train of abuses. To counter earlier narratives of Mary's life, her allies revised her biography in the context of nineteenth-century class and gender history. They rewrote Mary's narrative without the "patriarchal thumb" on the scale.

MARY IN FILMLAND

To understand how Hollywood has portrayed "Mary Todd" and then "Mary Lincoln" and the variations on the theme of the Bad and Good Marys, observe the context of moviemaking in 1920s and 1930s. For all his many human faults, director D. W. Griffith, in his racist and controversial epic *The Birth of a Nation* (1915), first set the standard for quality American filmmaking in terms of storytelling and film techniques. "He was the teacher of us all," legendary film producer and director Cecil B. DeMille said. "Not a picture has been made since his time that does not bear some trace of his influence."[22] James Agee described Griffith as a "primitive tribal poet" who was unsurpassed "in epic, and visual and lyrical and narrative visual poetry" in filmmaking.[23] Yet, even by 1930, for all his genius at moviemaking and his seminal influence on American film history, he was out of step with the new Hollywood in presenting women, if not race, on film.

Griffith, born in 1875, possessed a Victorian persuasion that had a lengthy half-life in his films. His preference was "for standard sentimental melodrama of the nineteenth century and cheap fiction" with an "adherence to a shallow, sentimental code of morality" and an "insistence on conservative sentimentality."[24] He maintained this adherence to romantic, sentimental cinema when he approached making a film of Lincoln's life. The Victorian cult of true womanhood provided Griffith's frame of reference. Yet, the appearance of a "new" kind of woman in the films of the 1920s and 1930s subverted Victorian restraints. This New Woman, which Griffith could not understand, was endlessly represented in films of the 1920s and 1930s, aided and abetted by new technology as the silent era gave way to talking movies—which also baffled him.

To stifle calls for federal regulation and to avoid the chaos of individual city and state censorship, Hollywood studios themselves finally adopted what came to be known as "The Code," that is, the Motion Picture Production Code of 1934, or Hayes Code, which lasted until about 1968. The studios self-censored scenes and dialogue deemed licentious, grotesque, unpatriotic, pedophilic, pornographic, deviant, sacrilegious, or blasphemous. Before that, the pre-Code films of the period 1930–34—*Safe in Hell* (1931), the story of a New Orleans prostitute, for example—were often amazingly frank in their depiction of sexuality. The films of the early 1930s depicted a cynical and sexualized world populated by young women freed from Victorian restraints. The New Woman dressed provocatively, smoked, danced wildly, had affairs, and got divorced. In *Other Men's Women* (1931), Joan Blondell, playing a waitress, has this exchange:

> MARIE (Blondell): (*taking off her apron*) Anything else you guys want?
>
> RAILROAD WORKER AT LUNCH COUNTER: Yeah, gimme a big slice of you on toast and some French-fried potatoes on the side.
>
> MARIE: (*taking out her compact and powdering her face*) Listen, baby, I'm A.P.O.
>
> RAILROAD WORKER AT LUNCH COUNTER: (*to the other railroad worker*) What does she mean, A.P.O.?
>
> MARIE: Ain't Puttin' Out!

Like *Other Men's Women*, Barbara Stanwyck's *Babyface* (1934) is still surprising in its explicit depiction of a woman who sleeps her way to the top. In this scene, Stanwyck, as Lilly Powers, argues with her father, who has pimped out his own daughter:

> NICK POWERS (Robert Barrat): You little tramp, you!
>
> LILY: I'm a tramp, and who's to blame? My father. A swell *start* you gave me. Ever since I was fourteen, what's it been? Nothing but men! *Dirty* rotten men! And you're lower than any of them. I'll *hate* you as long as I live!

F. Scott Fitzgerald observed that Joan Crawford in *Our Dancing Daughters* (1928) "is doubtless the best example of the flapper, gowned to the apex of sophistication, the girl you see in smart nightclubs, toting iced glasses with a remote faintly bitter expression, dancing deliciously, laughing a great deal with wide hurt eyes. Young things with a talent for living."[25] The Code appeared five years into the Great Depression. But, in truth, the "bad girl" of the pre-Code movies was more exploited than liberated. The Code later forced filmmakers to be not only more discreet but, ironically, more creative. They toned down the flapper–jazz baby's overt sexuality and transmuted the "bad girl" into the more interesting wisecracking "dame" of the 1930s and 1940s "screwball comedies" such as *It Happened One Night* (1934) and *The Awful Truth* (1937). Women in these comedies are a match for any man, friend or foe. *The Palm Beach Story* (1942) represents the rapid repartee, silly plot convolutions, and riffs on marriage and divorce characteristic of the genre:

PRINCESS CENTIMILLIA (Mary Astor): I'd marry Captain McGloo tomorrow, even with that name.

JOHN D. HACKENSACKER, III (Rudy Vallée): And divorce him the next month.

PRINCESS CENTIMILLIA: Nothing is permanent in this world— except Roosevelt.

The Depression also resuscitated the familiar figure of Hollywood's cult of true womanhood—in this case the strong, loving mother who anchors a family crushed by hard times. Who better embodied this figure than Ma Joad (Jane Darwell) in *The Grapes of Wrath* (1940)? World War II produced more diverse images of women. The Ma Joads remained onscreen, though now alongside Rosie the Riveters and a host of women directly or indirectly involved in the war effort—either as faithful wives tending the home front while their husbands go to war or as individuals rushing to take on a wide variety of roles either in the defense plants or in the military, often as nurses (*So Proudly, We Hail!,* 1943).

A bleak variation of the wisecracking "dame" emerged in the figure of the mid-1940s to mid-1950s *femme fatale* in those remarkable *film noir* crime movies that featured beautiful, fascinating women who lure men into danger. These are women who, if necessary, sleep their way to the top (or at least to the middle) or murder, sometimes out of greed for money or freedom from a man's control. Barbara Stanwyck went from pleasure-seeking temptress in *Babyface* to lethal seductress in *Double Indemnity* (1944). In this scene, the potential murderers circle each other like a pair of scorpions:

PHYLLIS DIETRICHSON: There's a speed limit in this state, Mr. Neff. 45 miles an hour.

WALTER NEFF (Fred MacMurray): How fast was I going, officer?

PHYLLIS: I'd say around 90.

WALTER: Suppose you get down off your motorcycle and give me a ticket.

PHYLLIS: Suppose I let you off with a warning this time.

WALTER: Suppose it doesn't take.

PHYLLIS: Suppose I have to whack you over the knuckles.

WALTER: Suppose I bust out crying and put my head on your shoulder.

PHYLLIS: Suppose you try putting it on my husband's shoulder.

Body Heat (1981), a *film noir* knockoff, reanimated the *femme fatale* in the age of twentieth-century feminism. Here the beautiful and cunning Matti (Kathleen Turner) responds to sad-sack lawyer Ned Racine's attempt to pick her up:

NED (William Hurt): Then you should have said—"I'm a happily married woman."

MATTY: That's my business.

NED: What?

MATTY: How happy I am.

NED: And how happy is that?

MATTY: You're not too smart, are you?

(Racine shakes his head "No.")

MATTY: I like that in a man.

Overt sexuality aside, imagine another Mary Todd or Mary Lincoln as a smart, politically engaged, sharp-talking companion to Lincoln—a feisty heroine for the modern age instead of the clichéd melodramatic Victorian shrew or the unstable neurotic. What if Hollywood had created a modern Mary in Lincoln films who represented a high-spirited woman in the likeness of Barbara Stanwyck or Joan Crawford or, as we will see, the smart Ruth Gordon who played Mary Todd Lincoln as a hard-faced shrew in *Abe Lincoln in Illinois?* This famous character actress was also a successful screenwriter. In the classic *Adam's Rib* (1949), Gordon created this piece of exquisite dialogue:

AMANDA BONNER (Katharine Hepburn): After you shot your husband . . . how did you feel?

DORIS ATTINGER (Judy Holliday): Hungry!

What if screenwriters had given Ruth Gordon as Lincoln's Mary something original and witty to say? How would this Mary have competed with the diaphanous spirit of Ann Rutledge? Sometimes they got close to creating such a Mary but then backed off. A Mary in genuine partnership with her husband on film would be a fascinating creature.

Regarding Mary, there was more than enough material beyond her emotional instability for an imaginative studio writer to work with—her unhappy childhood, her unconventional beauty, her first-class mind, her connection to the ruling elites, and her fascination even as a young girl with politics—"Miss Mary," age thirteen, alone and unannounced, the story goes, once rode her new poney to visit her idol Henry Clay. A contemporary provided this description of Mary Todd: "Although not strictly beautiful, [she] was more than pretty. She had a broad white forehead: eyebrows sharply but delicately marked, a straight nose, short upper lip and expressive mouth curling into an adorable slow coming smile."[26] In Louis Bayard's novel *Courting Mr. Lincoln* (2019), Mary stands before a mirror and accesses her reflection: "Arms: shapely. Shoulders: smooth. Complexion: good. Forehead: too broad. Cheeks: too ruddy. Face: a touch too round. Hair: chestnut with a hint of bronze. Eyes: blue, shading toward violet. Eyelashes: silky. Lips: curled. Teeth: small. Figure: full, with the tiniest suggestion of stoutness."[27] Carl Sandburg provided an equally impressionistic interpretation of her character: "She embodied a thousand cunning, contradictory proverbs men have spoken about woman as wildcat and as a sweet angel. She was vivid, perhaps too vivid."[28] What did Sandburg mean by "too vivid"? Was she too animated, too authentic, too intense, too outspoken in ways that would distract from his main character, the humble Abraham Lincoln?

Mary and Abe were an odd couple both in appearance and in social origins. She was five foot two and stout, he was six foot four and lean. (Lincoln joked that their comic disproportion of two feet was "the long and the short of it!").[29] She had twelve years of formal education; his fragmented schooling lasted less than twelve months. She came out of the Louisville version of American aristocracy; he was from the hardscrabble frontier. Her father was a banker, state senator, and slaveholder; his father was a failed dirt farmer.[30] She lived in a fine house on Aristocracy Hill; he grew up in a series of ramshackle frontier cabins and crude taverns. She was fashion conscious; he was famously disheveled. She, a coiled spring, easily took offense; he was self-deprecating. She sought solace in the Presbyterian Church and séances; he was a skeptic. She appeared at receptions decked out in sophisticated Paris-styled finery; he squirmed in formal attire.

In Griffith's 1930 biopic *Abraham Lincoln,* actress Kay Hammond[31] plays Mary Todd as a self-confident and high-spirited southern belle determined to marry the right man. But who is the right man? Mary, in real life as in the film, had her choice of beaus, among them the accomplished Stephen Douglas and the shy, young lawyer Abraham Lincoln. At twenty-one and unmarried in 1840, Mary was approaching being a spinster left on the shelf. At this point Douglas, quite the dandy, was the more successful suitor. An easterner by birth, he had come to the West to seek his fortune. Fortunate indeed, he found success in Illinois as a lawyer, judge, and state legislator. The great debates of 1858 with Lincoln for a US Senate seat and the presidential contest of 1860 lay in the future. This first contest is between the two over the hand of the sparkling Mary Todd. A prescient observer, Mary sees potential in Abe, the callow young lawyer (played by Walter Huston), over his rival, the elegant and accomplished Stephen Douglas (E. Alyn Warren):

The Scene: Springfield, Illinois. It is evening at the elegant home of Ninian and Elizabeth Edwards.

ELIZABETH EDWARDS (*Mary's sister*): My goodness, Mary Todd, just think! *He'll* be here in a few minutes . . . the catch of America! Stephen A. Douglas! Just think of being his wife!

MARY: Don't be in such a hurry, Sister. I'm not even engaged yet, much less married.

ELIZABETH: But if he *should* propose?

MARY: How do I know he's going further than anyone else in Springfield? When I pick a husband, sister, I'll pick a *man!* But I don't know what you're talking about. A lot of people seem to think a man named . . . ah . . . Abraham Lincoln is going even further than Mr. Douglas.

ELIZABETH: Why, Mary Todd, have you gone crazy! You compare an unknown cornfield lawyer with a brilliant cultured gentleman like Stephen A. Douglas! Why, if you just saw the two of them together.

THE MAID: Oh, he's here! Mr. Douglas is down in the parlor and he's asking for Mary!

ELIZABETH: Now, Mary, you must be very careful, and remember he doesn't like to have girls too bold.

MARY: Don't get so excited, sister, and don't hurry me. I'll take care of myself.

Later, as Mary and Douglas dance, an uncomfortable Lincoln, his coat sleeves too short, stands against the wall fiddling with his tie and ill-fitting vest. Mary giggles at his awkwardness. Though he is physically clumsy and socially graceless, Mary finds Lincoln amusing in his endearing clodhopper way and much more interesting than the pompous Mr. Douglas:

DOUGLAS (*dancing with Mary*): You glide through the dance like grace itself, Miss Todd.

MARY: Always the politician, Mr. Douglas!

DOUGLAS: Who wouldn't be a politician with so fair a constituent to win? (*as the dance ends*)—Exquisite!

MARY: The fan, Mr. Douglas?

DOUGLAS: No, the fair owner herself. May I look?

(*She hands him the fan*)

LINCOLN (*strides over to the couple*): Why, Mr. Douglas . . . I wonder if you'd do me a great favor?

DOUGLAS: Yes.

LINCOLN: And pray present me to this young lady.

DOUGLAS: Miss Todd?

MARY: Yes?

DOUGLAS: May I present one of the leading lawyers of Springfield, Mr. Abraham Lincoln?

MARY: Mr. Lincoln.

LINCOLN: Miss Todd, I wonder if you'd honor me with the next dance? (*Mary giggles*)

MARY: Why . . . why . . . I'd be delighted. (*Mary continues to giggle as they begin to dance. . . .*)

LINCOLN: Miss Todd, you thought my face was funny, and the way I dressed even funnier, but the joke's on you.

MARY: Why, I don't understand.

LINCOLN: Wait till you dance with me.

(*As the scene ends, Mary continues to giggle at his clumsy performance on the dance floor.*)

1939: HOLLYWOOD'S GOLDEN YEAR

A universal consensus deems 1939 as the greatest year in Hollywood's classic period. From the various dream factories that year emerged 365 films, including some of the most enduring productions. December 1939 saw MGM release *Gone with the Wind* (*GWTW*), which, despite its flaws, is the greatest of all the films of the classic Hollywood. It may, in fact, be the greatest American film ever made since it contains all the elements that made Hollywood the world's preeminent filmmaker. It took Griffith's racist stereotypes and the Lost Cause ideology and gave them a "respectable" re-imagining. *GWTW* reanimated the corpse of *The Birth of a Nation* and used

Technicolor (only one of eight films to use it in 1939) to create the compelling story of a determined woman's struggle through the hard times of the Civil War and Reconstruction. It was not as lethally vile as its 1915 predecessor but still misleading because of its benign depiction of slavery. As 1939 was also a good year for biopics (Richard Dix as Sam Houston; and Don Ameche as Alexander Graham Bell), 1940 continued to inspire and reassure an anxious public with uplifting stories of Great Americans: Don Ameche as Stephen Foster; Tyrone Power as Brigham Young; Mickey Rooney as the young Thomas Edison, Spencer Tracy as Edison the grown-up; Jon Hall as Kit Carson; and Pat O'Brien as Knute Rockne. In time of crisis America needed national heroes.

But in 1939, it is a woman who eclipses all the men on film: Scarlett O'Hara (Vivien Leigh) as *GWTW*'s protagonist—a woman of ambition, skill, ruthlessness, and courage who defines her own place in the world of men. This is another example of how screenwriters might have created a Mary Lincoln to be remembered. What if cinematic Mary had exhibited the same pluck and exceptionalism as Scarlett O'Hara? As film critic Roger Ebert observes, "Women are rarely allowed to be bold and devious in the movies; most directors are men, and they see women as goals, prizes, enemies, lovers and friends but rarely as protagonists."[32]

The range of films during that golden year of 1939 offered something for every taste. MGM's *The Wizard of Oz* gave the world images both memorable (a cowardly lion, a scarecrow, a tin man), terrifying (a wicked witch and her flying monkeys), and a still-famous song about a rainbow. *Gunga Din* valorized the British Empire in India. James Stewart portrayed a naïve politician in *Mr. Smith Goes to Washington.* Hollywood examined both sides of crime in *The Roaring Twenties* and *Another Thin Man.* The Wild West came alive in *Jesse James, Dodge City, Union Pacific,* and *Destry Rides Again* (with James Stewart and Marlene Dietrich playing fast and loose with the tropes of the American western). The Marx Brothers in *At the Circus,* W. C. Fields in *You Can't Cheat an Honest Man,* and Shirley Temple in *The Little Princess* (another of the eight Technicolor films produced that year) provoked laughs and smiles. Fred Astaire's dancing continued to dazzle in *The Story of Vernon and Irene Castle.* Drama and comic drama arrived in attractive packages: *Wuthering Heights, Goodbye Mr. Chips, Dark Victory, Only Angels Have Wings, The Women, Beau Geste, Of Mice and Men, The Adventures of Sherlock Holmes, Love Affair* (remade in the 1957 as *An Affair to Remember,* it became a clever plot device in *Sleepless in Seattle,* 1993), *Juarez, Midnight,* and *Ninotchka* (in which Garbo not only "talks" for the first time onscreen but actually laughs).

For the master filmmaker John Ford, 1939 was an exceptional year. He directed not only *Young Mr. Lincoln* but also *Drums along the Mohawk* and the far more influential *Stagecoach,* John Wayne's breakout film. In 1938, screenwriter Lamar Trotti found an early draft of *Young Mr. Lincoln* written by Howard Estabrook in the files of Twentieth Century–Fox. Estabrook was an actor, director, producer, and writer whose screenplay for *Cimarron* (1931) won an Oscar. The possibilities fascinated Trotti.

While working as a journalist in Georgia, he had covered a murder case closely resembling the Duff Armstrong trial, the central event of the film.[33] Trotti showed the early script to Darryl F. Zanuck, who then recruited John Ford for the production. According to Zanuck, Trotti was "practically an authority on Lincoln."[34] He conceived of Mary's first appearance in the story differently than Griffith.[35] But as in Griffith, "The idea of the picture," Ford said, "was to give the feeling that even as a young man you could sense there was going to be something great about this man."[36] For the famed film critic Pauline Kael, Ford's Lincoln is a "man so humane and so smart that he can outwit the unjust and save the innocent." He is "the Lincoln of our dreams."[37]

John Ford is so identified with masculine identity and how it manifests in a variety of settings, most notably in his western films, that the roles women play in his films are often relegated to footnote status. Film historian David Meuel, in his selective analysis *Women in the Films of John Ford (2014),* titles his concluding chapter "Dare We Call Ford a Feminist? The Director's Achievement in Context." Meuel asserts that "One of Ford's great strengths as a conveyor of women's experiences and perspectives is the great variety of female characters featured in his films. There is no one type of 'Fordian female' the way there is a 'Hawksian woman.'"[38] Meuel does not mention Mary Todd Lincoln at all and refers to Ann Rutledge only obliquely when praising Vera Miles's performance in *The Man Who Shot Liberty Valence* (1962): "Hallie [Vera Miles] and Link Appleyard [Andy Devine] ride out to Tom's [John Wayne] ranch and Link cuts a cactus rose for Hallie [which she puts on Tom's grave]. The music is Alfred Newman's 'Ann Rutledge' theme reprised from . . . *Young Mr. Lincoln,* a piece about lost, never-to-be-recovered love."[39]

Nevertheless, Meuel makes a strong point that the alcoholic Ford, despite being verbally abusive to women and, like Griffith, a relic of late Victorian attitudes toward women, managed to transcend some of the flaws in his own personality and in his own films. Five actresses in them were nominated for Academy Awards over the decades, four for Best Supporting Actress and one for Best Actress: Edna Mae Oliver for *Drums along the Mohawk* (1939), Jane Darwell for *The Grapes of Wrath* (1940), Sara Allgood for *How Green Was My Valley* (1941), and Grace Kelly for *Mogambo* (1953). Ava Gardner won the Best Actress Award for *Mogambo.* Meuel repudiates film critic Andrew Sarris's claim that, "As might be expected, the actresses are fairly marginal creatures in Ford's masculine cosmos."[40] Meuel asks us to consider the range of performances (among the many that could be cited) by Jean Arthur in *The Whole Town's Talking* (1935), Claire Trevor in *Stagecoach* (1939), Mildred Natwick in *She Wore a Yellow Ribbon* (1949), Joanne Dru in *Wagonmaster* (1950), Maureen O'Hara in *Rio Grande* (1950) and *The Quiet Man* (1951), Olive Carey in *The Searchers* (1956), Vera Miles in *Liberty Valence,* and even in Ford's last film, Anne Bancroft in *7 Women* (1966). At the end Meuel responds to his repeated question, "Dare we call Ford a feminist?" with an ironic, "Why not?"[41] He was certainly called worse things. The focus is on Mary's political ambition, not Lincoln's, when she first meets young Abe. Unfortunately, Ford could have developed Mary's character far more broadly. (John Cromwell, an experienced but far less talented director than John Ford, did much more with Mary than Ford did in *Abe Lincoln in Illinois*—a far less accomplished film than *Young Mr. Lincoln.*)

Trotti introduced Mary Todd in an early treatment of the script for *Young Mr. Lincoln.* The Scene: Independence Day celebration. A sidewalk on Springfield's courthouse square. A parade of Revolutionary War and Black Hawk War veterans representing US and Illinois history, including "two or three feathered Indians." Stephen Douglas and Mary Todd along with Ninian Edwards and his wife, Elizabeth, appear walking through the crowd. "Douglas is about Lincoln's age, but there is no greater contrast between two rivals. Whereas Lincoln is tall and angular, Douglas is short, about 5 feet 4—and stout. His [Lincoln's] is a boyish face." Douglas (as played by Milburn Stone) is aristocratic in manner and fashionable in dress: "A gallant champion of the ladies, he shines in society—whereas Lincoln (the young Henry Fonda) is shy and almost boorish. Mary is likewise short, rather plump, and exquisitely dressed. She carries a parasol over her head, and wears a gay, extravagant bonnet."[42] Before Lincoln arrives, Douglas woos Mary in an episode that touches briefly on her outspokenness and ambitions. Ford, however, removed the Douglas-Mary dialogue in the final cut, to focus on Lincoln. The deleted scene illustrates the potential for development in Mary's character:

MARY (*with a smile at Douglas*): Mr. Douglas, I've been hearing some mighty fine things about you—even down in Kentucky. I told my sister *you* were the *very* first gentleman I wanted to meet in Springfield.

DOUGLAS (*highly pleased*): You'll forgive me, ma'am, but all of Springfield has been warned not only against the beauty of Miss Mary Todd, but against the prettiness of her Southern speeches.

MARY (*pretending to be shocked*): Why, Mr. Douglas! Everybody who *knows* me, knows I'm awfully sincere. I just say what I mean.

DOUGLAS (*already in her coils*): So, I'm beginning to see, ma'am.

MARY: In fact, my family and friends always say I'm *too* frank about the people I like. They say I'm only interested in men I think will be famous, but I tell them it's just because I can only admire intelligent men.

DOUGLAS (*delighted*): The thought does honor to one so young.

MARY (*with a slightly disparaging laugh*): Sister says I'll never really be happy until I marry a man who'll be President. But I tell her I'd rather marry a good man with a good mind who has a chance to be famous, than to marry any other man, even though he had all the Negroes and gold in the world.

By changing the emphasis and dialogue, Ford refocuses on Lincoln's arrival at the parade:

ELIZABETH: Mary, this is Mr. Abraham Lincoln.

(*bows stiffly to Mary and then sits down on the curb by the side of the group who are seated on a dais*)

After the initial greeting, Douglas, seated next to Mary, ignores Lincoln. Mary, however, is fascinated.

> MARY (*leaning forward*): I've been hearing some mighty fine things about you, Mr. Lincoln.
>
> LINCOLN (*lightly*): Don't believe everything Douglas here says about me, ma'am. We kind of straddle different political fences.
>
> MARY (*with great earnestness*): Oh, but I haven't been discussing you with any other gentlemen. My sister told me about you. You're in the legislature, aren't you?
>
> LINCOLN (*looking away from Mary*): If you'll put that in the past tense, I'll plead guilty. I *was* in the legislature.
>
> DOUGLAS: Mr. Lincoln's practicing law with John Stuart, who beat me for Congress.
>
> LINCOLN: That's a mighty flattering way he puts it, ma'am, when what I'm really doing is wearing a hole in Stuart's best rocking chair.

Later, included in the film, Lincoln receives an invitation to a supper dance hosted by Ninian Edwards. As the scene opens, Young Lincoln is off center stage telling a funny story to three older men. Douglas, once again, is courting Mary:

> DOUGLAS (*gallantly*) Upon my word, ma'am, in all my experience I have never danced with a more graceful and charming partner. (*Mary is now seated. Douglas stands before her.*)
>
> MARY (*smiling graciously—inclining her head*): I'm awfully glad that you don't share Mr. Lincoln's aversion to feminine society.
>
> DOUGLAS: Oh, Mr. Lincoln's a great story teller. Like all such actors, he revels in boisterous applause.
>
> MARY (*laughs lightly and looks toward Lincoln*): And yet, Ninian says it was his wit that saved those two wretched boys.
>
> (*Here Mary is referring to an earlier scene in the film in which Lincoln as the defense attorney for two boys accused of murder dissuades a lynch mob.*)

DOUGLAS (*magnanimously*): Unquestionably, he has ability in handling an unthinking mob. Not even his enemies deny that he has a certain political talent.

(*Mary looks at Douglas and smiles enigmatically. Lincoln, surrounded by the group of admirers, glances across the room at Mary.*)

GRAY-HAIRED GENTLEMAN: Mr. Lincoln, are you by any chance a member of the well-known Lincoln family of Massachusetts?

LINCOLN: Not by any chance I know of.

GRAY-HAIRED GENTLEMAN: A very fine old family—very fine.

LINCOLN: Then I say the evidence is all against us belonging to it. No Lincoln I ever knew amounted to a hill of beans.

(*Mary Todd, her head high, her manners imperious, heads toward Lincoln and interrupts the group.*)

MARY: Mr. Lincoln (*the three men step aside as Mary interrupts the conversation*) In the part of the South I come from, it's customary for a gentleman to ask the visiting lady to dance with him. Wouldn't you care to ask me?

LINCOLN (*smiling*): I'd like to dance with you the worst way, ma'am, but since all the dancing I've ever done was behind the plow, I'm afraid I wouldn't cut much of a figure alongside a fancy stepper like Mr. Douglas here.

MARY (*with quiet force*): Mr. Lincoln, I shall be very glad to dance this dance with you.

(*She reaches out, takes his hand and draws him away. As they go, Douglas and the other men look after them. Douglas is far from pleased. As she goes into his arms, the music is still playing, couples are dancing.*)

LINCOLN (*hesitating*): You've heard of the old saying: "Don't let your left hand know what your right hand is doing. Just apply that to my feet, and you'll have a rough idea of what you've got yourself into.

You can discern Carl Sandburg's poetic hand in Hollywood's creation of the Abe and Mary story: "Miss Mary Todd was twenty-two years old, plump, swift, beaming, with ready answers slipping from a sharp tongue. . . . She had her gifts, a smooth soft skin, soft brown hair, and flashing blue eyes. With her somewhat short figure sheathed in a gown of white with black stripes, cut low at the neck and giving free play to her swift neck muscles, her skirt fluffed out in a slightly balloonish hoop, shod in modish ballroom slippers, she was the center of likes and dislikes." As for her manner: "Though her tongue and its sarcasm that came so quickly and so often, brought dislikes and likes, there was a shine and a bubbling, a foaming over of vitality."[43]

In the original script but missing in the final cut for *Abe Lincoln in Illinois*, Mary holds firmly to Lincoln's arm and they start off. Lincoln was right; he is no dancer. He stumbles and slides, and Mary almost loses her balance. They bump into other couples, thoroughly disrupting the dancing. Finally, Mary must stop. In the final cut, none of this occurs. Instead, when he engages with Mary, Lincoln is near speechless and excessively formal. He bows formally to her and leads her into the dance. His movements are stiff with long, looping strides—not disastrous by any means. Though Mary is used to more elegant partners, she finds his frontier awkwardness endearing.

Alas, the famous dance scene is an "amusing legend" about the first encounter between the two. In the event, she found this man fascinating: "He was in every respect—background, looks, manners, mentality—totally unlike any man she had ever met. She became almost immediately intrigued by him, and he by her."[44] Though the story is certainly not true, it makes for effective screenwriting. So effective, in fact, that Ford reimagined the moment in his classic western *My Darling Clementine* (1946). In the film, marshal Wyatt Earp (again, Henry Fonda) dances with the pretty Clementine (Cathy Downs). Fonda moves exactly as he did with Mary Todd as the young Abe Lincoln. He first bows stiffly and then leads her with long, looping strides to the sound of a fiddle. In both films they skip to the same lively tune, "Hello, Susie Brown."

After the dance, from *Young Mr. Lincoln:*

MARY (*laughing*): Mr. Lincoln, at least you're a man of honor. You said you would dance with me the worst way, and I must say you've kept your promise. This is the worst way I've ever seen.

LINCOLN (*smiling*): I warned you.

MARY (*determinedly*): Shall we go outside and talk instead of dancing, Mr. Lincoln?

(*She takes his arm and they move to the porch.*)

Once on the porch and alone with Mary, Lincoln ignores her and says nothing. He is sad and deep in thought. He thinks not of his angel mother, as in Griffith's film, but of Blessed Ann of New Salem. Remarkably, there is no dialogue; Trotti imagines what Lincoln is thinking: "As they come from the house and stroll across the porch, Lincoln has suddenly become absent-minded—almost indifferent. Mary shoots sly glances at him, taking his indifference for shyness. As they come to the porch bench, Mary disengages her arm, arranges her skirt, and sits down. Then Lincoln, almost forgetful of her, looks across the river. Mary looks up at him." At this point Trotti evokes the spirit of Ann Rutledge, as Lincoln is never free of the specter: "To Lincoln, the river means one thing only—Ann, the woman he has loved. Mary, of course, suspects nothing of this. To her Lincoln is just an awkward man—from a different sphere of life—ill at ease in the presence of a glamorous woman. She will set him at ease—will give him to understand that though great lady that she is, she is not inaccessible, if only the man will do her bidding." Though removed from the final shooting script, Trotti imagined another scene to end the film:

VOICE OF GOD: Well, young fellow, it looks like you're on your way! (*Lincoln straightens up quickly, looks around.*)

LINCOLN: What's that?

(*There is a chuckle, but no one appears.*)

VOICE OF GOD: Just me. (*As Lincoln continues to look around.*) Stop twistin' yourself all out of shape. You know who it is.

LINCOLN: (*grinning*) For a minute there, you had me fooled.

VOICE OF GOD: (*with a chuckle in it*) Mary Todd seemed right pleased, didn't she? (*as Lincoln nods*) Fine woman, Mary, but a little sharp-tongued and outspoken! Still, if you hadn't married her, there's no tellin' what'd become of you.

LINCOLN: Married her!

VOICE OF GOD: (*philosophically*) That's the trouble. We men never know what we'd amounted to if we'd married the other woman.

LINCOLN: (*agreeing*) Yes—I sometimes think if Ann had lived . . .

The Voice leads Lincoln into a discussion of his past and his future. As Lincoln peers into the distance he sees a train chugging along, draped in black, accompanied by a chorus of moaning—"The moaning rises in intensity until it seems to be the voices of grieving thousands." It was wise to exclude this ham-handed scene, but it does indicate the persistence of the myth of sweet Ann of New Salem versus Mary, the Witch of Springfield. Screenwriters could not let go of so simple and dramatic a contrast.

■ ■ ■

Before going to California to eventually write twenty-one scripts, eleven of them for John Ford, including *The Searchers* (1956), Frank Nugent wrote hundreds of reviews for the *New York Times.* On June 3, 1939, his short review of *Young Mr. Lincoln* appeared, followed on February 23, 1940, by a longer review of *Abe Lincoln in Illinois,* directed by John Cromwell. Nugent had already written enthusiastic reviews of *Stagecoach* and *The Grapes of Wrath.*

Nugent called *Young Mr. Lincoln* "one of the most human and humorous of the Lincoln biographies" and characterized Henry Fonda's Lincoln as "one of those once-in-a-blue-moon things: a crossroads meeting of nature, art, and a smart casting director." While Fonda's Lincoln "dominates the picture, Director John Ford and Scriptwriter Lamar Trotti never have permitted it to stand out too obviously against its background—the Midwestern frontier." Nugent concludes that the film "is not merely a natural and straightforward biography, but a film which indisputably has the right to be called Americana. . . . [I]t is a journey most pleasant to share."

Later, *Abe Lincoln in Illinois,* "a great picture and a memorable biography of the greatest American of them all," earned a longer review from Nugent. He identifies the place of the film in the context of its time: "There isn't, by jingo, a trace of jingo. . . . There isn't a touch of national complacency, of patronage or boastful pride. But Lincoln, and the film . . . about him, is a grave, sincere and moving and eloquent tribute to these United States and to what they stand for, and must stand for, in these and future times."

In Robert Sherwood's script, the ghost of Ann Rutledge continues to haunt Lincoln after his marriage to Mary. "Lincoln's commitment to Rutledge," film citic and historian J. E. Smyth states, "always questioned by professional historians, is central to *Abe Lincoln in Illinois* and is treated as the crucial event in Lincoln's life." [45] The contrast between Ann and Mary could not be clearer. Whereas Ann was all innocence, Mary Todd is all calculation. Ann was artless; Mary is designing. Mary Todd inhabits a world of accomplishment and sophistication, a refined society of elegant form and high fashion a world away from simple Ann and the country bumpkins of New Salem. Sherwood provides much more background than Griffith or Ford to the early relationship between Abe and the Todd family. He places emphasis on the difference in social class between Mary (Ruth Gordon), the high-spirited sophisticate, and Lincoln (Raymond Massey), the melancholy, down-to-earth, unambitious small-town lawyer—the sad, soulful hero of the common man. Massey was a hit in the role onstage and in film. Gordon, however, steals every scene in which they appear together. Never beautiful by Hollywood standards, Gordon was a "sharp-faced, middle-aged woman" in 1940 who, nevertheless, had commanding presence on the screen.[46] Gordon was forty-four when she played Mary, too old for the role. Mary Todd was twenty-one when she met Lincoln in 1840. Lincoln was ten years her senior. Cromwell insisted that Gordon have a severe Victorian look: "I want your hair Chinese black." Instead of dying her hair, Gordon wore a "Chinese black wig" custom-ordered through Max Factor, Hollywood's famous makeup artist.[47]

> The Scene: The law office of Lincoln and Herndon. Abe and his hard-drinking young law partner, Billy Herndon (Alan Baxter), are discussing the Todd family's invitation to a dance.

> BILLY: He [Ninian Edwards] wants you to meet his sister-in-law, Miss Mary Todd, who has just arrived from Kentucky.

> LINCOLN: You don't say so? Well, I am becoming a social success.

> BILLY: Yes, Mr. Lincoln you are. And I'm afraid you are enjoying it.

LINCOLN: Well, the Todd family are mighty high-class people. Spell their name with two Ds, which is pretty impressive when you consider one was enough for God.

It is unclear why Sherwood's Billy believes Abe is enjoying his social success. Lincoln gives no indication of this in the film. The real Herndon would have attributed Lincoln's success to what he called Lincoln's ambition (that "little engine that knew no rest") to move up in society, to leave behind the backwoods of his childhood and early youth, to find fulfillment in the law, the legislature, and, finally, the presidency.

The origin of Mary's ambition is exhibited but not explored. To fulfill her desires, she needed to attract a man such as Lincoln, someone, essayist Joshua Wolf Shenk concludes, who shared her politics and, she hoped, her ambition, her destiny. The ritual of courtship provided Mary her entrée into the exciting world of men and politics—her escape from the strait-jacket of female domesticity. Her "power was not in the vote but in the veto. What made Mary Todd ambitious—a dubious compliment for a Victorian female—was how hard she worked to solicit proposals that she could accept or reject. At some point she lit on Lincoln."[48] Gene Lockhart, a character actor perfectly cast, plays Stephen Douglas, Lincoln's loquacious rival. "My first day of shooting was the scene where Mary Todd, soon to be Mrs. Lincoln," Ruth Gordon wrote, "was visiting my sister in Springfield, Illinois."

The evening at the dance at the Edwards home, Douglas is flattering Elizabeth Edwards, Mary's sister. At that point, Ninian Edwards, Mary's brother-in-law, approaches Douglas:

NINIAN (Harvey Stephens): Good evening, Steve. Mary, my dear, may I present our most eloquent citizen, Mr. Stephen Douglas?

MARY: I'm honored.

(This gives Douglas the opportunity to turn on the charm.)

DOUGLAS: Miss Todd, your brother-in-law has described me as eloquent, but alas, I must prove him wrong, standing as I am in the presence of such penetrating intelligence, such devastating charm. I am rendered speechless.

MARY: I can hardly believe it.

(*Mary turns her attention away from Douglas when Lincoln enters the room. Abe hits his head on the crystal chandelier knocking a piece to the floor. He scrambles to pick it up. The guests laugh, but Mary merely smiles at his awkwardness. Lincoln smiles back.*)

LINCOLN: Ninian, I thought you were going to have that thing raised up.

JOSHUA SPEED (*Minor Watson plays the role of Lincoln's friend and roommate*):[49] It wouldn't have made any difference, he'd have knocked over something else. Mr. Lincoln is more at home in the backwoods than in a drawing room.

MARY: How do you do, Mr. Lincoln?

LINCOLN: So far, I haven't been doing so well. Thank you.

MARY: Never mind, Mr. Lincoln, I'm sure all the other gentlemen here envy you for being tall enough to break the chandelier.

DOUGLAS: Miss Todd, I want you to know that I resent that bitterly. Hello, Abe.

LINCOLN: Evening, Steve.

DOUGLAS: Still got the same old coat on.

LINCOLN: I got a little attached to it.

DOUGLAS: Seems to be a little short.

LINCOLN: It'll be longer before I get another.

(*Mary laughs*)

DOUGLAS: Abe is what you might call a self-made man.

LINCOLN: Well, I guess my parents ought to take some of the blame for it.

DOUGLAS: When I first knew him, he was behind a counter selling whiskey and rum and intoxicating the customers with his own raw humor.

LINCOLN: You see, Miss Todd, I was always behind the bar and Steve Douglas was always in front of it.

(*Mary smiles and turns to Douglas, anticipating his reply*)

DOUGLAS (*outwitted, frowning, and rubbing his chin*): Something tells me I shouldn't have started this.

(*Later in the evening Douglas engages Mary and the Edwards with stories of his political cleverness.*)

DOUGLAS: So, I said to Daniel Webster: "You may stand where you like in Massachusetts, but you'll meet your downfall out here in Illinois."

MARY (*sarcastically*): I can understand why they call you the Little Giant (*Douglas is taken aback*)

NINIAN (*spitting his punch back into his cup*): You better be careful, Stephen. Mary is just as ambitious as you are.

ELIZABETH (*encouraging Douglas*): My sister has made no secret of the fact that the man she marries will be the President of the United States.

DOUGLAS (*encouraged*): Well, I'm delighted to hear it, Miss Todd, for I have been looking for the perfect First Lady to be my consort at the White House and now I have found her.

MARY: Really? But you should give that out to the newspapers: Stephen Douglas consents to be become President.

(*Mary puts her posey up to her nose and abruptly walks away.*)

DOUGLAS (*flummoxed*): I . . . uh, seem to need a little more refreshment.

In Sherwood's script, as in Trotti's *Young Mr. Lincoln,* Mary Todd and Abe leave the dance floor and move out to the porch. But there is a difference. Here Abe thinks not of Ann Rutledge, as in *Young Mr. Lincoln,* but of his mother, Nancy Hanks. Mary and Abe sit together on a bench as he recalls his mother's death. We enter the scene in midconversation:

> MARY (*with a kind expression*): I'm sure your mother must have been a wonderful woman. How old were you when she died?
>
> LINCOLN: I was seven [he was actually nine at the time of her death]. The milk sick got her, poor creature. I helped Pa make the coffin, whittled it with my own jackknife. We buried her in a timber clearing beside my grandmother. I used to go there often to look at the place. I used to watch the deer run over her grave with their little feet. Funny, I could never kill a deer after that. Once I got a licking from Pa because when he was taking aim at a deer, I knocked his gun up. But this is no way to behave in society, talking about the backwoods I come from.
>
> MARY: It's just the way to behave, Mr. Lincoln. Please tell me more about the lickings you got.

(The scene ends as they laugh gently together.)

"THAT WOMAN SCARES ME"

Sometime in December 1840, Mary Todd and Abraham Lincoln announced publicly their intention to marry. Then on New Year's Day 1841, Lincoln called off the engagement. This was scandalous: engagement in the nineteenth century involved a promise of true commitment and personal honor for both men and women—especially for the man. In a small community such as Springfield, this was especially shameful. It could not be taken lightly. Remarkably, Mary left no record of the event. Was she too ashamed to commit her thoughts to writing? Her aunt Katherine Helm speculated that Lincoln, a man of little means at the time, was "panic stricken" at the prospect of having to provide for a woman of Mary's social class and material expectations. So, he used Mary's flirtation with Stephen Douglas as an excuse to end the engagement. There is another—shocking—version of the affair: William Herndon stated that Lincoln had decided that he really did not love Mary Todd, and he intended to write her a letter informing her of his decision. Joshua Speed, his closest friend, persuaded him to tell her in person. Yet, when confronted with Mary's tearful reaction, he reluctantly decided to go through with the wedding. Then, on January 1, to Mary's humiliation and the horror of her minister, family, and friends, he left her standing at the altar (so the story goes). Here is how D. W. Griffith imagined the event: as Mary and her guests await the groom's arrival, the scene shifts to Lincoln's law office. Abe and Billy Herndon are in conversation:

BILLY (Jason Robards Sr.): Did you get the license, Mr. Lincoln?

(*Lincoln removes the document from his tall hat.*)

BILLY: Well. She got you. I knew she would when she started out the first time.

LINCOLN: Now, Billy, don't bother me. I'm gonna be married and I'm scared to death.

BILLY: Oh, don't be alarmed, there's many a bite that's worse than a bride.

LINCOLN: But, Billy, that woman scares me. Well, she's even got the ridiculous idea that I could be President.

BILLY: Oh, don't take that seriously. Every spunky girl thinks her husband ought to be President.

LINCOLN: I know that, Billy. But it's a pity to fool her and she's a fine woman. Smart as pepper and pretty too.

BILLY: She'll be a great help, Mr. Lincoln but you got to keep climbing with her.

LINCOLN: (*resigned*) Yes, yes, I know.

The Wedding Day

BILLY: Well heaven's sakes, you've got to hurry.

LINCOLN: You go ahead. You go on over and I'll come later. I doubt there's a word in the dictionary that could tell how I feel. Say, Billy what does a man do when his head's all right but his legs are cowardly?

BILLY: My cure is to get drunk.

LINCOLN: My legs are too frightened to pay attention to liquor.

(*Billy leaves and Lincoln takes from a drawer a picture of Ann Rutledge.*)

LINCOLN: (*moaning*): Ann . . . Ann . . . Ann!

(*Back at the Edwards house, it is clear that Lincoln has left Mary at the altar.*)

MARY: (*greatly agitated*) Ran away? From me? On our wedding day? Can you imagine? That's what a Todd gets for engaging herself to a country baboon!

The left-at-the-altar story is a false. It never happened. A year and a half later Abe and Mary reconciled. She had endured the breakup reasonably well. For Lincoln it was a soul-killing period of despair. He was heartsick over the embarrassment he caused Mary. In a letter to his boon companion Joshua Speed in March 1842, he wrote of "the never-absent idea, that here is one still unhappy who I contributed to make so. That still kills my soul."

Griffith, again:

(*Lincoln is waiting as Mary enters the room in the Edwards house.*)

LINCOLN: I uh . . . I uh . . . Mary you don't have to bother about me anymore. I've settled down at last. I hope I can make your future all you desire.

MARY: We'll say no more about it. I really think after all, you really need me.

LINCOLN: You need a lot of patience to put up with me, Mary, but if anyone can do it, You're the one. I'm sure you're the one. Oh, Mary.

(*They embrace and the scene ends.*)

The reconciliation with Mary makes possible the redemption of the nation. Lincoln has surrendered to Mary's ambitions. "For all her faults," historian

Michael J. Gerhart judges, "Mary Todd, was fiercely in Lincoln's corner, calling their marriage 'our Lincoln party.' If Lincoln's confidence lagged, and it did, she was there to refuel their joint ambitions."[50] He has "settled down," that is, accepted his fate. He finds no joy in this, but he is reconciled.

In the film version of *Abe Lincoln in Illinois,* Lincoln makes one last visit to New Salem. As he roams the deserted hamlet, the ghost of Ann Rutledge appears briefly in the background. She says nothing. Then he hears the voice of Nancy Hanks: "The world passeth, but he that does the will of God will abide forever." The Man of Sorrow will marry at last, "a matter," in Lincoln's words, "of profound wonder." Marriage marks the beginning of his Mission. He accepts this burden: the sin and suffering of the nation. Abraham Lincoln will pilot the Union through a great sacrificial war, free the slaves, extend forgiveness to the defeated, and offer himself as a sacrifice on Good Friday 1865. Mary Lincoln is the *co-redemptrix*—the subordinate yet essential partner who shares in his suffering and death for the nation's redemption.

The fraught two-year courtship and controversial eighteen-year marriage of Abraham and Mary constitute a trove of assumptions and counterassumptions. They planned to be married on January 1, 1840. Lincoln then suddenly called off the wedding. Whatever the blow was to Mary's pride and to Lincoln's self-esteem, sixteen months later all seemed to be forgiven when they married on April 4, 1842, and Mary gave birth to their first child, Robert, exactly nine months later. (Was she pregnant at the time of the marriage?)

The Bad Mary image went largely unchallenged until the rise of feminist scholarship. Kay Hammond in Griffith's *Abraham Lincoln,* Marjorie Weaver in *Young Mr. Lincoln,* and Ruth Gordon in *Abe Lincoln in Illinois* defined this determined, manipulative, and essential Bad Mary.

MRS. LINCOLN
GOES TO WASHINGTON

The White House Years

"I shall become Mrs. President, or I am the victim of false prophets, but it will not be as Mrs. Douglas," Mary Todd said to her swain, the elegant Stephen Douglas, during her Springfield courting days.[1] True to her word, Mary arrived in Washington, DC, in 1861 as the wife of the president of the United States. Her ascension to the White House, however, would not be the triumph she expected. The animosity of the social elite, the hostility of the press, the death of her beloved son Willie, and the assassination of her husband turned her tenure as Mrs. President into four years of almost unremitting pain and suffering. In the history of Mary and Abe before and during the Washington years, Mary's role is to seduce him into marriage, drag him into public office, nag him about the condition of the White House drapes, and remind him that "We'll be late for the theater."[2]

PRELUDE—THE NOMINATION

According to Robert Sherwood, Humble Abe is so little interested in his political future that he fails to mention to his wife, Mary, that a delegation of Republican leaders will soon arrive to assess him and, if impressed, to offer him the nomination for the presidency of the United States. The scene opens with Mary complaining about Robert Lincoln's smoking. She forbids it. Abe quips, "Come, come, Mary, you mustn't be disrespectful of a Harvard man." She is not amused. After Robert leaves the room, Joshua Speed arrives and informs him that a delegation will arrive shortly. Lincoln is the heart of the film, as Frank Nugent points out: "His domination is unquestioned here only when Miss Gordon's Mary Todd is not gazing archly at Mr. Massey's Lincoln with eyes crackling with cold ambition, or flaring at him for not wearing his boots when the steering committee is coming to call, or defeatedly leaving the political headquarters when the returns are coming in, with the bitter taste of victory in a mouth that has become a thin, straight line."[3]

The Scene (in the film):

MARY: (*sharply*) What delegation?

ABE: Oh, some prominent politicians, ministers, some bankers—that sort of people.

MARY: Well, what are they coming here for?

ABE: Well, I don't precisely know—but I presume to see if I'm fit to be a candidate for President of the United States. (*Mary is, for the moment, speechless.*) I suppose they want to find out if we still live in a log cabin and keep pigs under the bed.

(*Joshua chuckles*)

MARY: (*in a fury*) And you didn't tell me!

ABE: I'm sorry, Mary, it skipped my mind.

MARY: You're being considered for the presidency, but it just slipped your mind.

MARY: Oh, if I'd only known. If you'd only given me time to prepare for them. Now they'll see us as we are—crude, sloppy, vulgar Western barbarians.

(*The sad, henpecked Abe slumps in his chair—a look of utter defeat on his face.*)

MARY: And living in a house that reeks of tobacco smoke and you in your filthy old carpet slippers. I declare, Abraham Lincoln, I believe you would have treated me with more consideration if I had been your slave rather than your wife! Go this minute and put some boots on!

ABE (*with a hangdog expression*): Yes, Mary.

(*Mary turns to Joshua.*)

MARY: I know, Joshua, you think as all the others do, I'm a bitter nagging woman—that I've tried to kill his spirit, and drag him down to my level.

SPEED: No, Mary. I think no such thing. Remember—I know Abe too.

MARY: He's always had some obsession of some future doom. And for 18 years, I've been trying to stir him out of it. But all my efforts have been like so many waves dashing against the Rock of Ages. And now the greatest opportunity is coming to him here, right into his own house. He must take it. He must see that this is what he was meant to be. But I can't persuade him of it. I thought that I could help to shape him as I knew he should be, and I've succeeded in nothing but in breaking myself.

In Sherwood's 1938 play, Mary's lament is much extended and more revelatory of her passion for Lincoln's success and her own utter disappointment that he will not accept the presidency as the joyous fulfillment of his destiny. What had happened to the ambitious, lively young Mary Todd? At the moment of his success, Mary Lincoln realizes the terrible price she has paid in lashing him forward. He expresses no joy, no celebration of a remarkable ascent from small-town Illinois lawyer to the nomination for president of the United States—only dark distress. Where is her victory? Where is her happiness? Where is her reward? In a remarkably bitter soliloquy, Mary pours out her fury and frustration:

MARY: There never could have been another man such as he is! I've read about many that have gone up in the world, and all of them seem to have to fight to assert themselves every inch of the way, against the opposition of their enemies and the lack of understanding in their own friends. But he's never had any of that. He's never had an enemy, and every one of his friends has always been completely confident in him. Even before I met him, I was told he had a glorious future, and after I'd known him a day I was sure of it myself. But he didn't believe it—or, if he did, secretly, he was so afraid of the prospect that he did all in his power to avoid it. He had some poem in his mind, about a life of woe, along a rugged path, that leads to some future doom, and it has been an obsession with him. All these years I have tried and tried to stir him out of it, but all my efforts have been like so many puny waves dashing against the Rock of Ages. And now opportunity, the greatest opportunity, is coming here, to him, right into his own house. And what can I do about it? He *must* take it! He *must* see that this is what he was meant for! But I can't persuade him of it! I'm tired—I'm tired to death! (*The tears now come.*) I thought I could help to shape him as I knew he should be, and, I have succeeded at nothing—but in breaking myself.

It is an astounding, unrestrained lamentation in which Mary unleashes a litany of complaints. Mary's hardness and unhappiness, theater scholar Thomas S. Hischak, concludes, foreshadows her eventual insanity. "In contrast, Ann Rutledge is a soft, selfless character who seems to be the embodiment of feminine perfection."[4]

Did Lincoln really fight against Mary's ambitions for him? No. Absolutly not. On the contrary, he took a deep interest and delight in state and national politics and a keen interest in the nomination. He was the master of his own political career. He sought the presidency, though legend and Hollywood would have it that the nomination sought him. There was no Humble Abe when it came to his ambitions. Mary Todd recognized it, and so did Billy Herndon, Mary's nemesis; Mary Lincoln rejoiced in it. His political life had suffered reverses in the past, but he was a political man to the marrow—a consummate political artist with uncanny skills. He had social aspirations as well. "Lincoln . . . had plenty of his own—to leave the log cabin of his birth and never look back, to marry a woman who could speak French and attended finishing school, to send his son to Exeter prep school and Harvard," Mark E. Neely Jr. writes about the myth and reality of Lincoln in the Ford and Sherwood films.[5] He combined ambition with a remarkable political acumen. He was a man on the make. He and Mary were not antagonists. If it is true that since girlhood Mary had planned to marry a man who would become the president of the United States, Lincoln had his plans as well: from "boyhood up, my ambition was to be president," he declared to his friend Ward Lamon.[6] Why, then, does Sherwood make Lincoln so reluctant to accept his destiny? It is because he needed a truly democratic hero—a man of, by, and for the people. Sherwood was not only a playwright and screenwriter; he was also a speechwriter for Franklin Roosevelt. J. E. Smyth observes, "Sherwood's Lincoln intones the creed of Roosevelt's New Deal democracy." *Abe Lincoln in Illinois* was "an ideological project, and Raymond Massey acknowledged that [the play's] reading of history was actively influenced by the author's and the audience's need to solve contemporary problems such as the impending war in Europe." This ambition was lost in translation to film, since "Sherwood's and Massey's Lincoln lacks the humanity, humor, and imperfection of the man portrayed in *Herndon's Lincoln.* Sherwood wanted his film, like the play, to be an impressive historical document, but it remains a document of the last antebellum days of the 1930s"—"a pompous history lesson."[7] FDR, a skilled politician like Lincoln, became the hero of the common man. Though, completely unlike Lincoln, Roosevelt descended from American aristocracy. The narrative needed a Democratic Champion of the Common Man who responds to the crisis of the Great Depression and war in Europe. Sherwood's Abe Lincoln had to be a homespun, simple man summoned to leadership. The real Lincoln was, of course, an uncommon common man.

This Lincoln shaped his own political future with determination and incomparable political skill.[8] When he won the nomination of the new Republican Party, "No one did more than Abraham Lincoln to make sure that *he* would be that candidate and victor," historian Michael S. Green concludes, "and the ability that he demonstrated in the process prepared him to lead the North to victory in the Civil War."[9] When Mary Lincoln accompanied her husband in his ascent to power, it was as the supportive if troubled companion and not as the essential driving force.

ELECTION NIGHT 1860—
"THIS IS THE NIGHT I DREAMED ABOUT"

The Scene (in the film): The Lincoln campaign headquarters, Illinois statehouse, November 4, 1860: Lincoln and Mary await the presidential election returns. Lincoln, with his tall hat on and wearing spectacles, is reading newspaper clippings. He finds the derogatory comments of opposition journalists amusing. Mary is seated wearing a bonnet, tippet, with her hands in a muff. She is anxious about the election reports and annoyed that Abe is so dismissive of the attacks printed in the newspapers. In his commentary on the story, Sherwood stated: "I have exaggerated the fact that [Lincoln]was forever pushed forward by his wife and friends. Certainly, they were always trying—they were expressing, however, unconsciously, the need of the people of their shuddering country for a leader who was a man of the people—but for a long time he successfully resisted them. When he did go forward, it was entirely under his own steam." Yet, "Lincoln's return to Mary Todd [following their breakup] is merely expressive of his acceptance of his destiny," he explained.[10]

Why is Lincoln so resentful of Mary? Sherwood's answer: "In this eleventh scene [the night of Lincoln's election victory in November 1860], is one speech that has been much criticized and deplored by good people who revere Lincoln's memory and who cannot believe that he ever cursed at his wife." Sherwood continues: "There is certainly overwhelming evidence of the fact that, in the years in the White House, he treated the obstreperous Mrs. Lincoln with an unfailing courtesy and tender consideration. This was his public behavior and, as far as anyone can know, his private behavior as well. . . . Nevertheless, I did not feel that concerning a part of the tragedy of Lincoln's life would be complete in its attempted honesty if I did not include the admission that on occasion, his monumental patience snapped." And this: "Usually he met her tirades with stony silence, or abrupt departure, or with laughter (the most infuriating response of all). Feeling that such an outburst from Lincoln to his wife was necessary, I placed it in this scene on Election Night, considering that this was the most appropriate moment, with the nerves of both so severely strained."[11] The author as screenwriter made it all up, but in his view, it made dramatic sense to create Mary's aria of bitterness and Lincoln's agony.

As the election results roll in, Mary is ever more anxious and angered when Abe reads with ironic humor the insults from opposition newspapers. Finally, enough is enough, and he orders her to leave. In the film, Lincoln is furious at Mary. In the play, he actually curses her—"Damn you! Damn you!" In the film the language is restrained, though not Lincoln's bitter anger:

MARY: (*addressing Lincoln and others in the room*) No. I won't go home! You only want to get rid of me. That's what you want ever since the day we were married—and before that. Anything to get me out of your sight. Because you hate me! And it's the same with all of you—all of his friends—you hate me—you wish I'd never come into his life.

ABE: [*"Damn you! Damn you!" in the play but deleted here.*] Why do you take every opportunity you can to make a public fool of me—and yourself! It's bad enough, God knows, when you act like that in the privacy of our own home. But here—in front of people! You're not to do that again. Do you hear me? You're never to do that again! But I still think that you should go home rather than stay here and endure the strain of this—this Death Watch.

MARY: This is the night I dreamed about when I was a child, when I was an excited young girl, and all the gay young gentlemen of Springfield were courting me and I fell in love with the least likely of them all. This is the night when I'm waiting to hear that my husband has become President of the United States. And even if he does—it's ruined for me. It's too late.

Frank Nugent observed in his review that Massey's Lincoln "wore his crown of thorns beneath a stovepipe hat and accepted his public life as a martyrdom."[12] As for Mary's character, "it was [to] Massey's fortune as an actor and to Lincoln's as a man that Mary Todd had to stand in the background for most of the film." Nevertheless, her role is essential. "Mary is in the anomalous position in the play [and the film] as in the myth, of being honored by a grateful country for prodding Abe into the presidency while being disliked for her lack of understanding and inability to inspire him with love."[13]

Sherwood's Lincoln, like Griffith's, is profoundly sad—affected not by inherent psychological issues, his famous melancholy, but by the loss of Ann, the oppression of Mary, and the Burden of History. Oh, for the simple life of New Salem with Ann. Now the Sad Man is caught up in the whirlwind of great events amid Mary's relentless harping. In an earlier scene set in Springfield, Abe exclaims, "I don't want to be ridden and driven upward and onward through life, with her whip lashing me, and her spurs digging into me!" Billy Herndon replies, "You're only using her as a living sacrifice, offering her up, in the hope that you will thus gain forgiveness of the gods for your failure to do your own duty!"

Theater scholar Winifred Dusenbury defines the role of Sherwood's Mary as the *deus ex machina:* It is impossible for the hero to combine both love with duty: "If Mary Todd had been beloved by Abe, it would have been necessary to alter the facts to make her, instead, his goad. The hero's is a lonely road. Mary Todd's function is not to alleviate but enhance Abe's isolation. She accomplishes this purpose perfectly because her own selfish ambition is the motivation which makes her drive her husband to success." Billy Herndon, in both play and film, appeals to higher motives—service to the nation. "But Billy does not succeed," Dusenbury notes, "therefore, Abe is in the position of attaining greatness to satisfy a selfish woman's ambition."[14] He is the reluctant, lonely, Sad Man forced into glory by "Mary's whip."[15]

MARY'S PARLOR POLITICS

Once Mary arrives in the nation's capital in 1861, she is a beset by a coven of critics—petty, snobbish, and cruel. The haughty Lydia Maria Child, an abolitionist and women's rights activist from Massachusetts, found Mary contemptible—a "vulgar doll" and a "fool" who, amid the human tragedy of the Civil War, only cared for "flattery, and dress, and parties."[16] Another Massachusetts patrician, Richard Henry Dana, described the First Lady as an "under-bred woman," "short and fat" with a "stubby face." She reminded him of someone's choleric "housekeeper."[17] On seeing Mary dressed in all her finery, Oregon senator James Nesmith snorted at the sight, appalled that "the weak-minded Mrs. Lincoln had her bosom on exhibition and a flower pot on her head" with "a train of silk dragging on the floor behind her of several yards in length."[18]

So, this was the new mistress of the Executive Mansion: a small-town hick who cooked "Old Abe's dinners and milked his cows," now happily exhibiting "her milking apparatus to public gaze."[19] Charles E. Strong, a prominent New York attorney, described her as a "vulgar old woman." On and on the criticism flowed over the president's lady—a "fleshly," "dowdy," "dumpy" little woman turned out in "low-cut dresses" with "flower-beds crowning her head," who exhibited to all the world the manners and look of a middle-class household's "servant woman."[20] (This image endures: essayist Adam Gopnik, writing in the *New Yorker* in 2020, reprising Mary's contemporary enemies, judged that Mary Lincoln was out of her element in the capital—"a bewildered Southern woman in an unmanageable role.")[21]

What was to be the fulfillment of her ambitions turned into a "pitiless searchlight of unfavorable publicity" and a "tidal wave of hate."[22] The "nice" people of Washington scorned Lincoln as well as Mary. He was a bastard by birth, an ape, a baboon, a hick, a rube, a yahoo, a race traitor, a coward, a warmonger, a ridiculous teller of dirty jokes, and much more. The two of them were no more than comical hillbillies come to high station—an embarrassment and danger to the nation. Charles Francis Adams of the imperious Adams dynasty observed that the Lincolns appeared uncomfortable among civilized people.[23] The joke, however, was on the capital snobs. Washington, DC, was a provincial backwater, a muddy hog wallow, in comparison to imperial London or Paris. Richard Lyons, 1st Viscount Lyons and British ambassador to the United States, found the city lacking any civilized refinement and culture: no gentlemen's clubs, no proper theater or opera, but saloons and whorehouses aplenty.[24] In any case, *the Comic News,* a London illustrated weekly, informed its readers that the Lincolns would not be long in Washington: Lincoln had purchased a plantation in the South and "as soon as circumstances permit, Mrs. L. will be sent away, and her place supplied by a bevy of African belles."[25]

Criticism of Mary Lincoln, however, went beyond ribald humor. Some accused her of being a Confederate spy in the White House; others charged that she was a traitor to the South. "I seem to be the scapegoat for both North and South," Mary wrote to Emilie Helm, her half sister.[26] Commenting on Mary's death in 1882, the *New York Times* admitted that "there were gossips among those in Washington who hated 'the new people' in the White House, who told abominable stories of 'that Ape,' as Lincoln was called, and who invented all manner of silly slanders about his wife" because they could not accept the fact that Mary, a southerner and Abraham Lincoln's "early choice and long-beloved companion," remained loyal to both her husband and the Union.[27]

Though they were outnumbered, Mary had her defenders. One Washington reporter observed that during the couple's first public reception at the Executive Mansion, Mary "made a pleasant impression upon every one [*sic*] who came near her. Had she been born and lived her whole life in the court of the Tuileries, she could not have shown more fitness for the position she so admirably adorns." George Bancroft, the aristocratic diplomat and historian, remembered Mary as "really well dressed," finding her "pleasant, affable, friendly and not the least arrogant."[28] *The New York Evening Post,* a Republican paper, had observed during the presidential election of 1860 that Mary Lincoln was a handsome, vivacious lady, "an interesting and sparkling talker" who "converses with freedom and grace, and is thoroughly *au fait* in all the little amenities of society."[29]

Mary Clemmer Ames, a contemporary journalist, deemed it an injustice to consider Mary "an ignorant, illiterate woman." On the contrary, "she was well-born, gently reared, and her education above the average standard to girls in her youth. She is a fair mistress of the French language, and . . . can write a more graceful letter than one educated woman in fifty. She has quick perceptions and an almost unrivalled power of mimicry." Her weaknesses were not ignorance or lack of refinement, "but a constitutional inability to rise to action of high motive." As such, "she was incapable of lofty, impersonal impulse" or to rise above "her own ambitions, her own pleasures, [or] her own sufferings."[30] (There is one beautiful scene in Griffith's *Abraham Lincoln* that, for an instance, softens Mary's character: It is the dead of night and Lincoln is deep in thought, pacing in an enormous room in the White House. He is barefoot and in his nightshirt. Mary, dressed in her nightgown and with her hair down, enters the room with a pair of slippers, kneels down, and slips them on his feet. It is an act of submission and love.)

Three productions imagine Mary Lincoln during the Washington years as a more fully formed and dynamic character, though one no less personally troubled—*Sandburg's Lincoln* (NBC, 1974/1976), *Gore Vidal's Lincoln* (NBC, 1988), and Steven Spielberg's *Lincoln* (2012). They may be off-kilter historically at times and retain the Bad Mary tropes, but their scripts are more complex than previous Hollywood treatments when it comes to Mary as the supporting character.

The six-part series *Sandburg's Lincoln* and *Gore Vidal's Lincoln,* a three-hour production based on Vidal's best-selling historical novel, present Mary Lincoln as emotionally troubled but also as intelligent and politically engaged. Though Vidal had little interest in Mary herself, this interpretation was his attempt to show "a more complex and modern portrait" of the couple.[31] In fact, Vidal had a low opinion of Lincoln literature and, especially, Lincoln scholarship and what he called "the screening of Lincoln." Hollywood films, he contended, have "been every bit as inadequate as the pros-ing of Lincoln. There was this actor Raymond Massey as Lincoln, at home in Illinois, quarreling with his wife; and there was the very young Henry Fonda as Lincoln, practicing law and burying, quite early in the film, Ann Rutledge, a minor blessing."[32] And then there was a "god-like presence in other films such as *The Littlest Rebel.*" Vidal at first conceived of his book as a screenplay and only later turned it into a novel. It aroused a fierce controversy.

Lincoln scholar Roy P. Basler is representative of the critics. Only half of the novel has any historical authenticity, he charged, and "another 25 percent of the book is made up of episodes that might have happened, but never as they are told by Vidal." Vidal's *Lincoln* was a mélange of specula-tion composed of facts of dubious reliability. Basler was especially critical of Vidal's portrayal of Mary's insanity. This, he found "most unbelievable even though she was indubitably at times on the verge of hysteria, if not actually insane." Specifically, he points to Vidal's account of Mary's behavior when she lashed out at General Edward Ord's wife for her presumption of riding next to the president during a review of the army. Basler argues that Vidal exaggerated the event "out of all proportion to the recorded facts."

As for Abraham contracting syphilis and then passing the disease on to his wife? Outrageous. He calls the accusations "pseudo-authenticities" reflecting "the 'ready for sex everybody' insouciance of Vidal's homosex-ual/transsexual novels *Myra Breckinridge* (1968) and *Myron* (1974)." Vidal's *Lincoln*, Basler concluded, is "'historical' fiction at its worst."[33] For his part, Vidal had no patience for what he called unimaginative historians obsessed by the hunt for obscure facts, devoted to "the Mount Rushmore school of history," who "like to think that the truly great man is a virgin until his wedding night; and a devoted monogamist thereafter."[34] In an interview in 2012, he doubled down on his assertion. "I am convinced Lincoln did have syphilis," he insisted, "and I'm convinced that Mary Todd died of paresis, contracted from him." "Long before he had syphilis or was married, he had this urge to be great."[35] He insisted he did not make much of this in the novel, but it is clear enough: In a conversation with John Hay (invented by Vidal but based on a reputed letter written on January 6, 1861, from the real Herndon), Herndon states, "They say there's a lot of syphilis here [wartime Washington], thanks to the army and all. God knows there was a lot of it in Illinois back in the thirties when Lincoln had it." Hay is appalled. Herndon goes on to elaborate: "Of course, he was a mere boy at the time. Your age I'd say. Yes. It was about the year 1835."[36]

Ernest Kinoy (an NBC scriptwriter whose contributions included *Dr. Kilroy, Route 66,* and *Naked City*) adapted *Vidal's Lincoln* for television and tamed the author's excesses. Abraham is still the sad Man of Destiny, and Mary the unstable yet loyal wife, but he eliminated Vidal's most egregious historical transgressions. Absent is any dialogue from the novel about venereal disease or Mary's "dismal teeth." Still, John Hay and Robert Lincoln visit a whorehouse. And Mary's outburst against Mrs. Ord as portrayed by Vidal made it to the small screen. In the novel and then as interpreted for the television series, "Mary rose in her place. She felt exalted. At last, she could strike at her enemies a mortal blow. 'You whore!' Mary said, delighted that she was able to control her voice well. Then, word by word, sentence by sentence, effortlessly, she told the slut what she thought of her and her behavior."[37]

On the whole and considering a screenwriter's rightful dramatic license, *Sandburg's Lincoln* and *Vidal's Lincoln* are largely true in spirit to Mary's role in Lincoln's Washington years. They are true as well to a woman's opportunities and limitations in the Civil War era. Though Victorian convention and law restricted their public role, women often transgressed these boundaries as key players in the reform movements in mid-nineteenth-century America—the abolitionist movement, the fight for improved treatment of the mentally ill, the suffrage movement, transcendentalism, utopian social experiments, and temperance. Even spiritualism provided women with agency and "a voice."

Mary was not unprepared for her new role as the nation's First Lady. Since the early days in Illinois, Mary Lincoln took a keen interest in politics. Now in the nation's capital, she continued to advise and to confront her husband in the arena where she held the most influence—the woman's realm of "parlor politics." When she arrived in Washington, she had every intention of making the Executive Mansion—her new home—a center of public life. Mary, despite her own inner demons, reveled in the world of elite society, political intrigue, and high fashion. In her own time and in important ways, Mary in Washington reflected aspects of the first wave of feminism in the mid-nineteenth century. A century later, the second-wave feminism of the 1960s and 1970s revised her historical image.[38] In its turn, Hollywood's New Mary represented the changing narrative from her deep unpopularity in the 1860s to the attempted academic rescue in Jean Baker's biography. Two stories illustrate this attempt to turn Mary Lincoln into a convincing human being. The first involves her rivalry with the Washington social and political diva Kate Chase Sprague. The second is about her relationship with the freewoman Elizabeth Keckley.

THE RIVALS: MARY LINCOLN
VERSUS KATE CHASE SPRAGUE

November 15, 1863. It was the event of the social season—a wedding to remember. The marriage of glamorous Kate Chase to the fabulously wealthy William Sprague IV, a Rhode Island manufacturer, Union officer, and Republican politician. More than five hundred guests attended. Enchanted, the New York Times reporter wrote: "The bride . . . is a lady possessed of those rare virtues of heart and mind which alone can be recognized and appreciated by all who are daily thrown in contact with her; and it is in the modest retirement of her own home that these graces sparkle and radiate like gems of dazzling splendor." The crystalline twenty-three-year-old Kate Chase, dressed in green silk and adorned with a wreath of orange blossoms, was "modest and retiring in her manner, yet blending withal a dignity and ease that singles her out to the least observant as a woman endowed with a nobility of heart, fitting for any position in life no matter how exalted." As the Marine Band played the "Kate Chase Wedding March" and serenaded the guests, "mirth and merriment were the order of the day." The guest list included members of the president's cabinet, General Henry Halleck, and foreign ambassadors, including Lord Lyons. At 8:30 p.m. President Abraham Lincoln arrived in his private carriage "without escort and alone." Arriving in his carriage, he greeted Kate with a gentle kiss. The First Lady did not attend, still in mourning over Willie, concerned about little Tad, who was sick with a fever, and, disinclined to congratulate her rival even on her wedding day.[39]

When Mary Lincoln arrived at the nation's capital in 1861, she rightly expected to be Washington's premier hostess, experienced as she was in the protocol of political life during the Illinois years. But Katherine Jane Chase, known as Kate, immediately challenged the First Lady's position. Kate was a force of nature. She "was without peer among American women in the boldness with which she played the political game for her father," her biographer writes.[40] A standoff ensued because Kate, the reigning star of Washington's political theater, was as ambitious for her father, Salmon P. Chase, as Mary was for her husband. As Chase's private secretary and chief advisor, she had worked behind the scenes at the Republican convention in Chicago in 1860 to get her father the nomination. She and her father continued to scheme against Lincoln when Chase, while serving as Lincoln's secretary of the treasury, maneuvered to take the party's nomination away from Lincoln in 1864.[41] As her father's special agent, she was a formidable opponent to the First Lady, whom Kate held in contempt. Years later, looking back on Kate's life, the New York Times observed: "There was magnetism in her personality. . . . She was a diplomat of uncommon tact, and within a short time the homage of the most eminent men in the country were hers." And more, "she was ambitious, and she wielded her power and the influence of her high social station as no other woman in this country . . . ever had. There was no secret about the chief ambition—it was to see her father President of the United States. To gratify this ambition, she made friends with the most powerful politicians, and planned with ceaseless adroitness to make them allies with her father."[42]

George Alfred Townsend, a widely respected correspondent who covered the Civil War and later the Lincoln assassination, highlighted the virtues of the romantic and fascinating Miss Kate for the New York Times in an extended obituary on August 27, 1899: "She had great charm and refined manners." "Her very tears in distress had the power of love." "She had the charm of constant ladyhood." "Her superiority was instantly felt." "No woman in Lincoln's court was more than an old nurse to her Juliet where she was not only the head of the table, but the place to bend the knee." Unconventional beauty reflected unconventional talents: her "complexion . . . freckled, from its sensitiveness, her eyes had the shine of darkest hazel, though they may have been black, pupils gray; her youth, dependence on men, and child quality never were withdrawn. To the last she could touch the heart by her plaintive voice, and amid her vicissitudes arouse the knighthood in boys and men."[43] Her intimate admirers included Lord Lyons and, in Vidal's story, Lincoln's private secretary John Hay. Gore Vidal provides this observation of Kate and her ambitious father: she was "a handsome ambitious motherless girl who acted as hostess to her father . . ., Salmon P. Chase, a handsome ambitious wifeless man, who was, in Abraham Lincoln's thoughtful phrase, 'on the subject of the Presidency, a little insane.'"[44]

The lives of Mary and Kate ran remarkably parallel after Mary left Washington. Like Mary Lincoln, Kate ascended to prominence in Washington and then suffered a humiliating decline following the war. Yet, Kate's fate was worse than Mary's. A scandalous affair with the powerful, poetry-reading politician Roscoe Conkling, a divorce from the abusive and alcoholic Sprague in 1882, the suicide of her twenty-five-year-old son in 1890, and a descent into poverty marked Kate's fall from grace.[45]

Sada Thompson as Mary and Elizabeth Ashley as Kate play the competing hostesses in *Sandburg's Lincoln.* In the "Sad Man Laughing" episode, Mary is angered at Kate and Salmon Chase's blatant political ambitions at the expense of her husband. At their first meeting at a White House reception, Kate plays the mean girl with a backhanded compliment on Mary's gown. Mary tries to ignore the insult, recalls that Kate has not been seen in public for some time. When Kate replies that she did not think anyone as unimportant as she would be a topic in the White House, Mary is ready: "We talk about many unimportant things here."

Three years later, in 1864, Secretary Chase and Kate visit the White House. Their attempt to wrest the nomination from Lincoln has failed, to Kate's distress. The Lincolns "welcome" father and daughter. Chase, practically grinding his teeth in rage, congratulates Lincoln on his renomination. As he offers "best wishes," a furious Kate, slowly and hesitatingly adds, "obviously." Lincoln and Chase leave to have a private chat. Kate informs Mary that "my father insisted that I come." Which prompts Mary's venomous reply: "Then your father can entertain you because I do not intend to." The First Lady turns her back and walks away.

"THERE IS NO JUSTICE ON EARTH": MARY LINCOLN AND ELIZBETH KECKLEY

In 2018, the *New York Times* announced the beginning of a series of retroactive obituaries entitled "Overlooked." "Since 1851," the editors wrote, "obituaries have been dominated by white men." The following year, the paper began a second series of reparatory essays devoted to "a prominent group of black men and women" whose deaths the editors had ignored. "It is difficult for me as a journalist," the editor Amisha Padnami, confessed, "to see important stories go untold. But perhaps more important, as a woman of color, I am pained when the powerful stories of incredible women and minorities are not brought to light."[46]

Among those incredible women and minorities were two fashion designers. Zelda Wynn Valdes (1905–2001) and Elizabeth Keckley (1818–1907).[47] Valdes was a dressmaker to the stars. Her clients included singers, dancers, and Hollywood actresses, among them Dorothy Dandridge, Josephine Baker, Mae West, Ella Fitzgerald, Eartha Kitt, Marian Anderson, and Joyce Bryant—known as the "Bronze Bombshell" or the "Black Marilyn Monroe." Hugh Hefner so admired Valdes's skills that he hired her to help design the first Playboy Bunny costumes in 1960. For her part, a hundred years earlier, Elizabeth Keckley dressed the Washington elite, including Mrs. Jefferson Davis and Mary Lincoln.

Shortly after Mary Lincoln's arrival at the nation's capital, she hired Keckley as her dressmaker. But Keckley became more than that; she became Mary's close friend, traveling companion, and confidant. The relationship lasted about seven years but ended abruptly when Keckley published her memoir, *Behind the Scenes or Thirty Years a Slave, and Four Years in the White House* (1868), the first White House tell-all book. Her revelations included Mary's political views, tensions in the Lincoln marriage, and the heartbreaking reaction of Abraham and Mary to the death of little Willie. Keckley intended the book as a defense of Mary's reputation following the "Old Clothes Scandal" in 1867 (Mary had caused a public scandal when she attempted to raise $10,000 to pay off debts through the sale of her used gowns, jewelry, even undergarments, among other items.)) Mary, however, was outraged by what she considered an invasion of her privacy. Elizabeth assumed that the special relationship with the president's lady, as well as the courtesy and respect given to her by Washington's elite, had lifted her to a position of near social equality with Mary and white society in general. It was a gross miscalculation. Attitudes and assumptions about race and class in American society trumped all presumptions of intimacy in the relationship. Reacting with ugly fury at what she saw as the "colored historian's" violation of her privacy, Mary severed the relationship. Race aside, the revelations in the context of Victorian social conventions would have caused offense whatever the goodwill of the author. Nevertheless, the affair destroyed the friendship. The *New York Times* did not publish its fulsome obituary of Elizabeth Keckley until 113 years after her death, but it did print a review of *Behind the Scenes* in 1868 that shared Mary Lincoln's reaction: "She would much better have stuck with her needle. We cannot but look upon many of the disclosers made in the volume as gross violations of confidence."[48] Robert Lincoln used his considerable influence to have the volume removed from bookstores and libraries.[49] The dressmaker had been effectively "canceled."

The focus on the memoirs as a primary source for understanding the Lincolns' inner life has obscured Keckley's own life and personal sacrifice. Born into slavery, subjected to humiliation, whippings, family separations, and rape, she emerged from years of oppression ("the savage efforts to subdue my pride") a woman of dignity, talent, ambition, and charity. After purchasing her own freedom, Keckley became a dressmaker to elite white women. She styled herself a *modiste,* a skilled artisan of custom-made gowns. Her son, George Kirkland, who passed for white, joined the First Missouri Infantry, a volunteer Union regiment, and died at the Battle of Wilson's Creek in 1861. In 1862, under her leadership, the Contraband Relief Association provided resources—to which the president and First Lady contributed[50]—to some forty thousand destitute enslaved persons who fled captivity and were then living in the filthy refugee camps around Washington. She later established a dressmaking school for freedwomen.[51]

In a scene in Vidal's *miniseries,* the family is adjusting to life in the Executive Mansion: Elizabeth Keckley arrives with a letter of reference from Varina Davis, the wife of Jefferson Davis. Critic Alan Bunce, writing for *the Christian Science Monitor,* praised Mary Tyler Moore's performance: "If you had any misgivings about Mary Tyler Moore as Mary Lincoln, a few seconds of her virtuoso performance should wipe them out. She seems to be having a ball—to the point of showiness once or twice—establishing the strong, turbulent personality of Mary. Southern accent at full throttle, she creates a shrewd ex-belle in readings of full nuance, bite, and furtive undertones that occasionally mock her listeners."

In the following scene, he judges Moore's acting "a marvel of skill" in her first encounter with Keckley: "She seems to bait the woman with terrible accounts of slavery—all the while bubbling about the dress to be made." The scene has a salient point, however: she, not her husband, understands the true horror of slavery. Lincoln opposes slavery on philosophical grounds and to save the Union. Mary opposes slavery "from her gut."

Moore's Mary Lincoln "traces a tragic figure who personifies a nation being torn apart by epic allegiances." Sam Waterston's "Father" and Mary Tyler Moore's "Mother" make "you feel you've been there—not always in the actual Lincoln presence, perhaps, but somewhere close to the human issues at the heart of the matter."[52]

The Scene: Mary's bedroom:

ELIZABETH (Ruby Dee): I am Elizabeth Keckley, Mrs. Lincoln. I am well recommended as a dressmaker. (*then seeing Mary in distress, Keckley pauses*) Are you all right, Mrs. Lincoln?

MARY (Mary Tyler Moore): What? Oh.

ELIZABETH: Is it the headache?

MARY: Ah, No, No, not *the* headache. No, that's very different. No, I can always tell when *the* headache is coming. Lights flash in my eyes. And no one understands except Mr. Lincoln. This is a quite ordinary headache. It will go away. So, you are the dressmaker?

ELIZABETH: Yes, ma'am.

MARY: Well, you see, next Friday evening we are obliged to give a reception and I shall need a new dress.

ELIZABETH: That's only three days from now. Have you the stuff for the dress?

MARY: Yes, the rose-colored moray. You worked for Mrs. Jefferson Davis?

ELIZABETH: Yes, Madame.

MARY: Well, how nice. I've known Mr. Davis for a very long time. I remember him years ago. Pale and elegant. He was, Lord, so young. He addressed the graduation at Transylvania University just before he went off to West Point so many years ago. Well, she writes you a fine reference indeed.

ELIZABETH: I was very fond of Mrs. Davis.

MARY: Then why didn't you go south with her?

ELIZABETH: I am colored.

MARY: But free.

ELIZABETH: I would never live in a slave state. Mrs. Lincoln, I must warn you. I am very political.

MARY: So am I. Though of course I must be very careful. The vampire press is already to spring on me. It is so comical. They say I am pro-Southern and Mr. Lincoln is an abolitionist. It is the reverse. Mr. Lincoln knows nothing of slavery except what he has heard from my family in Lexington. His views are merely philosophical and, of course, political. One of my first memories is of the slaves chained together and being marched to the auction block in the courthouse square, And the whipping post. Lord, I can hear the screams yet. And then there was this Judge Turner. Mrs. Turner was a large, *showy*, violent woman. She beat to death seven slaves that we knew of. When the judge died, he left in his will that his wife Caroline, that was her name, Caroline, was not to get any of the slaves. Well, she overturned the will. I have the pattern right here. *Leslie's* magazine. There was a boy. Richard. He was her coachman. He could read and write. Handsome. Brighter yellow boy. Brighter than you. One morning she chained him up and commenced to beat him to death. He was in such pain, he pulled *loose* of the wall, *seized* her by the throat and choked her to death. Of course, he was arrested by the sheriff, one of Mr. Lincoln's cousins, curiously enough, and hanged for murder.

ELIZABETH (*quietly*): There is no justice on earth.

MARY: There will be. People do not understand that I love my brothers and sisters, and my family. I've made choices in many things and I chose Mr. Lincoln. I'm glad of it. Can you make this dress for me for the reception on Friday?

ELIZABETH: Yes.

MARY: Good. Of course, we are from the outlandish West, as everybody says. And we are poor. You know that, don't you?

ELIZABETH: Yes, Mrs. Lincoln.

MARY: Then we understand each other. I think there may be more employment for you in our household. And remember, no matter what you may read in the press, *I* am the one who wants slavery destroyed.

ELIZABETH: They do not depict you as you are.

MARY: When do they ever? But this earth is only a passing show, Mrs. Keckley.

The dialogue in the introduction of Elizabeth Keckley to the story closely follows Gore Vidal's narrative but edits the conversation between Mary and Elizabeth. Mary's attitude toward slavery in the novel is far clearer a mix of abolitionist ideals, Old South Pollyannaism, moral evasion, and racism. In Vidal's novel, Mary says to Elizabeth: "Mr. Lincoln knows nothing about slavery, except what he heard from me and my family. . . . Yes, we had . . . and we have slaves. But we did not traffic in them, and they governed our lives and not the other way around. Nelson was the butler. He made the finest mint juleps in Kentucky, so everyone said, while Mammy Sally brought us all up and gave us the most thorough spankings you could ever imagine! I see her yet."[53] The scene with Elizabeth Keckley implies that Mary knew firsthand about the Turner murder. She had been married to Lincoln for two years by then and was living in Springfield, Illinois. Nevertheless, her story about the psychopathic Mrs. Turner is reasonably accurate. The August 24, 1844, *Lexington (KY) Observer & Reporter* printed this ad:

500 DOLLARS. REWARD! Runaway on Thursday (22d last) from the residence of Mrs. C.A. Turner. RICHARD. He is about 24 years of age, of yellow complexion, and about 6 feet high. He can read and write, and is a very sensible and plausible [*sic*] negro. He was raised in Fleming county, Ky. By James Jones, who this year brought him to Lexington, and sold him. Mrs. TURNER was found strangled in her house, and from all the circumstances it is believed Richard murdered her, as she was his mistress, and he left immediately after the occurrence.

The accompanying newspaper article went into more detail: "Mrs. Turner was reproving the negro man [her carriage driver] for some bad conduct the evening before, when he seized and strangled her, before she could be rescued from his murderous grasp." The article concluded: "He cannot escape." Indeed, his escape lasted only two days. The Fayette Circuit Court sentenced the man to be hanged on November 19, 1844. (Some speculation asserts that Richard did not choke Mrs. Turner to death but killed her with an axe.)[54] In 1841, Mrs. Turner had filed a petition in the Court of Chancery accusing her husband of abuse. She claimed that over their twenty-year marriage she had had to endure "unspeakable cruelties." In one instance, he ordered one of his slaves to seize and drag her to the plantation "jail," where Mr. Turner kept his "Ungovernable slaves." This "indignity and violence" hastened her decision to move out of their house. Further, he denied Caroline access to her private possessions and her children. He even sold off her body servant Polly. In her suit, she demanded restitution from her husband's "sizable estate," valued at over $200,000 (over $6.5 million in 2022). The court dismissed her case in 1843. Caroline does not mention that at one point Fielding had her committed to an asylum. Nevertheless, she emerged victorious in the end, outliving her husband and untimately gaining control of the estate.[55]

There is another angle to the Keckley story. In 1935, a journalist, David Rankin Barbee, wrote an article distributed by the Associated Press claiming that *Behind the Scenes* was a hoax and that, shockingly, the author, Elizabeth Keckley, in fact never existed. John E. Washington, a member of the capital's Black elite, instantly came to Keckley's defense against the outrageous claims. From Washington's collection of personal recollections of Black men and women who knew the Lincolns—butlers, cooks, barbers, bodyguards, and others—he revealed long-neglected sources for understanding the Lincolns and their relationship to Black Americans. His informants also reflected on their memories of Mary Lincoln. "From my interviews with the old folks," Washington wrote in *They Knew Lincoln* (1942), "I found that she was beloved as no other white woman in public life and that they thought of her as their earthly Holy Mary." Further: "I found that the old people believed that because of the attacks from without and trouble from within, Mrs. Lincoln sought Mrs. Keckley as a friend to look out for her comfort and sympathize with her, and she relied upon her more than her family."[56]

Spiritualism also formed another connection between Mary Lincoln and Elizabeth Keckley. Distraught over the death of Willie, Mary sought consolation through the ministrations of mediums. In the following scene from the Vidal series, Mary arranged a séance with Mrs. Margaret Laurie. Having just survived an attempted assassination on his way to the Old Soldiers' Home,[57] Lincoln enters the room:

MRS. LAURIE: There is danger. Danger! There is a dark cloud hovering over us. Danger!

MARY: (*in a low but emphatic whisper*) Father, do come in.

LINCOLN: Well, I . . . This I take it is the famous oracle, Mrs. Laurie?

MARY: Actually, it's her control that I have been speaking with. The Emperor Constantine.

LINCOLN: Oh, Good evening, Emperor.

MARY: He's been with Willie. So, have I. On the other side. Willie wants to know if Tad has learned to ride his pony. Ah. . . . and he finally met little Eddie.

LINCOLN: How nice for the hostler.

MARY: Don't joke, Father. The Emperor has some good advice.

MRS. LAURIE: (*channeling Emperor Constantine*): Beware of a small man with a large nose.

LINCOLN. Mr. Chase is a large man with a small nose. So, that rules him out.

MARY: It's Seward, who else?

LINCOLN: Molly. Mr. Seward has an important nose. But he is by no stretch a small man. And he has become one of the few friends that the administration and I have got.

MARY: The Emperor feels he has been a bad influence on you and so do I.

(*At this point a bodyguard arrives at the door and informs Lincoln that he has retrieved his hat.*)

LINCOLN: Excuse me, Emperor (*He turns and leaves the room to speak with the messenger.*)

This scene is not beyond historical possibility. Mary Lincoln had a documented connection to the spirit world of the nineteenth century through Mrs. Margaret Ann Laurie (spelled "Laury" in Vidal's novel) and her husband, Cranston Laurie, a post office employee. The Lauries were famous, or infamous, for their entrée to the other side. They and their children exhibited "mediumistic" abilities that involved speaking with the dead through séances and "spirit art." They even conjured an elevating piano. The evidence does not mention the Roman emperor Constantine, but Pinkie, the spirit of an "aztic" princess, is mentioned. Mary also attended sessions at the Lauries' residence in Georgetown. She met with Margaret in the White House seeking peace of mind following Willie's death. The evidence for Abraham Lincoln's participation in spiritualist events is contradictory. No hard facts exist. The Vidal script missed a chance to include a much more fascinating character from the world of nineteenth-century spiritualism—Nettie Colburn, a twelve-year-old wonder who could purportedly commune with the departed. At Mary's request little Nettie "went under control" for an hour and a half during a session with Mary. "This young lady must not leave Washington, I feel she must stay here, and Mr. Lincoln must hear what we heard. It is all-important and he must hear it," she is reported to have said. Nettie was able to summon a certain "Old Dr. Bamford," who had interesting things to say about the Union army and its commanders. Sometimes she was accompanied by Belle Miller, Cranston's daughter, a physical-medium, and her "waltzing" piano.[58]

If the evidence for Abraham Lincoln as spiritualist is more than uncertain, clearly Mary, in her sorrow and despair, found solace in charlatans. Here is a possible connection to Keckley: Historian Nancy Gray Schoonmaker argues that the origins of Mary's interest in the matter go back to her Kentucky days and the influence of the people owned by the Todd family. As a lonely child, Mary found "comfort" in the "African convictions that the barrier between the world of the living and the world of spirits was permeable." Years later, Mary "fell into easy conversation with Elizabeth Keckley in the hours they spent together." And Elizabeth, drawing on her African traditions, urged Mary to seek contact with Willie, whose death had taken him to the other side.[59]

Keckley appears again in Spielberg's *Lincoln* as the president struggles to pass the Thirteenth Amendment to the Constitution. The screenplay, part fact and part fiction, takes as its subject the politics of persuasion, compromise, bribery, and high moral purpose that led to the legal excision of slavery in America. Here Lincoln has a brief conversation with Elizabeth Keckley (Gloria Reuben):

The Scene [according to the script]: Exterior, The portico of the White House. The carriage has pulled up, and Mary is entering the White House. Lincoln helps Mrs. Keckley down from the carriage. She hesitates before proceeding in. Then she faces Lincoln.

ELIZABETH KECKLEY: I know the vote is only four days away; I know you're concerned. Thank you for your concern over this, and I want you to know: They'll approve it. God will see to it.

LINCOLN: I don't envy Him his task. He may wish He'd chosen an instrument for His purpose more [wisely] than the House of Representatives.

KECKLEY: Then you'll see to it. (*Lincoln looks at her, considering.*)

LINCOLN: Are you afraid of what lies ahead? For your people? If we succeed?

KECKLEY: White people don't want us here.

LINCOLN: Many don't.

KECKLEY: What about you?

LINCOLN: I . . . I don't know you, Mrs. Keckley. Any of you. You're . . . familiar to me, as all people are. Unaccommodated, poor, bare, forked creatures such as we all are. You have a right to expect what I expect, and likely our expectations are not incomprehensible to each other. I assume I'll get used to you. But what you are to the nation, what'll become of you once slavery's day is done, I don't know.

KECKLEY: What my people are to be, I can't say. Negroes have been fighting and dying for freedom since the first of us was a slave. I never heard any ask what freedom will bring. Freedom's first. As for me: My son died fighting for the Union, wearing the Union blue. For freedom he died. I'm his mother. That's what I am to the nation, Mr. Lincoln. What else must I be?

This is a remarkable bit of dialogue, in which a Black woman, by the sacrifice of her child, symbolically becomes a mother of the nation. In creating Elizabeth Keckley on film, actress Gloria Reuben[60] said, "I take a great deal of responsibility for all the characters that I portray. But when the character is someone that actually lived, I want that portrayal to be as true to life as possible." And to find "what might be lying beneath the surface."[61] Historian Cory Rosenberg argues that the African Americans in Spielberg's film "only appear on screen when the director wishes to up the emotional ante of a given scene: "Keckley and the other black characters are in the largely 'set dressing,' though, in context, white abolitionists themselves at the time also used 'black bodies' primarily as supporting actors in their crusade against slavery."[62]

TWO INTERPRETATIONS OF MARY

Sandburg's Lincoln (1974) is best known for Hal Holbrook's Emmy Award–winning performance. The remarkable makeup and Holbrook's adoption of a high, squeaky voice effectively evoked Lincoln's looks and tone. For her part, Sada Thompson's Mary Lincoln was a nuanced interpretation aided by her having a passing likeness to Mary herself. Like Mary, Thompson had dark hair and was slightly plump. She later caught national attention for playing another wife and mother, Kate Lawrence, the staid, upper-class matron in *Family*, a long-running ABC television series (1976–80). The series depicited the life, trials, and tribulations of Kate and Doug and their three children. (The backstory to the program includes a passing reference to a son who died.)

Television critic Cecil Smith noted that Kate was the heart of the family but with a twist on the 1950s and 1960s interpretation of the suburban American wife and mother on the small screen: "She's not Mother Knows Best—God knows!—she's quick-tempered, outspoken, and often wrong."[63] That sounds a great deal like another family matriarch—Mary Lincoln. What makes the portrait of Mary ring true is how Thompson evokes her nervousness, obsessions, love of family, intelligence, and political acumen. Thankfully, the writers avoided the tired, hackneyed images of her as the nagging, shrewish antagonist to the ever-patient Man of Sorrow. Sada plays Mary as a complex and conflicted woman thrust into the tremulous climate of Civil War Washington's political, military, and social life. She is good-hearted, for example, when she reprimands the arrogant Robert Lincoln for objecting to the visit of General Tom Thumb and his wife to the White House.

But she is outrageously ignoble when she unfairly and publicly humiliates General Edward C. Ord's wife for presumptuously riding next to Lincoln during the president's review of the troops at City Point in March 1865.

One of the most moving portraits of Mary Lincoln (via Sada Thompson) occurs at the end of the episode titled "The Last Days" in *Sandburg's Lincoln*. It is the afternoon of April 14, 1865. Before getting ready to attend the theater that evening, the couple take a carriage ride through Rock Creek with only about a half dozen soldiers as an escort. Lincoln initially sits in stoic silence. Mary remarks that his look frightens her; she only saw it once before when Willie died in 1862. "We must be more cheerful," Lincoln finally says. Mary asks what they should do once they leave the White House in 1869. Go back to Springfield, Lincoln suggests. His mood brightened. He can be lawyer again or a judge or a farmer. Of course, he will hire someone to run the farm itself. Mary smiles.

They leave the carriage and the escort behind, sitting down by the creek. Lincoln suggests they go to California, where he can pan for gold. He may be the president of all the states, he says, but he has never seen most of them. Mary, with great empathy, suggests Europe—especially Shakespeare's England, and France—which neither has ever seen. Lincoln says he would like to see the Holy Land and walk where Christ walked. They get ready to go back to the carriage, and Mary ends the calm moment between husband and wife. "It's getting late," she says. "We must get ready for the theater tonight." This is a loving couple. Mother and Father are relaxed—no hectoring, no shouting—these two people have endured a long period of personal suffering and come out of the storm stronger.

Mary Tyler Moore rivals Sada Thompson in her interpretation of Mary Lincoln in the 1988 television adaptation of Gore Vidal's novel about the Lincoln war years. Moore became a star in a situation comedy that ran from 1970 to 1977 playing thirty-year-old Mary Richards, a single, high-spirited young woman who becomes the associate producer of the six o'clock news at the fictional WJM TV station in Minneapolis. The show broke ground in the age of second-wave feminism by depicting an independent career woman, freed of husband and children. For all the talk of Mary Richards's liberation, it had limits. The show "textually repositions 'Mary'—the single, professionally minded independent woman—into romantic and familial categories so that she emerges as a self-sacrificing, nurturant figure of True Womanhood."[64] It was likewise for Mary Lincoln. Like most women of her time, she was never truly independent. And, like Mary Tyler Moore's Mary Lincoln, the romantic and familial categories bound her into the role in both life and on film as the self-sacrificing and nurturant figure of domesticity.

Reinhart writes that Moore "sympathetically portrays Mary as an intelligent yet unstable woman whose life is coming apart at the seams due to the loss of her son."[65] She pushed against the boundaries but never escaped them. Although the great Ruth Gordon in *Abe Lincoln in Illinois* presented Mary as a forceful, compelling character, the script did not let her transcend the image of Mary the Shrew. Moore (as well as Thompson) brought to life a quick-tempered, smart, and outspoken Mary Lincoln who is framed in reference to her devotion to her husband and her love for her children.

In a remarkable and purely imaginative scene in the Vidal series, Mary visits Lincoln's office, where he is conversing with Secretary of War Stanton. Mary notices a map showing the movement of the armies of Robert E. Lee and General Gordon Meade. Here Vidal provides Mary with a certain agency—a degree of engagement or initiative missing in all other productions:

MARY: This town here is significant because of all the roads?

STANTON: There *are* a lot of roads, yes.

MARY: (*pointing with her fan*). Oh, but look. The main road here to Baltimore. One here to Philadelphia; and this one to Harrisburg. Why this town is at the very center of everything in Pennsylvania.

LINCOLN: You know, Molly, you may be right. I can't say any of us here at the highest command post of all ever noticed much of anything except a town called Gettysburg.

MARY: *Someone* must have known. These places are not chosen at random, *are they?*

LINCOLN: I have a hunch they are, Molly. You see, General Meade was here (*pointing to the map*) and Lee was here and they have just gone and met between these two places.

MARY: Well let us hope that we do not lose this all-important town.

So, until Mary drew it to their attention, neither Lincoln as commander in chief, nor Stanton as secretary of war, nor Henry "Old Brains" Halleck, the commanding general of the Union army, recognized the strategic importance of Gettysburg.Though no such conversation took place, the scene does illustrate Mary Lincoln's liberation from the hackneyed role of nagging housewife. In another scene, she accompanies her husband to the front lines outside Washington to observe the rebel positions. The officer escorting them is wounded when the enemy opens fire. Lincoln and Mary take cover. She is furious:

MARY: Well, give me a gun and I'll start shooting.

LINCOLN: Mother, you amaze me.

MARY: I mean it. No, I mean it. I was a marvelous shot as a girl. I could kill a squirrel at thirty yards—through the eye.

LINCOLN: You *are* bloodthirsty.

MARY: If only I could get rid of hoops and stays and fans and really fight.

The dialogue above derives in spirit from a real-life scene from the recollections of the artist Francis Carpenter, who spent six months in 1864 at the White House painting the famous cabinet portrait entitled *First Reading of the Emancipation Proclamation of President Lincoln.* He recalled an incident on July 12 during President and Mrs. Lincoln's visit to one of the outer works defending the capital. Rebel sharpshooters made the outing especially dangerous: The president and his lady "were imprudently exposed,—rifle-balls coming, in several instances, alarmingly near! . . . I saw no one who appeared to take this more to heart than Mrs. Lincoln, who was inclined to lay the responsibility at the door of [Edwin M. Stanton] the Secretary of War." Some two or three weeks later, Stanton made light of the incident. "Mrs. Lincoln," he joked, "I intend to have a full-length portrait of you painted, standing on the ramparts at Fort Stevens overlooking the fight!" Mary was up to the challenge: "That's very well, and I can assure you of one thing, Mr. Secretary, if I had had a few *ladies* with me the Rebels would not have been permitted to get away as they did!"[66]

In *Abraham Lincoln: Vampire Hunter,* the feisty Mary shows up at the Battle of Gettysburg, where her husband and the Union army are defending against a Confederate army of the undead. She shoots Vadoma, the demon who had murdered both Nancy Hanks and Willie Lincoln. Since only a silver bullet can kill a vampire, Mary had loaded her Spencer carbine with a silver pendant—a miniature cavalry sword on a necklace once worn by Willie.

Mary Tyler Moore's Mary Lincoln is not only an astute military strategist, she is a tiger as well for the Union cause. But then Bad Mary's unhinged jealously shows up. On a visit to meet her husband to review the troops at City Point in 1865, based on a true event, Mary, who arrives late to the parade, observes that Mrs. Mary Ord (Fay Greenbaum) the wife of the commanding officer, General Edward C. Ord, is riding next to *her* Lincoln. She is insane with anger, calling Mrs. Ord a "whore," a "scarlet woman," and a "camp follower" who makes her living on her back. At that moment "The Headache" appears. Sick with pain, Mary falls into the arms of the general and his wife. Sada Thompson also enacted the Ord Affair in the Sandburg-based series. In that production, after her outburst, she and Lincoln remove themselves to a tent, where Mary apologizes, and Lincoln tenderly holds her in his arms. The scene in *Gore Vidal's Lincoln* is close to the event described in the novel when Mary is overcome during her outburst by her terrible migraine: "Mary felt as if she were floating over the landscape like a cloud, a thundercloud."[67]

Fast-forward to 2012 and Steven Spielberg's Oscar-winning portrait of the last four months of Lincoln's life: Spielberg's approach to the subject is hagiographic, as in all Lincoln films. And, again, he is the Man of Sorrow. The scripts never really change. "When exploring the four exceedingly bloody and hard years of the Civil War," he wrote, "it's impossible not to see Abraham Lincoln as our very own phoenix, emerging from unimaginable devastation to insist that we can be better than we have been, to show us that it's possible to transform the bloodiest war in American history into a means even if a tragic means, by which a great proposition, that all men are created equal, has been tested and found true."

Spielberg created this *Lincoln* from the perspective of a mid-twentieth-century liberal. In his commentary, he recites the progressive litany of the 1960s: "No one can understand the triumphs of the [civil rights] movement's most glorious, inspiring moments, such as the Selma march or Martin Luther King's speaking at the Lincoln Memorial, from the horror of the four little girls being blown up in a church, or the three young men murdered in Mississippi." He emphasized that "the beauty and the memory of Dr. King is indelibly stained with his martyr's blood. As the civil rights workers know, just as the soldiers on Omaha Beach on D-Day knew, democracy offers the promises of reason, justice, happiness, liberty, and peace, but often terrible sacrifice is required before these promises can be realized."[68]

In this way, he connects the civil rights movement, Martin Luther King, and the legacy of the Greatest Generation to the story of the Great Emancipator. In a study of the biopic and American national identity, film scholar R. Barton Palmer argues that Spielberg's film is "another version of the medium's long tradition of moralizing biography, making room for sequences depicting Lincoln's stormy but loving marriage to Mary Todd . . . in which he shows tolerance and love for a woman generally acknowledge to be difficult."[69] He loves his wife and his sons. He is devoted to emancipation. If Lincoln was the Great Heart of the Age of Griffith, when he stood for reconciliation between brothers North and South, he is now the Great Emancipator in the Age of Obama. It was a long journey for Mary Lincoln as well. Now, Sally Field's Mary "is a woman with interest in both Houses [Congress and the Executive Mansion], historian Andrea Foroughi observes. "Even as it acknowledges the political restraints this nineteenth-century wife, mother, and first lady faced, *Lincoln* presents family relations and gender politics in a way that its twentieth-century audiences will recognize."[70]

Spielberg originally intended to make a war movie based on the last three years of the Civil War. He wrote a preliminary script between 2001 and 2002. Over the time it took him to bring the film into production, his intention changed as the mood of the country did as well. This could not be another battle-and-leaders approach. This could not be another *Gettysburg* (1993) or *Gods and Generals* (2005). It would be (it had to be) about race and politics. The focus narrowed to the last four months of the Lincoln presidency. He wanted to tell a Lincoln story, but the president's character, he judged, would be "lost" in a film about titanic battles. Instead, the story now centered on Lincoln, his cabinet, and the politics of emancipation—a much reduced, more intimate drama and a more relevant topic. Spielberg ultimately rejected his own script and hired Tony Kushner, who researched and wrote the final Lincoln screenplay.[71] "I shared Steven's divided loyalty between Lincoln's light and darkness," Kushner noted. "Daniel Day-Lewis incarnated it. Almost everyone who's spent time with Lincoln concludes, as

Carl Sandburg did after his epic effort to encompass the man, that to truly describe Lincoln, you must 'put in mystery without end. Then add mystery.'"[72] The same can be said of Mary Lincoln.

"DAMAGED GOODS":
STEVEN SPIELBERG'S MARY LINCOLN

It had been seventy-two years since a major motion picture about Lincoln appeared, Spielberg stated in a promotional interview. It was time for a fresh approach. Irish actor Daniel Day-Lewis became the new Lincoln, and Sally Field the new Mary. Out of respect to their memory and to keep the actors in character on the sets, he addressed Day-Lewis as "Mr. Lincoln" and Field as either "Molly" or "Mary Todd." (Mary, no doubt, would have insisted on being called "Mrs. Lincoln.")

Regarding his approach to the character of Molly, Spielberg states, "The most important thing was to be fair. We've all read different accounts of Mary, and how her condition might be defined in modern psychology. There have been stacks of authors who were for her, and stacks of authors who were against her. We knew one thing, based on the facts; Mary was the engine of Lincoln's ambition." She stood by him in political defeat confident of his eventual success: "Without Mary, when Lincoln lost the Senate to Stephen Douglas, he probably would never have imagined that after that Senate loss, he could next go for the highest office in the land. Mary supplied the motor that put Lincoln in the direction of his destiny. She just believed in him, and he believed in her belief in him." And her mood swings: "He looked to her as a guiding force, a light, but also as damaged goods. He knew when she was being rational and politically savvy, and when she was being emotionally irrational. At those times, he did his best just to simply let her go through moods and those manic moments, just sit with her for hours and hours and hours and let her vent until she came out of a fog. In that sense it was one of so many burdens during his presidency."[73]

Spielberg and Kushner both credited historian Doris Kearns Goodwin's best-seller *Team of Rivals: The Political Genius of Abraham Lincoln* (2005) as the principal source of their story.[74] Journalist Timothy Noah, however, propounds an alternative thesis about the origins of *Lincoln*. He argues that the real source was not Goodwin's narrative history that begins with Lincoln's early life, but a more focused history of the politics of emancipation by Brown University historian Michael Vorenberg entitled *Final Freedom: The Civil War, the Abolition of Slavery, and the Thirteenth Amendment* (2001).[75] Kushner replied to Noah that he drew upon some twenty to thirty books, including Vorenberg's, but insisted that Goodwin's was the key. "No book that I read was as significant," he replied to Noah. "Doris's book is a magnificent account of Lincoln as a master politician that is the Lincoln I really wanted to write about," he emphasized. It was the book "to which I am most indebted."[76] Kushner also conversed with thirteen other historians. Whatever the case, the Goodwin book has little to say about the politics of the Thirteenth Amendment but, interestingly, much more about Mary Lincoln.

In the most intense family scene in Spielberg's film, Mary excoriates her husband over Willie's death and, having vehemently opposed their son's joining the army, Robert's possible death as a soldier. The death of another child would not, could not be endured. Lincoln lashes out angrily: "Just, just this once, Mrs. Lincoln, I demand of you to try and take the liberal and not the selfish point of view." Mary responds "with a mocking smile," "and if I refuse to take the high road . . . will you threaten me again with the madhouse as you did when I couldn't stop crying over Willie, when I showed you what heartbreak, real heartbreak looked like, and you hadn't the courage or countenance to help me ?"

Lincoln explodes, denouncing Mary's "grief, your grief . . . inexhaustible grief." He continues: "And his mother won't let him near her, 'cause she's screaming from morning to night pacing the corridors, howling at shadows and furniture and ghosts! I ought to have done it, I ought to have done it for Tad's sake, for everybody's god-damned sake I should have clapped you in the madhouse!"

> MARY: "THEN DO IT! Do It! Don't you threaten me, you do it this time! Lock me away! You'll have to, I swear, if Robert is killed!"

"WILL YOU BE OUR MOLLY?"

When director Steven Spielberg considered Sally Field for the role of Mary Lincoln, he asked Daniel Day-Lewis to approve the casting. After Day-Lewis met with Field, Spielberg asked her, "Will you be our Molly?" Yes, she replied ecstatically. But how would she interpret the character? She said that Catherine Clinton's biography of Mary Lincoln had been the most helpful to her. Over dinner, she and Clinton discussed the project: "Instead of giving me her own opinions as to what was going on with Mary," Field recalls, "she simply stated the facts, said what everyone else thought they meant, and then let me draw my own conclusions." She had found the information in Clinton's book on Mary's married life especially helpful. "Most of my scenes were with Daniel [Day-Lewis]," she explained. "When you're playing someone with a long married life, there has to be a connection, an intimacy, that you can't fake. You have to find that place where human beings know each other so well, and their physicality together becomes incredibly important. You really have to know where they are sexually. Do they touch each other, or is there just an unconscious intimacy between them? All of that plays even if you never speak about it, even if the scenes are about something else. Catherine's book was especially good for me because it gave me that sort of information."[77]

To get Mary's accent just right, the actor borrowed research tapes from the film's dialect coach of elderly women from the area around Lexington, Kentucky, Mary's birthplace. The recordings dated from the 1980s, "when the women [themselves] were in their eighties, so they weren't that far removed from the Civil War," Field explained. "Even though the accents had become a little more homogenized, you could still hear a little of the way people used to speak in that part of the country." Besides Sally Field, two others added their talents to creating the role, Kathleen Kennedy and Joanna Johnston.

Producer Kathleen Kennedy praised Field for her unconventional interpretation of Mary Lincoln. Sally Field could have easily played Mary as the shrew; instead, she sought (as Moore and Thompson did) a more nuanced approach. "In many respects," Kennedy states," Sally Field had one of the most difficult roles in the movie. A lot has been written about Mary Lincoln and how incredibly distraught and depressed she was, not only because of the loss of two children, but also because, at this point in the story, the war had been raging for years and there is so much sadness throughout the country. She experienced this sadness in her own family, and she watched the country go through it as well. Sally could have taken that and done something very predictable, but instead she found an incredible amount of restraint. So much of what Mary went through was overwhelming, but you understand the need for her to be the first lady and to support her husband."[78]

Costume designer Joanna Johnston sought to interpret Mary through her gowns, knowing how important fashion was to the First Lady: "At the start of this project, I knew nothing about Mary Todd, except that she was an off-looking creature who spent a lot of money on clothes and seemed to annoy everyone. But as I learned more about her, I became incredibly fascinated by her character. She seemed to be a very misrepresented person and was probably rather extraordinary." "When," she explained, "you study her, you learn that she was incredibly conscientious about the way she dressed, and she had a very particular style. That's why such a great volume of work went into Mary Todd—because she had such a huge closet in her life, and we needed to get a sense of her."[79]

THE GRAND RECEPTION

Spielberg's *Lincoln.* The Scene [according to the script]: January 15, 1865. The enormous White House room is splendid, decked out with garlands of flowers, tall candelabra burning, flags from army divisions. An orchestra plays. Lincoln is uncomfortable and tugs at his gloves. Approaching Mary in the reception line are Congressmen Thaddeus Stevens [Tommy Lee Jones], James Ashley [David Costabile] along with Senators Benjamin "Bluff" Wade [Wayne Duvall] and Charles Sumner [John Hutton]. Historian Cory Rosenberg observes that "Sally Field's Mary Todd Lincoln is haggard, domineering, and effective from the first shot. Her vitriolic speech and explosive temper are let loose in tempests of alternating rage and sorrow when alone with the president, and in dagger-sharp barbs and invectives pronounced through a forced smile while in public":[80]

MARY: Senator Sumner, it has been much too long.

SUMNER: (*interjects*) "Oh, who can look on that celestial face and . . .

(*Cutting him off, Mary pretends to recognize Ashley.*)

MARY: And . . .?

ASHLEY: James Ashley, ma'am, we've met several times.

(*She ignores him and greets Stevens.*)

MARY (*Her Southern accent becomes more lustrous.*): Praise Heavens, praise Heavens, just when I had abandoned hope of amusement, it's the Chairman of the House Ways and Means Committee!

(*Stevens bows to her.*)

STEVENS: Mrs. Lincoln.

MARY: Madame President, if you please! (*Mary laughs.*) Oh, don't convene another subcommittee to investigate me, sir! . . . I'm teasing! . . . Smile, Senator Wade.

WADE (*not smiling*): I believe I am smiling, Mrs. Lincoln.

STEVENS: As long as your household accounts are in order, Madame, we'll have no need to (*slight laugh*) investigate them.

MARY: You have always taken such a lively, even prosecutorial interest in my household accounts.

STEVENS: Your household accounts have always been so interesting.

MARY: Yes, thank you, it's true, the miracles I have wrought out of fertilizer bills and cutlery invoices. But I had to! Four years ago, when the President and I arrived, this was a pure pigsty. Tobacco stains in the Turkey carpets. Mushrooms, green as the moon, sprouting from the ceilings! And a pauper's pittance allotted for the improvements. As if your committee joined with all of Washington waiting, in what you anticipated would be the comfort in squalor, further proof that my husband and I were prairie primitives, unsuited to the position to which an error of the people, a flaw in the democratic process elevated us.

(*Lincoln, suddenly without anyone in line to receive, looks to see the backlog forming behind the radicals. He notes the exchange but says nothing. Robert sees him looking.*)

MARY (*continuing*): The past is the past, it's a new year now and we are all getting along, or so they tell me. I gather we are working tighter! The White House and the other House? Hatching little plans together.

(*Robert leans to her.*)

ROBERT: Mother?

MARY: What?

ROBERT: You're creating a bottleneck.[81]

MARY: Oh! (*to Stevens*) Oh! I'm detaining you, and more important, the people behind you! How the people love my husband, they flock to see him, by their thousands on public days! They will never love you the way they love him. How difficult it must be for you to know that. And yet how important to remember it.

(*She gives him a slight, lethal smile. He holds the look; his poker-face yields to a barely perceptible smile, amused and perhaps a little admiring.*)

The last conversation between the Lincolns in Spielberg's opus takes place during a carriage ride on the afternoon before the assassination. The Lincolns are discussing traveling after Lincoln leaves office. Lincoln suggests visiting the West by rail; Mary asks about going "overseas." Lincoln suggests, "The Holy Land . . . Jerusalem. Where David and Solomon walked. I dream of walking in that ancient city." They lapse into silence until Mary, sadly, interjects: "All anyone will remember of me is I was crazy, and I ruined your happiness." Lincoln responds, "Anyone thinks that doesn't understand, Molly." Mary's last words in the scene suggest a vision of how the future will regard her: "When they look at you, at what it cost to live in the heart of this, they'll wonder at it. They'll wonder at you. They should. But they should also look at the wretched woman by your side, if they want to understand what this was truly like. For an ordinary person. For anyone other than you." Lincoln responds: "We must try to be happier. We must. Both of us. We've been miserable for so long." (In Gore Vidal's television series, the last carriage ride dialogue is just three lines. Mary says to Lincoln:

"I know I have not made it easy for you." Lincoln gently responds, "I have not taken care of you as I should" A pause, then, "I am happy.")

Mary's final scene in the Spielberg's *Lincoln* is at her husband's deathbed. It was the last day of shooting. Field recalls the emotional moment for the cast: "Mary kisses her husband's hand good-bye, and she's ushered out of the room while he lies there, dying. By that time, I don't think any of us knew the difference between the film and reality, including Steven."[82]

■ ■ ■

The traditional portrayals of Mary Todd recycle through every depiction of her until the 1970s. Typically, In *Abe Lincoln in Illinois,* she lapses into a savage soliloquy when Lincoln, at the last moment and with some humor, tells her that a delegation of party officials is coming to their house to offer him the nomination for president. She scorches Lincoln for his lack of ambition. In truth, if not in Hollywood, Lincoln was hugely ambitious for the presidency and carefully and, one might say, cunningly maneuvered his way into the nomination.

Thompson, Moore, and Field offered nuanced depictions of Mary Lincoln. They made her more believable by providing a counterpoint to the mawkish traditions of Hollywood film. These new interpretations were welcome revisions to the clichés embedded in the Bad Mary tropes, and they serve as antidotes to the venom of her critics.

REDUX

The Last of Mrs. Lincoln

History is "the charting of economic and political weather," English biographer Michael Holroyd observes: "What is missing [from history without biography] . . . is the individual on whom the weather rains and shines and without whom, without her, history is a remote thing."[1] During her life and her afterlife in public memory, literature, and film, Mary Todd Lincoln encountered more rain than sunshine.

Even in death Mary could not escape public ridicule. On July 18, 1882, two days following her passing, the *New York Times* published a patronizing obituary that encapsulated the image of the widow Mary: It was her "hard fate that she was translated [*sic*] while in the maturity of life, to a sphere of which she was not wholly fitted." She was a woman "invested with a certain historic and tragic interest," and who, although she "was not a woman of exquisite refinement nor of a high intellectual development," was, nevertheless, "a devoted, loyal, and affectionate wife."[2]

Consider the sorrows of Mary Lincoln: Over her lifetime she suffered agonizing personal tragedies, chronic ill health, and public scorn. An often-absent father, a distracted mother who died when Mary was eight, and a wicked stepmother shaped her childhood. Her relations with her siblings were often strained. Shortly after her father died of cholera, Mary's second child, Edward, died from "consumption" (tuberculosis) at age three. The third son, Willie, died of "bilious fever" (perhaps typhoid) at age eleven. Several close friends and Todd family members died in the Civil War. She witnessed her husband's murder. Her fourth son and constant companion during her widowed years, "Taddie," died at eighteen (tuberculosis, pleurisy, pneumonia, or, possibly, congestive heart failure). Only the eldest son, Robert, from whom she was alienated for seven years, lived through adulthood. In 1863, she sustained a traumatic, coma-inducing brain injury as the result of a carriage accident. As a consequence, the injury possibly led to spells of uncontrolled or inappropriate behavior. In midlife and especially during her declining years, evidence based on varying degrees of reliability indicates that she suffered or imagined to herself to suffer from a wide variety of medical conditions.

Mary Lincoln's list of real or imagined ailments is truly formidable: gynecological problems, tuberculous, pleurisy, myxedema, boils, diabetic gangrene, insomnia, migraine headaches, neuralgia, posttraumatic stress, vitamin deficiency, narcissistic personality disorder, depression, delusions, dementia, hallucinations, persistent cough, "weak lungs," mood disorder, choral hydrate overdoses, sensitivity to light, incontinence, nervous breakdowns, pernicious anemia, and tabes dorsalis. The last is a slow degeneration of the nerve cells and fibers that carry sensory information to the brain. It can be a consequence of syphilis, though Mary's health records contain no evidence of this.[3] A fall from a stepladder in 1876 caused an "inflammation of the spinal cord and partial paralysis of lower part of her body."[4] If any of this reflected attention-getting hypochondria, the pain and disabilities were no less real to her.[5]

Was she crazy? Film scholar Dennis Bingham in his study of the Hollywood biopics mentions *An Angel at My Table* (1991), a film based on the life of New Zealand writer Janet Frame, who, misdiagnosed with schizophrenia, found herself committed to an asylum and in danger of being lobotomized: "Frame's story is an extreme example of how someone who deviates from the expectations of women can be judged—and she will be judged in some way—as mad."[6] This could be the script for a revisionist depiction of Mary Lincoln that portrays her as the victim of a patriarchal system unable to accept a woman of independent thought. On the other hand, an interpretation holds that she was, clearly, bipolar[7]—a condition revealed by her wired personality characterized by agitation, euphoria, sleep deprivation, instances of unusual talkativeness, racing thoughts, mood swings, and distractibility.

Margaret Stuart Woodrow, Mary's cousin and childhood friend, remembered Mary as "very highly strung, nervous, impulsive, excitable, having an emotional temperament much like an April day, sunny all over with laughter one moment, the next crying as though her heart would break."[8] In a mid-December 1869 letter to her friend Sally Orne, Mary reflected on her decline and on happier times: "Tomorrow is the anniversary of my birthday—I will be 46—and feel 86."[9] Over the years, whittled down by tragedy and illness, physical and emotional frailty, and by personal and political enemies, Mary aged rapidly. "Sick in mind & worn out in body, my present state, has become unendurable. . . . I am racked with pain," she reported to a friend in 1870.[10] When Mary was fifty-four, in 1872, a photograph of her illustrates her physical decay: "a pulpy, square-jawed woman" with "glassy and clouded eyes."[11]

There is another photograph from 1872. Obsessed by the memory of her husband, she visited the "spirit photographer" William H. Mumler, an infamous grifter who took advantage of the bereaved. He operated out of the studio of the famed Civil War photographer Matthew Brady. According to Peter Manseau, historian, museum curator, and novelist, "the pictures she left with that day would become the most famous spirit photograph of all." It shows Mary sitting, dressed all in black. A ghostly image of her beloved "Mr. Lincoln" stands behind her with his hand on her left shoulder: "To some, the photograph . . . is evidence of her gullibility or her madness. To others, it suggests not just the psychological damage done to one woman, but the suffering of the nation that she represents in her grief. To her, it was simply the kind of comfort that made all other meanings irrelevant."[12]

Her obsessions and depression never ceased. Her life became an earthly purgatory. During her confinement in the asylum in 1875, she attempted suicide by poison—what she thought to be a concoction of laudanum and camphor. A photograph taken in 1880 shows her to be "little and thin, wrinkled and gray . . . [and] "look[ing] like an old woman."[13]

■ ■ ■

Gore Vidal said that when he wrote the conclusion to his novel *Lincoln,* "it seemed quite natural to end with the assassination. There would have been no point in continuing with Mary Todd's story. That didn't interest me anyway. Historical novels seem to follow their own designs, their own self limits."[14] Theater and television writer James Prideaux, however, extended the limits of the Lincoln story and treated Mary Lincoln as a woman in her own right in his 1972 play *The Last of Mrs. Lincoln,* which PBS released as a filmed theater production in 1976. Here Mary is the protagonist who gets to tell her own story. In the opening scene, a certain "Senator Austin" (Denver Pyle) visits Mary Todd Lincoln (Julie Harris) while she is staying in a lonely, self-imposed exile in Frankfurt, Germany. The year is 1868. The scene begins with the usual courtesies. Then the tone changes. Tension rises quickly as Austin voices a litany of complaints against Mary: She allowed her half sister, Emilie Helm, a Confederate widow, to stay in the White House during the war. She has been outspoken on political matters. She has criticized the United States Senate for refusing her an appropriate pension. She is an embarrassment. She should shut up:

SENATOR AUSTIN: I had hoped in the intervening years you had learned the wisdom of silence.

MARY: When I see injustice, I feel it my duty to speak.

SENATOR AUSTIN: The duty of a president's wife is to smile and dispense tea ... nothing more.

MARY: Oh? Is she to show no interest in the affairs of her country?

SENATOR AUSTIN: Interest is one thing, interference is another.

MARY: Is that an accusation toward *me,* Senator?

SENATOR AUSTIN: You may call it what you like. You tampered with political appointments. You attempted to influence the president.

MARY: Well, I admit I did my share of talking.

Julie Harris knew how to reanimate women from the past. During her career, in addition to Mrs. Lincoln, she played the writer Isak Dinesen, Florence Nightingale, Nora Joyce (the wife of James Joyce), Dora Carrington (of the Bloomsbury literary group), Fanny Osbourne (the wife of Robert Louis Stevenson), movie actress June Havoc, Queen Victoria, and, most famously, Emily Dickinson in the Emmy-winning, one-woman play *The Belle of Amherst* in 1976. On her interpretation of Mary, Harris asks rhetorically, "Would it have helped the image of Mary Lincoln—whose downfall came about by her love of beautiful things—to have had an Aristotle Onassis in her widowhood-by-assassination—instead of badgering Congress over a small pension?" She concludes: "That never could have happened with this woman. Jackie Kennedy had not the necessity to love the one man in such a way that when he was taken, there could be no other life." Drawing on the research of Ida Tarbell, Harris concluded: Lincoln "wasn't born a saint, he had to work at it." And on his relationship with Mary, "a man at Mary Lincoln's funeral said that she and the President were like twin trees that were struck by the same lightning bolt—though one took a long time to die."[15]

The Last of Mrs. Lincoln opened in December 1972 at the American National Theater in New York City. It reappeared four years later on the Public Broadcasting System's Hollywood's Television Theatre. The story focuses on Mary Lincoln during the post-assassination years in America and Germany. Although it is not a Hollywood feature film, it is by far the best dramatic treatment of this complex woman—and the only one to present a retrospective of her life.[16] This is Mary's Passion Play. And it provides her with a voice and a greater degree of agency. The author sees her as a smart although deeply conflicted woman obsessed by money worries, intrusions of a scandal-hungry press, her pension dispute with the US Senate, her status as the former president's wife, her memories of dead children, and her husband's murder. Yet, this is a woman who fought against the injustices of history. The principal characters in the drama are her sister, Elizabeth; her dressmaker and confidant "Lizzie" Keckley; her invalid son Tad; and Robert, her eldest and emotionally remote son. She is also haunted in her mind by the ghost of Ann Rutledge.

In the story Mary resembles Tennessee Williams's Blanche DuBois in his play A Streetcar Named Desire (1947), a sad, exploited, unstable woman relying on "the kindness of strangers" to survive. Like Blanche, Mary is mentally and physically frail. "I've just got to get away" to a place, Blanche laments, "where I'm not regarded as a lunatic. Sometimes I think I'll have to spend the rest of my life in the company of strangers."

Hollywood's Mary was, of course, always the story's secondary character, the second banana, never the protagonist. In two acts, Prideaux (who also scripted the episode "Mrs. Lincoln's Husband" for Sandburg's Lincoln) puts Mary center stage, where she gets to tell her story. The New York Times critic John J. O'Connor applauded Harris's performance: Her "conception and execution of the role are similar to a multicolored mosaic. As Mrs. Lincoln, she lightly flits from Southern graciousness to bitter determination, from a kind of [Blanche] DuBois distractedness to a calculating charm."[17] Though "pounded by tragedy" and a regiment of enemies, she maintains her dignity and her unconditional devotion to her husband. In the play's last scene, she is living in her sister Elizabeth's home in Springfield, where she married Abraham Lincoln so long ago. She is near death. The memories flood back of Ann Rutledge; of her first dance with Abraham Lincoln; of election night in 1860; and of herself as Mrs. Lincoln. For once, Mary herself gets to tell her story in all of its tragic complications. These are the things she carries in the chambers of her consciousness:

ANN RUTLEDGE

MARY: How dare he [Herndon] say that! I wrote letters, I asked friends about it. She was the fiancé of someone else and dearly loved by him. Mr. Lincoln knew the family. I know that he lived in their home in New Salem, and they were very good to him. When their daughter died, you may be sure Mr. Lincoln grieved. His great heart was always touched by death. But he told me many times that I was the only woman he ever loved.

THE FIRST DANCE

MARY (*Shakes her head and speaks haltingly to her young friend David Baker*): I want to . . . talk to you. I want to tell you something. It was . . . in this room. A party. There was music. I had been dancing. I was sitting . . . on the sofa. To get my breath. I looked up . . . looked up . . . and I saw him. I saw him . . . coming toward me . . . this strange . . . beautiful . . . man . . . coming toward me. I knew . . . in that moment . . . what my life . . . was meant to be. I saw . . . what nobody else . . . in the world . . . could see . . . I saw shining through . . . his beautiful eyes . . . the look of God. "Miss Todd" . . . he said . . . "I want to dance with you . . . in the worst way." And he did.

THE ELECTION OF 1860

I rush to the window of the house at the corner of Eighth Street and Jackson in Springfield, Illinois, and, my, the bells get louder and louder, and I look down the street to where the crowd is coming, cheering and throwing their hats in the air. And in the center of the crowd, taller than anyone, walks Mr. Lincoln, the expression I know so well on his face, sad and tired but a slight smile, and everyone trying to shake his hand. His face is lit by torchlight. My heart is beating so fast I have to hold on to the window frame. I rush down the stairs to meet him at the door and I can't help the tears running down my cheeks. People pour in and I don't hear what they say. It's only when he comes in and stands above me and I feel his hands on my shoulders, and he says to me, "Well, mother, I am to be the president," that I understand what has happened. "I am very glad Mr. Lincoln," I say.

ON BEING MARY LINCOLN

ELIZABETH (*Priscilla Morrill, coming forward with the tea tray*): I asked you to remember that you were a Todd. All our lives I've had to remind you that you were a Todd.

MARY: I'm no longer a Todd, Elizabeth, I'm a Lincoln.

ELIZABETH: You wouldn't have been if you had listened to us. But you went ahead and married beneath you.

MARY: I think it should be clear now that I married *above* me.

LEWIS BAKER: Mr. Lincoln was . . .

ELIZABETH: Mr. Lincoln was not a gentleman!

MARY: You are quite right, Elizabeth, Mr. Douglas was a gentleman. Mr. Lincoln was a saint!

Robert Lincoln (Michael Cristofer), in the last line in the story, says of Mary Lincoln: "Tad . . . used to tell of my mother that she was a great lady. Perhaps she was not that. But I hope when you write of her, you will say this: as she would have wished and let it be her epitaph. She had a great love." Surely Mary experienced true love and, from time to time, a certain happiness, yet genuine joy always evaded her.

CODA

Shirley Temple and Marilyn Monroe
in Lincoln's Legacy

If Abraham Lincoln as The Studious Boy in *The Blue Bird* dreaded his future, Shirley Temple looked forward to another hit in 1940. Alas, it was not to be. The movie received tepid applause. *New York Times* reviewer Frank Nugent called it "brilliantly Technicolored, scaled to the dimensions of a World of Tomorrow and replete with Shirley Temple. As a children's show we suppose it is quite acceptable."[1] Worse than being merely "acceptable," it lost money. If this was the advent of Abe's screen career, it was the beginning of the end of little Shirley's. What happened to the golden moppet? Audiences disliked her in the role of a bratty child. More seriously, at age eleven, although still uniquely pretty, she had lost a bit of that baby-face cuteness so endearing to her legions of fans. In fact, when Shirley's *The Little Princess* came out in 1939, Darryl Zanuck had been so concerned that the kid was approaching "that awkward age" of puberty that he suggested that the studio publicity department reset her birthday from 1928 to 1927.[2] So, in 1940, she was eleven going on ten, "the most improbable child in the world," according to the *New York Times*.[3]

Though by 1940 Miss Temple had clearly arrived at her sell-by date, she continued to hold a special meaning for audiences in the tormented age of the Great Depression—though Abe still had the war years to look forward to. Franklin D. Roosevelt had joined them to form the dynamic trio—iconic, hopeful images in the America of the 1930s who helped make life bearable for an anxious generation. Beset by the greatest economic catastrophe in the nation's history and the war clouds gathering in Europe, Americans took comfort in the image of Abraham Lincoln as the Great Humanitarian; Shirley Temple as the spunky, self-reliant kid; and FDR as the cheerful, indispensable political leader—the holy trinity of American civic faith.

In a series of some forty-five movies in the 1930s, Shirley Temple demonstrated onscreen a remarkable resilience in the face of numerous hardships—usually a missing father. "It is a sidelong proof of how far the Depression had eroded confidence in the 1930s that it took Shirley Temple to reassure so many," says David Thomson. "For the characteristic situation," in each film, "is not just a child leading her life under adult shadows, but a Lilliputian moralist in ringlets, tap-dancing into your heart [or Abraham Lincoln's] and then delivering the sententious message that sorts out all the confusion."[4] Her role in "virtually all of these films is to soften hard hearts (especially of the wealthy), to intercede on the behalf of others, [and] to effect liaisons between members of opposed social classes."[5]

Temple began her film career in a series of ten-minute, one-reel comedies entitled *Baby Burlesks* (*sic*) in 1932–33. Produced by Educational Films (a company title that was surely an ironic invention), the movies often featured little children imitating sexualized adult behavior. The seminude, shockingly provocative preschoolers acted out satires of politics, film stars, and film genres, including war films and the Tarzan movies. What stands out today, however, is the disturbingly sexualized performances of half-naked children. "From the waist up, we costumed as adults. From the waist down, we wore only diapers secured by a safety pin large enough to have come off a horse blanket," the adult Shirley remembered."[6] In *War Babies* (originally *What Price Gloria?*), Shirley appears as a "bar girl" in a takeoff of *What Price Glory?* (1926), a comedy–war film in which Dolores del Río played an innkeeper's daughter in love with an American marine. ("'Me, monsieur?' I said coyly, as one diaper-clad doughboy yanked me to his side," she wrote in her autobiography.)[7] For her role in *Polly Tix in Washington* (1933), a call girl dressed in a black off-the-shoulder gown, the little "vixen" is "a strumpet on the payroll of the Nipple Trust and the Anti-Castor Oil Lobby." Her role, Shirley Temple recalled fifty years later, "was the task of seducing a newly arrived bumpkin senator." ("Aw, c'mon, Senator, you can be had.") The child actress was directed to display "aggressive charms" and perform "kootchy dances." The adult Shirley lamented, "Being a child star is a complicated life, especially if you are four years old."[8]

From the beginning, something weirdly ambiguous attended the amazing tike with the cunning of an adult. Preschoolers acting as adults may have amused an audience then, but today such role-playing seems closer to child pornography. Surely, some viewers found these antics not only cute but also arousing. In *Glad Rags to Riches,* Temple, as a saloon singer, parodies Mae West in *She Done Him Wrong* (1933), while *Kids in Africa* casts her half-naked in a dangerous jungle.

Nine minutes and forty-five seconds into the *Polly Tix in Washington* episode, we meet a Senate candidate on the "Clodbuster" ticket who is running a campaign against castor oil. The castor oil lobby offers him bribes of wealth and fine clothes—all of which he rejects: "Not for Sale." The lobby then turns to its secret weapon: Miss Polly Tix (Were the writers thinking, "Polly Turns Tricks"?). The scene: Five-year old Shirley Temple is attired in a bra and panties as the lobbyist purchases her services to "entertain" the senator and convince him to change his vote. She sashays into the senator's office, announces that she is "Polly Tix," and plants a lingering kiss on the senator's lips. The senator tries to resist, then declares, "I think you're the most beautiful woman I've ever seen." More deep kisses from Polly, who announces, "I'm expensive." The senator says he is a poor man. "You can have any luxury if you'll vote for my bill," Polly counters. One of these luxuries is a giant cake that she unveils and tempts him to taste. The senator resists. Polly persists, eating a piece of cake and declaring, "this is lovely." As the senator attempts to eat the cake, two of his supporters, including his daughter, try to pull him away. A tug-of-war with Polly ensues. "Why don't you leave my father alone!" the daughter shouts to Polly. "He's not your kind. You're not a good woman." Polly tells her she is crazy, displays an armful of glittering jewelry, and asserts, "You have to be good to get stuff like this." Again, dazzled by Polly, the senator goes for the cake and receives yet more kisses. Finally, the senator pushes her away. The lobbyist appears and asks, "Is it fixed?" and offers Polly more jewelry. She refuses and declares, "I love him." Enraged, the lobbyist tries to strangle her. The senator and his aides come to the rescue and chase the villain off. More kisses. The film ends with the senator asking one of his aides what he is looking for. He answers, "prosperity." Beyond being child actors, these were New Deal propagandists in diapers.

So, there was more to Shirley's image than the little kid who defies the odds. So improbable was Shirley's presence onscreen that a rumor circulated that this was no supernaturally inspired child at all. This was a talented thirty-year-old midget.[9] "Until 1937," she wrote, "my film image had been someone cuddlesome and cute, a matchmaker and problem solver, a child unsinkable and indestructible, always a paragon of purity." A more mature Shirley appeared in *Wee Willie Winkie* (1937). Her character sang only one song, did not dance, and, more importantly, exhibited hints of the emerging physical maturity so evident by 1940. By 1937, she had begun, Shirley later stated, "to turn one shoulder on childhood." She saw her performance in Ford's adventure film as progress or growth in her acting career. "Not everyone ... was content to hold me static," she noted. Concerned about Hollywood's increasing influence on modern culture and Shirley Temple's not so subliminal erotic appeal, the Vatican newspaper, *Osservatore Romano,* sent a representative, one Father Silvio Massante, to interview the tiny actress. In her autobiography, Temple reflected on the interview with amusement: Was she familiar with the paintings of Botticelli, he asked? Did she know any Italian words? Would she like to visit Italy? "And her religious instruction?" he inquired of her mother. As he was leaving, he stopped, looked down at his shoes, turned toward Shirley and her mother, and said: "In Italy, as in some other countries of Europe there is the perception that she is no child at all," he stated. Now he was satisfied—not so for British novelist and journalist Graham Greene in his take on what transcended messages of true grit in the face of economic hardship in her films—adult sex appeal. To make this assertion so public was dangerous.

Criticizing the child wonder and national mascot was an act of near blasphemy. In a review of *Captain January* (1936) in *Night and Day* (Britain's answer to the *New Yorker*), Greene wrote: "The latest Shirley Temple picture is sentimental, a little depraved, with an appeal interestingly decadent. ... Shirley Temple acts and dances with immense vigor and assurance, but some of her popularity seems to rest on a coquetry quite as mature as Miss [Claudette] Colbert's and on an oddly precocious body as voluptuous in grey flannel trousers as Miss [Marlene] Dietrich's."[10] Shirley was seven years old at the time.

Inspired by his anti-American sentiments and with ill-considered flippancy, Greene doubled down on the topic of little Shirley's sexuality in his review of *Wee Willie Winkie.* John Ford (who became the godfather to Shirley's first child) directed the film—a huge critical and commercial success. It sparked Greene to ruminate on the nature of her success: her innocence was really a disguise—"her appeal is more secret and more adult," her persona enhanced a "neat and well-developed rump, " a "dimpled depravity," and a "childhood skin-deep."[11]

Now consider, Greene continues, "the owners of a child star"; "her appeal is more secret and more adult"; "trousers with the mature suggestiveness of a Dietrich" (an echo from the review of *Captain January*); "wearing kilts, she is completely totsy"; her "dimpled depravity"; her "middle-aged men and clergymen" admirers; "the sight of her well-shaped and desirable little body."[12] Not only was he flippant, he was also more than a little cruel. For this attack on Hollywood's wee moneymaker, Greene would pay a price—literally. Curiously, considering his later attack, his initial reaction to Shirley Temple had not been critical at all. In reviewing *The Littlest Rebel* for the *Spectator* in 1935, Greene wrote, "Miss Temple appears in a very sweet and very simple tale of the American Civil War which culminates, as these dramas always do, with an appeal to Abraham Lincoln to save somebody— in this case a father, in *The Birth of a Nation* a lover. I had not seen Miss Temple before as I expected there was the usual sentimental exploitation of childhood, but I had not expected the tremendous energy which her rivals certainly lack."[13] Two years later, he penned the controversial article about the pint-sized actress. *Night and Day* promoted the piece with the headline "Sex and Shirley Temple." Predictably, Fox studio reacted with outrage to the insult to their box-office prodigy.

Greene fled to Mexico to avoid a summons, as his publisher, *Night and Day* magazine, faced a lawsuit from Shirley's handlers at Fox. They accused the reviewer and the journal of saying that the studio pimped the little girl—"procuring" Temple "for immoral purposes." The presiding judge called the review a "gross outrage" and ordered Greene and the magazine to pay £3,500 in damages.[14] This was an enormous fine at the time, and it forced the magazine into bankruptcy. Greene had to pay £500 personally as well. Not satisfied with just the money, Shirley's team also wanted an apology. "I found a cable waiting for me in Mexico City," Greene recalled, "asking me to apologize to that little bitch Shirley Temple."[15] He kept a copy of the lawsuit on his bathroom wall, he wrote, "until the wall was removed" during the Blitz. After the trial, the judge sent the court records to the archives of the director of public prosecutions, "so that ever since that time I have been traceable on the files of Scotland Yard."[16]

For her part, Shirley held no grudge, writing in her autobiography in 1988 that the affair had no meaning to her as a child. Her little 1937 self would not have understood at all what in the world dear Mr. Greene was apologizing for. Her revenge was sweet in other ways: "Suddenly unemployed as a film critic, Greene was released permanently into the ranks of eminent novelists," she noted, "and finally, the saucy publicity tweaked British box-office interest, for *Wee Willie Winkie* prospered gloriously. Important from my standpoint, the Royal Tribunal also confirmed me childless and nine years old."[17]

For all his ill-considered effrontery, Greene was on to something about Shirley and the cinematic seduction of adult men, including President Lincoln. In her films, as she "sang sexy love songs to handsome male costars, she was under the direction of grown men—a point Temple herself confessed in her autobiography: "Before long, acting in *Baby Burlesks* demonstrated some fundamental lessons in movie life. . . . Starlets have to kiss a lot of people, including some unattractive ones. . . . Often starlets are required to wear scanty costumes and suffer sexist schemes. . . . Like a girl scout, starlets must be cheerful and obliging, particularly to directors, producers, and cameramen."[18] (Actor Gary Cooper nicknamed Temple "Wiggle-Britches.")

Child abuse accompanied the sexualization of the little actors. *Burlesks* director Charles Lamont, frustrated when the children misbehaved on the set, banished them to the dreaded six-by-six-foot "Black Box" room. "Two boxes [set on wheels] were available for us, one to be used for sound mixing. The other was empty, save for a large block of ice, its diabolic, dark interior waiting expectantly for some troublesome child," Temple claimed. A "block of ice provided the only place to sit."[19]

Later, with Shirley under contract to Fox Film Corporation, the executives knew they had a potential star in their hands. In May 1934, they released *Stand Up and Cheer.* Her impact was enormous.[20] *Bright Eyes* (1934), in which she sang "On the Good Ship Lollipop," began her reign as the number-one box office draw in America. She earned a "Juvenile Oscar" in 1935 and had her tiny handprints and footprints added to the forecourt of Grauman's Chinese Theater. A stable of nineteen writers known as the "Shirley Temple Story Development Team" created eleven original screenplays and adaptations of classic stories for her over the next three years.

Who better to appreciate the hope and optimism she generated in the middle of the Depression than her co-counterrevolutionary FDR? According to Hollywood lore, Roosevelt said: "It is a splendid thing that for just fifteen cents, an American can go to a movie and look at the smiling face of a baby and forget his troubles."[21] Importantly, for that age of anxiety, David Thomson observes, the child was "the solace and inspiration for an essentially adult audience."[22] In 1935 "Shirley" was the second-most-popular child's name in America—forty-two thousand parents christened their babies after the dimpled wonder.[23] "Over the course of her film career," film critic Champ Clark writes, "Shirley Temple faced down every damn desperate hardship placed in her way during very desperate times. No mother or father . . . check. Evil head mistress . . . check. Bleak poverty . . . check. The grim orphanage . . . check. But indomitable Shirley always kept it positive—even through the occasional tears. No matter what the odds, she always had animal crackers in her soup, with monkeys and rabbits doing loop the loop."[24]

Shirley Temple, "Abraham Lincoln," and Franklin Roosevelt led the American people through the Great Depression—two Hollywood creations and one media-savvy politician. Her fame, if not her movie career, lasted beyond the Great Depression. *Washington Post* columnist Martha Sherrill detected a brief Shirley Temple revival in 1995, when Walmart and Blockbusters ran special promotions for her movies: "She escapes from orphanages, sliding down ropes made of bedsheets. She dances with bachelor millionaires and street bums. She's a rebel, a stowaway, a poor little rich girl. She wears pants and sailor suits, and the shortest coat-dresses imaginable. She holds her own against the meanest battle-axes, and climbs into the laps of the grouchiest of old men, wrapping her dimpled arms around their necks and petting their thin hair." The wonder child "appeared like a vision in the movie houses of the Depression and altered the atmosphere like the opening of a window on a sickroom to an exhilarating breeze."[25] Some sixty years after her glory days in Hollywood, Shirley Temple was still a miniature box-office hero using her superpowers for good in the world—overcoming all obstacles, free of all prejudice, treating all equally from the plantation butler to the president of the United States.

Was it not inevitable that this preternaturally gifted child would pull Hollywood's Abraham Lincoln into her orbit? *The Littlest Rebel* (1935) was the kiddie version of the sectional reconciliation and racial themes embedded in D. W. Griffith's *The Birth of a Nation.* In the latter film, two petitioners from the South travel to Washington to plead for mercy from Abraham Lincoln, "the Great Heart." Ben Cameron (Henry Walthall), the epitome of the mythical "Confederate cavalier," had displayed magnificent courage and compassion on the battlefield, even pausing during a heroic charge against the federal lines to offer water to a badly wounded Union soldier, an act that provokes cheers from the troops of both sides. Afterward, a prisoner of war, he lies recovering from wounds in a Union hospital, when a "secret influence" declares him to be a guerrilla. A military court sentences him to hang. Making their way to Washington, his mother (Josephine Crowell as the plantation mistress) and his beloved Elsie Stoneman (Lillian Gish), a northern girl, realize their only hope is Abraham Lincoln (Joseph Henabery).[26] "We will ask mercy from the Great Heart," declares Mrs. Cameron. Looking old, weary, and on the verge of tears, Lincoln, of course, pardons her son, sending the mother and Elsie racing back to the hospital to declare, "Mr. Lincoln has given back your life to me." Later, as the war ends and Lincoln is assassinated, Cameron's father (Spottiswoode Aitken) cries out, "Our best friend is gone. What is to become of us now?" Ben Cameron has the answer: he creates and then leads the Ku Klux Klan to the rescue of white womanhood and the honor of the South.

WHEN ABRAHAM LINCOLN MET SHIRLEY TEMPLE

Twenty years later, the seven-year-old juggernaut of infant talent replaces Mrs. Cameron and Elsie Stoneman in the heart of Abraham Lincoln. In *The Littlest Rebel,* Shirley Temple is Virginia "Virgie" Cary, daughter of a "Cavalier" gentleman of the Cloud Cuckoo Land that was the Old South in Hollywood memory. The film was part 2 of Shirley's Southland-themed triptych. *The Little Colonel* (1935), released nine months before *The Littlest Rebel, is* set during Reconstruction. Shirley acts as the agent of North-South reconciliation when her grandfather, an unreconstructed rebel, disowns her mother when she marries a northerner. In a third film, *Dimples* (1936), she plays Little Eva in a New York stage version of *Uncle Tom's Cabin.* At the conclusion of the play, the curtain comes down and then rises again to reveal the cast of supporting players in minstrel makeup and costume—announced as "New York City's first minstrel show." Shirley, in white top hat, tie, and tails, sings and dances to the accompaniment of banjos and tambourines. Critic Frank Nugent again: this version of Harriet Beecher Stowe's classic "is the Little Old New York version, the locale more specifically being the Bowery and the time just before the Civil War (although we might refer to it as the War Between the States out of deference to the film's producer, the Georgian Nunnally Johnson").[27]

In *The Littlest Rebel,* Confederate Captain Henry Cary (John Boles) has gone to war but sneaks back from time to time through Union lines to visit his daughter Virgie and his wife (Karen Morley). Perfectly synched with the Lost Cause myth, before the father leaves for the first time, Virgie and "Uncle Billy" (Bill Robinson), the family's faithful slave, discuss the reason for the war. The child and her devoted retainer are confused about the meaning of it all:

> UNCLE BILLY: No one knows why there will be a war. There's a man up north who wants to free the slaves.
>
> VIRGIE: What does that mean?
>
> UNCLE BILLY: I don't know myself.
>
> VIRGIE: It's funny, isn't it?

"Funny?" No, not really. Meanwhile back at the old plantation, Captain Cary's last visit corresponds to the death of his wife. Fortunately, a sympathetic Union officer, Colonel Morrison (Jack Holt), lends the rebel a blue uniform so he can make his way back home undetected. (This is the "Brothers' War," in which both sides are honorable and brave.) Thus disguised, Cary tries to make it through the lines to get Virgie safely to Richmond. The scheme fails when the Yankees discover the plot. Captain Cary is arrested and condemned to death as a spy. The determined Virgie and the loyal Uncle Billy travel to Washington to seek the president's mercy. (In Hollywood's Civil War, "the Great Heart" appears to have little to do except sit around the White House listening to pleas for clemency.) They finance their trip with a sidewalk routine in which they sing and dance to the tune of "Polly Wolly Doodle," reflecting the tropes and cadences of the minstrel tradition.

More importantly, it gives the audience what they came to expect from a Shirley Temple film, singing and dancing either alone or with a "faithful" servant.[28]

Lincoln (Frank McGlynn Sr.) welcomes them to his office, even shaking hands with Uncle Billy, who reacts with amazement to this gesture.[29] ("I'se a slave!" he reminds Lincoln in a deleted bit of dialogue.)[30] That a Black man would show deference to a white man was not at all unusual in the films of the era. But cultural historian John F. Kasson discerns a deeper meaning in the exchange: "It is the film's one explicit, if fleeting suggestion of the dignity and freedom owed to African Americans," though "it was intended to emphasize Lincoln's magnanimity rather than Uncle Billy's equality."[31] Later, in real life, "Uncle Billy" actually met a US president. "At last a golden opportunity to press for African American inclusion did emerge when Robinson met President Franklin Roosevelt," Kasson notes. "Not allowed to plead for his people to President Lincoln as Uncle Billy in *The Littlest Rebel,* when Robinson stood face-to-face with Roosevelt, he seized the moment: 'By the way Mr. President, I see you got some kind of New Deal going,' he said undoubtedly smiling, 'when you shuffle those cards, just don't overlook those spades.'"[32]

In *The Littlest Rebel,* Lincoln is sitting at his desk peeling an apple that he shares with her. (A theater owner in Detroit proclaimed that whoever "included the apple incident between Lincoln and Shirley deserves a medal.")[33] At one point, Virgie snuggles up so closely to Lincoln's chest that it borders on a love scene. After a brief exchange where Virgie's charm makes his great heart even greater, President Lincoln declares: "Your father and Colonel Morrison are going free."[34] Hollywood's Lincoln will free the slaves, pardon the rebels, and heal the nation—the Great Emancipator, the Great Heart, and the Great Humanitarian consubstantial. As the film ends, Virgie and Uncle Billy sing and dance "Polly Wolly Doodle" for a combined audience of appreciative Union guards and Confederate prisoners. The theme of the book that inspired the movie is clear: "The enmity between North and South is dead; it sleeps with the fathers and the sons, the brothers and the lovers, who died in a cause which each believed was just. Therefore, this story deals, not with the right or wrong of a lost confederacy, but with the mercy and generosity, the chivalry and humanity which lived in the hearts of the Blue and Gray, a noble contrast to the grim brutality of war."[35]

In Hollywood's version of the novel, Shirley sweet-talks (seduces) Lincoln into issuing the pardon, as the other women in the life of Abraham Lincoln—Nancy, Sarah, Ann, and Mary—had inspired, motivated, agitated, or seduce him into action. We see embodied in this memorable passage the quintessential Temple acting technique, the faithful slave trope, the Lost Cause myth, and North-South reconciliation—a perfect fit for a nation in crisis in the 1930s. Reconciliation spurred unity and common purpose for a nation in trouble. Sociologist Barry Schwartz judges that "Moving pictures of Lincoln . . . did more than express Depression-era sentiment; they organized it, made it conceivable, intelligible, communicable, and public."[36] At some point in the 1930s Abe and Shirley had to meet. Here Abraham Lincoln displays his essential decency and humanity, opening his office to the common people. And here is Shirley in all her seductive glory:

The Scene: When Virgie and Uncle Billy arrive at the White House, they wait outside the president's office with a group of petitioners, among them wives, mothers, sweethearts, a wounded soldier—even a Union general. All are seeking the favor of the Great Heart.

SECRETARY: (to Virgie): You may go in now.

VIRGIE: Thank you, sir. (Virgie takes Billy's hand.) Come on, Uncle Billy.

(Lincoln bids them to enter as "The Battle Hymn of the Republic" plays in the background.)

LINCOLN (cheerfully): Come right in. Miss Virginia Cary and Uncle Billy?

VIRGIE (Lincoln stoops shake her hand. Shirley bobs a curtsy.): Yes, sir.

UNCLE BILLY: Yes, sir, Mr. President.

LINCOLN: How do you do, my dear?

VIRGIE: Very nicely. Thank you, sir.

LINCOLN: (cheerfully) And how are you, Uncle Billy?

According to the script: Lincoln offers his hand to Uncle Billy. Made speechless by the gesture, Uncle Billy stands and looks at it. Then realizing the significance, he wipes his hand on his own coat. He looks up and smiles. He slowly accepts Lincoln's hand and shakes it. In a gesture deleted in the final cut, the directions read: "the colored man looks at the hand Lincoln gripped, in awe."

LINCOLN: Let me see. Judge Van Allen told me about this case.

UNCLE BILLY: Yes, sir. He's the gentleman the soldier man sent me to.

LINCOLN (*to Virgie*): Come over here. Tell me all about it. (*Takes Virgie's hand and sets her on his desk*) There. Now . . . that's nicer.

(*Lincoln begins to peel an apple.*)

VIRGIE: My daddy and Colonel Morrison are in prison . . . and they're going to shoot them.

LINCOLN: Your father is a captain in the Confederate Army.

VIRGIE: Yes, sir.

LINCOLN: Arrested as a spy.

VIRGIE (*angered and with a pout*): My daddy isn't a spy!

LINCOLN: Do you know what a spy is?

VIRGIE: I know it's something bad, because they shoot you for it . . . and my daddy couldn't do anything bad.

LINCOLN: I don't see how he could either . . . with a little one like you.

(*Lincoln hands Virgie a slice of apple.*)

VIRGIE: Thank you kindly, sir.

LINCOLN (*smiling*): Tell me about it.

VIRGIE: My daddy went away to the war . . . and then the Yankees came around to our house . . . and sometimes my daddy came home.

LINCOLN: Was he in uniform?

VIRGIE: Yes, sir.

LINCOLN: What color?

VIRGIE: Gray.

LINCOLN: I see.

(*Lincoln hands another slice of apple to Virgie.*)

VIRGIE: Thank you, sir. Then there were so many Yankees around
. . . my daddy couldn't come home anymore. Then they burnt down
our house, and my mommy got sick . . . and had to go to bed in Uncle
Billy's cabin.

(*Lincoln holds out another slice to Virgie.*)

VIRGIE: No, that's yours. I had the last piece.

LINCOLN: That's right.

UNCLE BILLY: We had nothing to get her medicine with, Mr.
President. The soldiers took most everything we had.

VIRGIE: And Mommy kept asking for my daddy. All the time she'd ask.

(*Lincoln attempts to eat another slice of apple.*)

VIRGIE: No, that's mine. You had the last piece.

LINCOLN: I beg your pardon.

VIRGIE: You forgot. That's all. So Uncle Billy went and brought my
daddy back home. The next day, my mommy went away.

(*Virgie begins to cry.*)

LINCOLN: There, there. Don't cry. You're a great big girl. You mustn't
cry.

VIRGIE: I won't.

(*Lincoln takes Virgie onto his lap.*)

LINCOLN: What happened next?

VIRGIE: Then the Yankees came, and my daddy had to hide in the garret. Then Colonel Morrison came in. He talked to me. He's awfully nice. He has a little girl, too, just my age. Then he found Daddy, and Daddy told him . . . about wanting to take me to my Aunt Caroline in Richmond . . . so I could get enough to eat.

UNCLE BILLY: That's why the colonel give Massa Cary the pass, sir— just so he could bring Miss Virgie where she could be taken care of.

LINCOLN: I see. Now, on this trip . . . before your daddy was captured . . . did he write down anything on paper or anything?

VIRGIE: No, sir.

LINCOLN: Did he ever stop and look at the Yankee soldiers . . . or count them or look at the cannons?

VIRGIE: No, sir. He told me that if we got to Richmond . . . and anyone asked me what I had seen . . . I was in honor bound not to tell them.

LINCOLN: He told you that?

VIRGIE: Yes, sir. Because Colonel Morrison asked him not to see anything . . . and my daddy gave his word, and they shook hands.

(Lincoln takes Virgie off his lap.)

VIRGIE: Mr. President?

LINCOLN: Yes, Miss Virgie?

VIRGIE: You won't let them shoot my daddy and Colonel Morrison, will you?

LINCOLN: *(he pauses, writes a note, and then hands it to his secretary)*: John, rush this by special courier to General Grant.

SECRETARY: Yes, Mr. President.

LINCOLN: *(handing Virgie a slice of apple)* Is this yours?

VIRGIE: No, it's yours. I had the last piece.

(Virgie climbs onto Lincoln's lap)

LINCOLN: There, there now. All your terrible fears are over. Your father and Colonel Morrison are going free.

VIRGIE: Thank you!

As an adult, Shirley recalled the experience of filming the scene with fondness: "After all, as a child I lived a storybook world; it was like living in books instead of reading them. I was Heidi in Switzerland, Wee Willie Winkie in India, the Little Princess in England, and I got to sit on Abraham Lincoln's knee."[37] It was the most expensive Temple project to date and a box-office smash. It recovered half of its production costs alone on the day it premiered—a hit not only in America but in London, Paris, and Berlin as well.

There is a fascinating footnote to the film's history: in a scene in *The Littlest Rebel,* deleted in later drafts, Lincoln, inspired by his meeting with the seductive little Virgie and the humble Uncle Billy, begins composing the Gettysburg Address.[38] Inspiring Lincoln's famous address, however, proved beyond even Shirley's powers of persuasion. "If you ever even suggest that Shirley Temple was the inspiration for the Gettysburg Address," actor and screenwriter Raymond Griffith exclaimed, "they'll throw rocks at us."[39] Nevertheless, her connection to Lincoln continued long after the child-star years had passed; at Shirley Temple Black's estate auction in 2016, her autographed edition of Carl Sandburg's four-volume *Abraham Lincoln: The War Years* (1939) sold for $1,300.

In 1935, *New York Times* reviewer Andre Sennwald said of the movie's underlying theme, "You may have got the mistaken notion . . . that the War between the States was filled with ruin, death, rebellious slaves and horrid Yankee barbarians. *The Littlest Rebel* corrects that unhappy thought and presents the conflict as a decidedly chummy little war."[40] *Variety* noted as well in its December 1934, preview: "Shrewdly playing both sides, as between the north and the south, the script (from the play by Edward Peple)[41] throws a lot of dialog to the Confederacy. 'I'm not a rebel, my daddy says so!' Virgie states defiantly, 'I'm a confederate!' All bitterness and cruelty has been rigorously cut out and the Civil War emerges as a misunderstanding among kindly gentlemen with happy slaves and a cute little girl who sings and dances her way through the story."[42]

In 1935, the success of Franklin Roosevelt's New Deal coalition depended critically on the support of entrenched southern Democratic congressmen and senators. In the North, in the South, and in Hollywood, the spirit of the Lost Cause dominated the popular memory. No one at that time demanded the removal of rebel statues and memorials. When she sat on Abraham Lincoln's lap to save the life of a Confederate soldier, Shirley Temple contributed as much as anyone to the spirit of a national reconciliation vital to the South's self-respect, self-image, and support for Franklin Roosevelt's political and policy success.

Three years after the opening of *The Littlest Rebel,* Shirley met FDR. She found him uncomfortable in her presence. Unlike the cinematic Lincoln, Franklin Roosevelt felt intimidated by the youngster, and he did not invite her to sit on his lap. It was an awkward meeting, saved only by the child's preternatural self-assurance: "For a long moment he just held my hand and stared silently at me, waiting for me to say something. Looking sideways, I spotted a sailing-ship model. Noticing my glance, he asked if I liked boats." At his point, she turned on the charm. I like fishing better, she replied and then they talked about her missing tooth. Finally, she asked him for his autograph ("For Shirley from her old friend."). Leaving the Oval Office, she ran into the secretary of the treasury, Henry Morgenthau. "Did he like you?" he asked. "I don't know," she replied, "but I like him."[43] Though the attribution may be a Hollywood myth, Roosevelt, declared, "As long as we have Shirley Temple, we'll be all right."[44]

IN LOCO PARENTIS:
WHEN ABE MET MARILYN

It is unclear when Abe and Marilyn Monroe first met. According to one story, the affair began at Emerson Junior High School, Los Angeles. Fifteen-year-old Norma Jeane Baker[45] wrote a paper on Abraham Lincoln and earned an A. She was good at writing essays and won a fountain pen for "Dog, Man's Best Friend."[46] Norma Jeane "developed a passion for Abraham Lincoln when she studied his life in class," feminist biographer Lois Banner writes: "She identified with his improvised upbringing in rural Kentucky and the death of his mother when he was young; she liked his democratic attitudes and his identification with ordinary people. His physical appearance—dark and rugged—appealed to her. He became another father figure to her."[47] Marilyn had a crush on Abe: "He was such a great guy. When I see a man like that, I would love to sit on his lap."[48] (Little Virgie had anticipated Marilyn's wish thirty years earlier.)

Joyce Carol Oates, in *Blonde: A Novel*, about Monroe, imagines a schoolday scene: "For her English teacher, Mr. [Sidney] Haring, she'd written essays on Mary Baker Eddy, the founder of Christian Science, and Abraham Lincoln, 'America's greatest president,' and on Christopher Columbus, 'a man not afraid to venture into the unknown.' She showed Mr. Haring some of her poems, carefully written in blue ink on sheets of unlined paper.

Into the sky—so high
I know that I will never die

I know that I would never be blue If I could love you.

If there is a way
For those on Earth to say—'I love you!'
And make it always true.
As God tells us 'I love you' and you—and you'
and always it is TRUE.

Mr. Haring smiled uneasily and told her the poem was 'very good'—the rhyming 'perfect'—Norma Jeane blushed with pleasure." They would often talk in his office after school, and he would drive her home. One time they spoke of Franklin Roosevelt and Abraham Lincoln: "Haring happened to mention that he didn't trust FDR, and that he didn't trust any politician on principle. Norma Jean flared up, saying no, no, that wasn't right—'President Roosevelt is different' . . . Norma Jean said, excitedly. 'President Roosevelt is a great man! He's as great as Abraham Lincoln maybe.' 'And how do you know that?' 'I have faith in him.'"[49]

There is another origin story—one Marilyn told herself in her reputed autobiography. She was trying to make it in Hollywood, alone and lonely. One night at a restaurant, she began a conversation with an older man, a certain Bill Cox from Texas: "He talked chiefly of the Spanish-American War and of Abraham Lincoln. These two topics were very exciting to him." She had never heard of the Spanish-American War—"I must have been absent from school the week it was studied in my history class." He went on to tell her all about the war and its causes. "And he also told me of the life of Abraham Lincoln from his birth onward." Later, "walking with Bill in the lighted Hollywood streets and hearing stories about the Spanish-American War and Abraham Lincoln, I didn't feel lonely and the sidewalk wolves didn't 'hi baby me.'" Bill went back to Texas. Sometime later, she received a letter from Bill's wife. He had died. "The Hollywood streets seemed lonelier without Bill Cox and San Juan and Abraham Lincoln," she remembered.[50]

Starting in 1926 (the year of Norma Jeane's birth), Lincoln, the Savior of the Union and the Great Emancipator, acquired once again the mantel of the supreme humanitarian, tempering the awe-inspiring monumentality of the magisterial Lincoln statue in the Memorial in Washington. Historian Nina Silber recounts how Lincoln multiplied, then multiplied again as every political, racial, and cultural faction in the 1930s—left, right, and center—co-opted Lincoln's image to promote their causes. Sandberg stands right at the beginning: "A good deal of this attraction to Lincoln, as a living and breathing human being, could be traced to the work of Carl Sandburg."[51]

Silber points out as well that Sandburg "imbibed this 'common man' portrayal of Lincoln and seemed more enthralled with Honest Abe's 'commonness.'" In 1911, he described Lincoln as "a shabby, homely man who came from among those who live shabby and homely lives."[52]

WHEN CARL MET MARILYN

Before he became the most famous among the legion of Lincoln biographers, Sandburg was one of the first serious American movie critics. In that role, he demonstrated an enthusiasm for Hollywood movies and an appreciation for film as an art for the masses. Between September 1920 and January 1928, he wrote approximately two thousand film reviews and essays, some only a few sentences, others more substantial. He reviewed the films of Mable Normand, Clara Bow, Mary Pickford, Joan Crawford, and Gloria Swanson. He also wrote about Charlie Chaplin, Harold Lloyd, William S. Hart, Lon Chaney, Rudolph Valentino, Douglas Fairbanks, Will Rogers, Tom Mix, W. C. Fields, and Buster Keaton. Sandburg commented as well on the talents of directors John "Jack" Ford and D. W. Griffith. Further, he examined related topics with a keen sense of the power and potential of moviemaking: the role of the cameraman, production costs, the need for film preservation, censorship (in the pre-censorship age), musical scores, the authenticity of war films, attempts at 3D projection, sports films, the wonder of special effects, among much else; his movie notes and reflections amount to a virtual history of early Hollywood. So, later, when Sandburg came within Marilyn's orbit, he was hardly naïve about the film industry.[53]

By the time Sandburg met Marilyn, she was rich and famous. Her childhood, however, had been tragic—shabby and sorrowful like Lincoln's. Her mother spent much of her later life in and out of psychiatric care. She claimed she did not know which of her several boyfriends was Marilyn's father. Norma Jeane went for a time to an orphanage and from one foster home to another. It is not complicated or complex psychology to understand her need for a father figure. What is curious, however, is her finding the lost father in the person of Abraham Lincoln. About Marilyn as his girlfriend in *All About Eve* (1950), actor George Sanders observed, "She played a very dumb would-be actress who I was taking around. Even then she struck me as a character in search of an author."[54] Eventually, she did find an author, playwright Arthur Miller, and then a surrogate father figure, President Abraham Lincoln. According to the story, in 1951, in a conversation with Miller, who became her third husband, the pathologically insecure Marilyn complained, "Most people can admire their fathers but I never had one. I need someone to admire." Miller later wrote to her, "Carl Sandburg has written a magnificent biography. If you want someone to admire, why not Abraham Lincoln?" The same day she received Miller's letter, Monroe biographer Donald Spoto notes, she bought Sandburg biography as well as a lithograph of Lincoln.[55] Marilyn was an autodidact who read widely if not deeply into fiction, poetry, philosophy, history, and the occult.

Marilyn later said: "I need someone to admire. My father is Abraham Lincoln. . . . I mean I think of Lincoln as my father. He was wise and kind and good. He is my ideal, Lincoln. I love him." As for Miller, two attributes caught Marilyn's attention—his intellect and his physical resemblance to Lincoln. "Doesn't Arthur look wonderfully like Abraham Lincoln? I'm mad for him." When Marilyn married the playwright, the inscription on her ring, in imitation of Mary Lincoln's wedding band dedication, read "A. to M. June 1956. Now is Forever."[56] (Mary's band: "A.L. to Mary, Nov. 4, 1842. Love is Eternal.")

Marilyn was not the first Hollywood star to fall in love with Abraham Lincoln. Actress Jean Arthur, who starred in *Mr. Deeds Goes to Town* (1936) and *Mr. Smith goes to Washington* (1939), married one Julian Ancker in 1928. It lasted one day, ending in in an annulment that caused a brief scandal. Jean made a mistake, she claimed. It was a case of misidentification, Arthur joked long after her career ended: "Julian looked a bit like Abraham Lincoln and that's probably why I fell in love with him."[57]

When exactly Marilyn and Carl Sandburg met is unclear. One story has it that they first encountered each other when Sandburg was working on the script for *The Greatest Story Ever Told* in 1959–60. (United Artists released the film in 1965.) Later, in 1961, she and Sandburg spent an afternoon together at the New York apartment of photographer and filmmaker Len Steckler. Sandburg was eighty-four at the time; Marilyn was thirty-five. (She would be dead in nine months.) Steckler remembered that she "was three hours late but had an excuse. She had been at the hairdresser, trying to get her hair color to match Carl's [silver gray]."[58] Sandburg observed, "She was not the usual movie idol. There was something democratic about her. She was the type who would join in and wash dishes even if you didn't ask her."[59] Like Lincoln and Sandburg, Marilyn was of the people. And for her a dual attraction born much earlier in Sandburg's life and career beckoned: "Just as significant of any writing Sandburg produced about Lincoln was his likeness to the subject—The tendency to equate Sandburg with Lincoln" Marilyn was not the first Lincoln admirer to see the connection between the author and his subject, "and Sandburg never resisted the comparison."[60] In 2011, a visitor to the Carl Sandburg Home National Historic Site remembered seeing "a cool picture of Sandburg with Marilyn Monroe" on display.[61]

Three photographs document her fixation with the sixteenth president. Two publicity shots taken on the same day in 1954 show the star at age twenty-eight, kneeling and facing backward on the front seat of a black Cadillac convertible. In her hands, she holds a large framed portrait of Lincoln, a copy of a lost ambrotype of Lincoln taken on August 26, 1858, by P. T. Pearson in Macomb, Illinois, the day before his historic debate with Stephen Douglas in Freeport.[62] James Mellon, an authority on Lincoln photographs, calls it "Possibly the most revealing portrait of the beardless Lincoln."[63] One shot with the same image of Lincoln shows Marilyn expressing a little-girl's pout. In the next image, she exhibits a coy smile. It is not Marilyn (clad in a tight, front-tied pink blouse) that attracts the eye; it is the large formal picture of Abraham Lincoln.

Marilyn later reflected on the moment in her "imaginary memoir" as invented in 1980 after her death by novelist Norman Mailer: "So, I told him [Milton Greene, her photographer] about my love for Abraham Lincoln, which I hadn't told anyone else (but Arthur Miller, who held my big toe once for hours as we talked). The truth was that I was afraid everybody would laugh themselves to death at the thought of me having a crush on such a famous President." She continued, "I truly adored Abraham Lincoln. I used to have dreams that I was his illegitimate great-granddaughter. 'Why not legitimate?' asked Milton. Before it was over, I let him talk me into taking a picture with my great-grandfather in my Cadillac car. I must have been in love with Milton right that minute to do something so revealing."[64]

How Marilyn imagined her relationship to Abraham Lincoln is muddled. Sometimes, he was the father, sometimes the grandfather, or, in this conversation, the great-grandfather. Whatever the genealogy, she adored Mr. Lincoln. There is another curious connection: in Maurice Zolotow's biography of Marilyn Monroe, there is a photograph of James Dougherty, Marilyn's first husband, standing in front of a bungalow that he and Marilyn lived in Van Nuys, California, in 1953. It looks remarkably like the images of Lincoln's legendary log cabin.[65]

The peripatetic glamour queen kept the 1858 portrait of Lincoln above her bed at her various residences: Doheny Drive in Beverly Hills, a Waldorf-Astoria suite, and the apartment on East Fifty-Seventh Street where she lived during her marriage to Arthur Miller.[66] The picture also hung at the hacienda-style home on Helena Drive in Brentwood, California, where she committed suicide.

She also collected a small library about Lincoln that she kept in her bedroom. She also hung a copy of the Gettysburg Address on the wall. And next to her bed, she kept her mother's photograph and a small framed picture of Lincoln. Feminist writer Gloria Steinem observed, "Marilyn nourished her habit of hungry but random reading and tried to fathom everything from biographies of Abraham Lincoln, her childhood hero, to such abstract treaties as [Mable Ellsworth Todd's 1937] *The Thinking Body,* a study of the symbiotic relationship between body and mind. She never stopped feeling inferior because she had not finished high school, and she never stopped trying to make up for it."[67] Hollywood journalist and Monroe biographer Maurice Zolotow interviewed Marilyn in 1955 in her home: "'Look, it's so hot, why don't we have this talk in the bedroom. It's air-conditioned,'" she said. "A huge print of Lincoln hung above the bed," he recalled, "Marilyn was clad in velvet toreador pants and a white jersey blouse. She uncoiled herself prone across the bed, her head peering up at me." Despite the air-conditioning, "I found the room—or rather myself—growing unbearably hot."[68]

"IT TAKES A LOT TO UPSTAGE ABRAHAM LINCOLN": MARILYN GIVES A SPEECH

On August 6, 1955, Marilyn made an appearance in tiny Bement, Illinois. A picture taken by her friend and photographer Eve Arnold shows the actress in a tight white dress ascending the ramp to an airplane—in her arms she holds an illustrated children's book, *Lincoln: A Picture Story of His Life* (1952), by Marilyn's friend the Hungarian immigrant Stefan Lorant, a photojournalist and filmmaker. The book was a prop; at that time she was actually reading Sandburg's Lincoln biography.

Carleton Smith, head of the National Arts Foundation and an Illinois native, invited Monroe to visit the historic village of 1,500 people. Apparently, Smith had at one time paid a large hotel bill for Marilyn, and she returned the favor by agreeing to attend a centennial celebration. The real purpose seemed to be to parachute Monroe into the middle of Bement's celebration for a publicity stunt—she was to open a Lincoln exhibit, unveil a bust of the great man, judge the Lincoln Beard Contest, visit a nursing home, and give a short speech. The focus of the event was the historic Bryant Cottage. According to local folklore, on July 29, 1858, Lincoln met Stephen Douglas at the home of Francis Bryant in Bement to arrange the format for the seven Lincoln-Douglas debates.

For Marilyn, her appearance was more than a publicity stunt; it was a chance to connect to the memory of her fantasy father. Unsurprisingly, the villagers that day were less interested in Abraham Lincoln than in Marilyn Monroe. The presence of the Hollywood sexual wonder woman overwhelmed them. (The population swelled to 28,000 during the event.) In front of the Lincoln bust, Marilyn Monroe, the icon of mid-twentieth-century American sexuality, declared: "I think of Abraham Lincoln as my father. He was a good and wise man." Sixty years later, on the anniversary of Marilyn's visit, a commentator noted, "It takes a lot to upstage Abraham Lincoln."[69]

"IF YOU GO ANY FURTHER, MR. LINCOLN, YOU'RE GONNA MISS THE PARADE"

Lincoln showed up again in 1956, when Marilyn Monroe and Don Murray had the lead roles in the film version of *Bus Stop*, directed by Joshua Logan and based on the play by William Inge. Murray is Beauregard "Bo" Decker, a Montana ranch owner on his way to the World Rodeo Championship in Phoenix. Bo falls in love with Chérie (Monroe), a "tinseled floozie," a "semi-moronic doll."[70] Bo wants to marry her and take her to Montana and life on his ranch—a cowboy's wife. She rejects the idea. Here is where Lincoln enters the story. The morning of the Phoenix rodeo parade, Bo makes one final try at courting Chérie. She is sleeping as he enters her bedroom. Logan wanted to film Monroe and Murray naked under the sheets. The studio forbade it. (Murray claimed that Monroe was in fact naked and he kept covering her up with the bedsheet.)

> BO (*sitting on the bed*): And do you know I can say the Gettysburg Address?
>
> CHÉRIE (*sleepy and under the sheets*): Come bustin' in here like a wild Indian. Sometime . . .
>
> BO: Chérie?
>
> CHÉRIE: Well, what?
>
> BO: "Four score and seven years ago, our fathers brought forth on this continent a new nation, conceived in liberty and dedicated to the proposition . . ."
>
> CHÉRIE: Bo?
>
> BO: ". . . that all men are created equal. Now we're engaged in a great civil war, to determine whether that nation or any nation . . ."
>
> CHÉRIE: Bo, listen . . .
>
> BO: ". . . so conceived and so dedicated can long endure."
>
> CHÉRIE: Bo . . .
>
> BO: "We are met here on a great battlefield of that war."
>
> CHÉRIE: I hate parades. I'm not goin'.

BO: "The world will not long remember, nor little note, what we say here, but it will never forget what they did here."

CHÉRIE: Bo?

BO: "Rather it is for us, the living . . ."

CHÉRIE: Please let me sleep.

BO: ". . . to be so concentrated and so dedicated . . ."

THE LANDLADY (*on entering the room*): If you go any further, Mr. Lincoln, you're gonna miss the parade.[71]

Lincoln and Marilyn make another appearance in *My Week with Marilyn* (1999), a film based loosely on the memoirs of British writer and filmmaker Colin Clark. He had worked as the third assistant director on Laurence Olivier–Marilyn Monroe comedy *The Prince and the Showgirl* (1957). The film re-creates the time when the producers assign him to be the minder for the chronically unreliable Marilyn. Consider the following scene as described in the script:

MARILYN'S BEDROOM. NIGHT.

(*Marilyn will not answer knocks on her door. People are worried that she is ill or worse, that she has attempted suicide. Unable to get her to answer, Colin gets a ladder and climbs through an open window. He tumbles in through the window with a clattering thump.*)

COLIN (Eddie Redmayne): Marilyn?

(*A shaft of moonlight reveals Marilyn lying naked across the bed, her body partly covered by the sheet. Half-empty pill and champagne bottles are scattered all over her dresser; there is also an old photograph in a silver frame of her mother Gladys.*)

COLIN: Marilyn?

(*For a second, he fears the worst, but then suddenly she groans and sits up, looking at him blearily.*)

MARILYN (Michelle Williams): Oh hi, Colin.

COLIN: Are you okay? Everyone was worried about you.

MARILYN: Phooey.

(*She pats the sheets at her side and settles down sleepily on the pillow.*)

MARILYN: Get in.

(*She is instantly back asleep. Colin fumbles his way to the door. He searches for the key on the side table and quickly finds it. He goes to unlock the door, but then pauses, looking back at Marilyn. He puts the key back and bends down to whisper at the keyhole.*)

COLIN: It's me. She's fine but I'm going to keep an eye on her. I'll sleep on the sofa.

MILTON (Dominic Cooper): (*Off screen*) Come on, Colin, open up.

COLIN: (*After a second*) I can't find the key. (*Pause*) You can all go to bed now.

PAULA (Zoë Wanamaker): [Marilyn's acting coach] (*Off Screen*) Colin, open this door! She needs me . . .

(*Colin goes back to the bed and gazes at the sleeping Marilyn, his expression suffused with a tenderness we have never seen in him before. He pulls up the sheet so that it covers her nakedness, then tentatively lies down to rest his head on the pillow. He falls asleep.*)

(*Colin wakes with a jolt as the light snaps on, blinding him.*)

MARILYN: Colin? What are you doing here?

(*Marilyn sits up, the sheet clutched to her chest, her expression panicky and disoriented. Colin hurls himself off the bed.*)

COLIN: I came in through the window . . .

(*He realizes this doesn't sound reassuring.*)

COLIN: Milton thought you were sick.

(*She stares at him in puzzlement then breaks into a dazed smile.*)

MARILYN: The window? Is there a balcony, like in Romeo and Juliet? How romantic. (*Pause*) But I'm not sick. What makes them think that?

(*She reaches instinctively for the pill container on her bedside table.*)

COLIN: Please don't take any more pills.

(*She frowns, clutching the pill bottle in one hand. He reaches out and pries it gently from her grasp. As he puts it back on the side he glances at the framed photograph.*)

COLIN: Who's that?

MARILYN: My mom.

(*Marilyn's expression softens as she looks at the picture.*)

MARILYN: They took her to the sanatorium when I was a kid. I grew up in other people's homes, mostly.

(*Alongside her mother's photo is another framed picture, this time of Abraham Lincoln. Colin frowns.*)

COLIN: Abraham Lincoln?

MARILYN: I don't know who my father is so it might as well be him. Why not? I can pick any father I want.

(*She smiles, then looks at Colin wistfully.*)

MARILYN: (*cont'd*) Do you have a home, Colin? A real one?

COLIN: Yes, I do.

MARILYN: And a mother and father who still live together?

COLIN: Yes.

MARILYN: And do they love you?

COLIN: I'm sure they do.

(*He nods. She smiles sadly.*)

MARILYN: You're lucky.

(*Her eyes fill with tears. She looks up at him anxiously.*)

MARILYN: Do you love me, Colin?

(*He stares at her. She looks lovely but desperately vulnerable.*)

When she divorced Arthur Miller, she took the photograph and a bust of Lincoln with her. She also treasured her terra-cotta bust of Sandburg. Berniece Baker Miracle, her half sister who lived with Marilyn for a time in Manhattan, recalled that she first saw it sitting on the floor of the new apartment in 1957, when Marilyn was still arranging her furniture, books, and decorations.

> MARILYN: "Yes! It's Carl Sandburg—isn't he wonderful? . . . What do you think—should you meet him as you come in, or should he be near his poetry?"
>
> BERNIECE: "I think he'd look good anywhere."
>
> MARILYN (*laughing*): "Thank goodness he's not too heavy. I keep carrying him from room to room. I want him everywhere!"

In addition to the Lincoln picture, she usually kept a copy of the Gettysburg Address on the wall wherever she moved: "It was her first love affair with a President of the United States."[72] (As the insecure and ambitious Mary Todd loved Abraham Lincoln, so did the insecure and aspirational Marilyn Monroe. Mary and Marilyn are soul sisters joined by their love for the enigmatic Lincoln.) Could Marilyn have been thinking of Abraham Lincoln when she sang "My Heart Belongs to Daddy" in *Let's Make Love* (1960)?

I wanna be loved by you, just you,

And nobody else but you,

I wanna be loved by you, alone!

I couldn't aspire, To anything higher,

Than to feel the desire,

To make you my own,

Ba-dum-ba-dum-ba-doodly-dum-boo![73]

"HAPPY BIRTHDAY, MR. PRESIDENT"

The Lincoln-Monroe affair had other bizarre connections. The Abraham Lincoln Presidential Library Association Foundation received a loan in 2018 to purchase the eclectic private collection of Louise Taper, a historian, Lincoln enthusiast, and film producer. The catalogue included a Lincoln stovepipe hat and the gloves he wore the night of the assassination. Included among the one thousand items was an unusual object, a black long-sleeve dress worn by Marilyn Monroe. To help pay for the Lincoln objects, the foundation later sold the dress for $50,000. Though they also tried to sell Marilyn's bust of Carl Sandburg, the bidding failed to meet the reserve value.[74]

In a separate auction, Ripley's Believe It or Not paid $4.8 million for the sheer, crystal-emblazoned dress she wore the evening of May 29, 1962. Adlai Stevenson, who attended the birthday celebration for John F. Kennedy when she wore the dress, described it as composed of "skin and beads."[75] Some claim that the designer sewed her into the dress.The gown originally cost $1,400. Marilyn wore the outfit for a Democratic super fundraiser (a "GalaAllStarShow" sponsored by New York's Birthday Salute to the President, Inc.) at Madison Square Garden in New York City. Seventeen thousand guests each paid from $10 to $1,000 (over $8,000 today) for a seat at the arena.[76] The celebration lasted four hours. "Wouldn't it be fun if Marilyn Monroe could sing 'Happy Birthday to the President?'" Peter Lawford (a B-grade actor, a member of Frank Sinatra's Rat Pack, and now Kennedy's brother-in-law and liegeman) proposed.[77] It would be the highlight of the evening. Television comedian Milton Berle hosted the event.[78]

It was a Camelot moment—a gathering of the liberal Democratic nobility and their vassals—political heavyweights and lightweights, fanboys, court jesters, and Kennedy family retainers along with a constellation of stars, including Jack Benny, Frank Sinatra, Henry Fonda, Harry Belafonte, Shirley MacLaine, Jimmy Durante, Mike Nichols and Elaine May, Peggy Lee, Miriam Makeba, Ella Fitzgerald, Bobby Darin, Danny Kay, Robert Morrill, Maria Callas, and Leontyne Price.

The highlight of the festivities featured Marilyn singing a parody of "Happy Birthday" to Kennedy.[79] He had a special place in her thoughts; she believed the young president would become, like Abraham Lincoln, the nation's savior. "This man is going to change our country," she predicted to her psychiatrist in 1962: "No child will go hungry. No person will sleep in the street and get his meals from garbage cans. People who can't afford it will get good medical care. Industrial products will be the best in the world. No, I'm not talking Utopia—that's an illusion—but he will transform America today like FDR did in the '30s." Further, she predicted, "He'll do for the world what he'll do for America transform it for the better. I tell you, doctor, when he has finished his achievements he will take his place with Washington, Jefferson, Lincoln and FDR as one of our greatest presidents."[80]

Rose Kennedy, the matriarch of the Kennedy clan, agreed with Marilyn. "Jack," she observed after seeing the television debate with Richard Nixon in 1960, "really looks, acts, and sounds like young Lincoln."[81] In a postmodernist interpretation of Marilyn's image and obsessions, feminist scholar and Monroe observer S. Paige Baty states, "Abraham, Bobby, John, and Marilyn are made to constitute a representative American legacy. Two assassinated presidents, and one assassinated candidate are here placed with a fatherless/childless woman, born somewhere between Hawthorne and Hollywood, the daughter of a schizophrenic film-cutter who dreamt of a 'wise and good' father, always keeping by her bed a portrait of Abraham Lincoln."[82] She was "a daughter of the republic, who died in 1962," who "chose a father of the 1860s" who "could make her whole again, as he had the divided Union." In her "longing for home there's no one waiting . . . and nowhere left to go but history."[83]

For the gala birthday celebration, Marilyn "dressed in a body stocking covered with 2, 500 sequins, which looked as if they were just stuck to her skin because the net was flesh colored."[84] Some suspected that she wore no underwear that evening. The French-born Hollywood designer John Louis had made a similar costume for Marlene Dietrich. Now, from a concept by Bob Mackie, he turned to Marilyn. "So," Louis recalled, "I designed an apparently nude dress—the nudist dress—relieved only by sequins and beading."[85] There were subterranean rumors, muffled by the press at the time but with hard evidence later, that Marilyn had an affair with Jack Kennedy.[86] Stricken with stage fright, dreadfully anxious that she would panic before the president, she rehearsed the song for three hours at her apartment, read *The Little Engine That Could* ("I think I can, I think I can") for encouragement, got drunk, arrived late (as was her habit), and then waited offstage.

The arena went dark, and then a spotlight focused on Marilyn Monroe. Lawford leaned into the microphone next to Marilyn and announced: "Mr. President, on this occasion of your birthday, this lovely lady is not only pulchritudinous but punctual. Mr. President—Marilyn Monroe!" Gazing at Marilyn, Kennedy sat back with his feet propped on the rail, a grin on his face, a cigar in his mouth.[87] (Jackie was absent and may have watched the event on television. She was not amused.) "Mr. President," Lawford continued, "because, in the history of show business, perhaps there is no one female who has meant so much, who has done more, Mr. President, than the late Marilyn Monroe!" She walked onto the stage and he removed her short mink rap to gasps from the audience. When the spotlight hit her, she appeared glistening and nude. She paused briefly, then, in her breathy, sex-kitten voice, and without accompaniment, she began:

Happy birthday to you
Happy birthday to you
Happy birthday, Mr. President,
Happy birthday to you

(*. . . and then to the tune of "Thanks for the Memory"*)

Thanks, Mr. President
For all the things you've done
The battles that you've won
The way you deal with U.S. Steel
And our problems by the ton
We thank you so much

(*Marilyn waving her arms up and down and shouting*)

Everybody, Happy Birthday!

The audience roared and, encouraged by Marilyn, followed with another chorus of "Happy Birthday," as two chefs rolled out a six-foot birthday cake with forty-five candles. Kennedy responded with his characteristic wit: "Thank you. I can now retire from politics after having had, ah, 'Happy Birthday' sung to me in such a sweet, wholesome way."[88] (He talked briefly with Marilyn at the afterparty as Bobby Kennedy hovered nearby.) Phil Moore, Marilyn's voice coach for *Gentlemen Prefer Blondes* (1953), said that when she sang, "She always sounds as if she's just waking up. You'd be surprised what kind of effect that has on male listeners."[89] Andrew Sarris, the film critic who advanced the auteur theory of moviemaking, penned a review of the event for the *Village Voice·* He was not kind: "Nothing is sadder than the degeneration of demonic talent into responsible citizenship." As for Miss Monroe, "Why not have Marilyn burst out of the cake next time? Superidea [*sic*]: why not have a real orgy next time.?"[90] Marilyn's electrifying appearance at the birthday party came only eighty-five days before her suicide on August 4, 1962.

There is another angle on the Marilyn Monroe story. After co-starring with her, Laurence Olivier observed: "There are two entirely different sides [to Marilyn]. You would not be too far out if you described her as a schizoid. The two people could not be more different."[91] As in Mary Lincoln's case, two personalities, the Bad and the Good, vied for dominance.

The Good Marilyn was the principal architect of her own popular image and professional career. She knew what she was doing when she created "Marilyn Monroe." There is a revealing bit of dialogue in *Gentlemen Prefer Blondes* in which Monroe as the gold digger Lorelei Lee has this exchange with her prospective millionaire father-in-law, Mr. Esmond, Sr. (Taylor Holmes):

ESMOND: Say, they told me you were stupid. You don't sound stupid.

LORELEI: I can be smart when it's important. But most men don't like that.

Like Lorelei, Marilyn Monroe could be smart when it was important. She was curious about the world (despite her limited education) and politically aware—a liberal advocate who attracted the attention of the FBI. She took acting, singing, and dancing seriously. She studied at the Actor's Studio with Lee Strasberg, famous among the method-acting advocates. She even set up her own movie production company to promote her career. She played in twenty-nine films between 1946 and 1961, including the classic comedy *Some Like It Hot* (1959). This was the Good Marilyn. Like Mary Lincoln, who challenged the nineteenth century's cult of true womanhood, Marilyn challenged Hollywood's cult of domesticity of the mid-twentieth century. In feminist interpretations, they were rebels against the restraints of the American homemaker. The Bad Marilyn was the Copacabana School of Acting alumna who drove movie directors to distraction with her inability to show up for work on time or to remember her lines. According to movie legend, it took fifty-nine takes for her to say correctly, "Where's that bourbon?" in *Some Like it Hot*.

Consider the sorrows of Marilyn Monroe: in addition to the lost father, the unbalanced mother, the foster homes, the orphanage, and the failed marriages, she suffered from Meniere's syndrome, endometriosis, insomnia, acute exhaustion, viral infections, depression, and drug addiction.[92] Unlike Mary Lincoln's failed attempt at suicide, Marilyn carried through with it.

Marilyn Monroe (the Good and the Bad) and Shirley Temple (there was only the Good Shirley) were seductresses, and not only of older men but of the nation as well. In an obituary for Shirley Temple Black in 2014, entertainment writer Alanna Bennett concludes that "generations of women spent their childhoods wanting to be Shirley Temple, and their adolescence or adulthood yearning to be Marilyn Monroe."[93] According to Gore Vidal, "The Sandburg–Mount Rushmore Lincoln is a solemn gloomy cuss, who speaks only in iambic pentameter, a tear forever at the corner of his eye— the result, no doubt of being followed around by the Mormon Tabernacle Choir, which keeps humming 'The Battle Hymn of the Republic' while the future ambassador Shirley Temple Black curls up in his lap."[94]

Abraham Lincoln and Shirley Temple, is it possible? Abraham Lincoln and Marilyn Monroe, is it possible? The intersection between a man who died in 1865 with "America's Little Darling" of the 1930s and the "Blonde Bombshell" of the 1950s comprised a web of connections, both on and off the screen. Shirley Temple was part of an idealized relationship—Abraham Lincoln/Shirley Temple/Franklin Delano Roosevelt—that inspired and consoled the nation in a time of economic collapse and the prelude to the biggest war in history. To label Temple a "child" star shortchanges her seemingly preternatural ability to beguile the country.

Later, another star who could seduce the people, including a living president of the United States, found in Abraham Lincoln the father she never had; the father she longed for; the father who would be as kind to her as he was to little Virgie. Shirley would sit on Lincoln's lap and turn on the charm; Monroe would, we assume, during their brief affair in March 1962, sit on JFK's lap.

Marilyn Monroe was more devoted to Lincoln than was Shirley Temple. Little Shirley could not really appreciate her public role in the heroic triumvirate confronting depression and war. For her part, Monroe carried that tormented memory of the infantine Norma Jeane and her fantasy of Abraham Lincoln. Like Marilyn, Americans, in no small measure through the imagination of Hollywood, created an Abraham Lincoln that fulfilled their collective desire for a political savior—that kindly, forgiving Man of Sorrow who bore the burden of the nation's sins and let us sit upon his lap—"and Jesus called a little child unto him."

CONCLUSION
Fade Out

George McDonald Fraser, screenwriter and author of a series of comic historical novels, said of Hollywood's history of the world: "Although films have sometimes blundered and distorted and falsified, have botched great themes and belittled great men and women, have trivialized and caricatured and cheapened, have piled anachronism upon solecism on downright lies—still at their best they have given a picture of the ages more vivid and memorable than anything in Tacitus or Gibbon or Macaulay, and to an infinitely wider audience."[1] Hollywood's history of Lincoln and the women he loved is both vivid and memorable, though blunders, distortions, falsifications, and romanticism abound—remember how high that corn grew on Hollywood's back lot? Willian Herndon, who claimed to have revealed the real Lincoln, and Carl Sandburg, whose romantic magnum opus on Lincoln is still, after almost a century, "the most influential and popular life of Lincoln ever produced,"[2] created the template for filmmakers.

The memories of Lincoln's friends and acquaintances from New Salem and Springfield remain controversial. Contemporaries remembered his comical awkwardness around young women. Yet, if he was conflicted about his sexual desires, he seemed no less interested in pursuing female relationships. After all, he proposed marriage to three or four women, if we can believe certain recollections.

Abraham Lincoln was famously circumspect about his early years, and evidence about the women he loved and who loved him in return is fragmentary. There is no consensus about Lincoln's inner life. Much of what is known is speculation. The death of his mother when he was nine years old certainly contributed to his lifelong melancholy. Or perhaps he inherited the trait from her. Both are possible. He appreciated stepmother Sarah's love and care. He was, however, not deeply attached to her or to his father or to other members of his family either immediate or extended. He hated the hard, unforgiving life of frontier farming and the unrewarding prospects such a life afforded. Whatever his relationship to Ann Rutledge, mere affection or eternal love, following her death, he moved quickly into an unfulfilled courtship with Mary Owens. Although it is clear that he would have married her if she had accepted him, Lincoln responded to her rejection with sarcasm and ridicule.

His relationship with Mary Todd Lincoln remains a subject of intense debate. Their courtship was rocky from the start, and she may have seduced him into marriage. Their life together was either a living hell or a passionate companionship. Good Mary was difficult to live with yet lovingly devoted to her husband and her boys. This was the high-spirited Mary Todd who challenged the patriarchal restraints of the day and then the beloved Molly who created an enduring political and sexual bond with her husband. Bad Mary was a hard-bitten shrew—an unhinged, self-absorbed woman—spoiled, unprincipled, lacking in dignity, self-control, and common sense.

Those who have searched out Lincoln's inner world and the women who inhabited it form no consensus. What the public knows about Nancy Hanks, Sarah Bush Johnston, Ann Rutledge, Mary Owens, and Mary Todd Lincoln is a gaggle of small-town recollections, speculations, romantic inclinations, poetry, serious scholarship, present-mindedness, and Hollywood invention.

In composing America's hymn of Abraham Lincoln, along with other harmonies of Railsplitter lore, D. W. Griffith, Stephen Vincent Benét, Edwin Burke, Lamar Trotti, Robert Sherwood, James Agee, A. J. Edwards, and others were often off-key. Yet, the false notes mattered little to audiences; the movies were better than real life. The story of Lincoln on film demonstrates no attempt to present other than the sad, mythical hero. Even the television adaptation of Gore Vidal's novel left out what he intended as a shocking revision of the Lincoln myth.

Influenced by and parallel to the work of Lincoln scholars and popular writers, especially William Herndon and Carl Sandburg, Hollywood studios brought Lincoln's story to life for generations of moviegoers: Joseph

Henabery, Frank McGlynn Sr., Walter Huston, Raymond Massey, Hal Holbrook, Sam Waterston, and Daniel Day-Lewis became the Man of Sorrow. Ann of New Salem could be fragile as Mary Howard or as serene as Joanne Woodward—and Mary Lincoln as conniving as Kay Hammond, as hard as Ruth Gordon, as haunted as Julie Harris, or as smart yet tormented as Sada Thompson, Mary Tyler Moore, and Sally Field. These are the lost loves and the troubled Mollies of popular memory.

Hollywood both created and enhanced the popular image of Abraham Lincoln, of Nancy, of Sara, of Ann Rutledge, and of the Bad and Good Marys. Films based on biography and the moviemakers' imaginations found anchor in the issues and cinematic approaches of their own times—the ideological and cultural relationships between films and society reflecting the competition between the filmmakers' romantic narratives and the varieties of historical truth.

Given the universe of material about Lincoln and its endless variations, this study narrowed the focus on Lincoln mythmaking to Hollywood films and a basic theme: how moviemakers imagined the women in Lincoln's life and afterlife and how these women explained and enhanced the myth of Lincoln as the Child of Destiny and the Man of Sorrow. In *The Better Angels,* mother Nancy says of her boy, "He's got a gift. Can't turn our back on what God has given us."

NOTES

Introduction: Hollywood and the Women in Lincoln's Life

1. Mentor Graham described Offutt as "an unsteady, noisy, fussy, and rather brutal man, wild and unprovidential" (quoted in Mark E. Neely Jr., *The Abraham Lincoln Encyclopedia* [New York: McGraw-Hill, 1982], s.v. "Denton Offutt").

2. Carl Sandburg drew his inspiration from Ida Tarbell. Best known for her muckraking *History of the Standard Oil Company* (1904), she was a "popularizer" but also a dedicated Lincoln scholar and Carl Sandburg's chief inspiration. Her *Life of Lincoln* (1900) was the product of impressive original research. She argued that Nancy Hanks "was legitimate and the descendent of a respectable old family," and "she never completely rejected the Ann Rutledge romance" (Neely, *Lincoln Encyclopedia,* s.v. "Ida Tarbell"). "Few persons realize Miss Tarbell's influence upon Carl Sandburg. She was his prime mover" (Benjamin Thomas, *Portrait for Prosperity: Lincoln and His Biographers* [New Brunswick, NJ: Rutgers University Press, 1947], 187).

3. Thomas, *Portrait for Prosperity,* 291.

4. Ibid., 285.

5. For an authoritative survey of anti-Lincoln writings, see John McKee Barr, *Loathing Lincoln: An American Tradition from the Civil War to the Present* (Baton Rouge: Louisiana State University Press, 2014).

6. Herndon quoted in Douglas L. Wilson, "William H. Herndon on Lincoln's Fatalism," *Journal of the Abraham Lincoln Association* 35, no. 2 (2014): 11.

7. Eugene W. Chafin, *Lincoln: Man of Sorrow* (Chicago: Lincoln Temperance Press, 1908), 18.

8. Merrill D. Peterson, *Lincoln in American Memory* (New York: Oxford University Press, 1995), 218.

9. Carl Sandburg, *Abraham Lincoln: The Prairie Years, 2 vols.* (1926; New York: Charles Scribner's Sons, 1948), vol. 1, 190.

10. Joshua Wolf Shenk, *Lincoln's Melancholy: How Depression Challenged a President and Fueled His Greatness* (New York: Houghton Mifflin, 2005), 228.

11. Kelly Miller, "I See and Am Satisfied," in *Negro Poets and Their Poems,* ed. Robert Thomas Kerlin (Good Press, 2022), chap. 5, Kindle.

12. Biopics are a continuing Hollywood tradition, but they were especially popular during the so-called classical period of Hollywood moviemaking (1930–60). Biographical films promoted the meaning of the American Dream and the role of the "great man" and, sometimes, of the great woman in history.

13. If the commercial spirit behind filmmaking needed any validation, that motive became perfectly clear when the online megaretailer Amazon bought the MGM studio and its film catalogue for its movie-streaming services in March 2022.

14. Alex D. Reid, "Writing Secondary Characters." Arcstudio.com, https://www.arcstudio pro.com/blog/writing-secondary-characters.

15. For a brief overview of the subject, see Lehrman Institute: Abraham Lincoln's Classroom, "Lincoln and Women," https://www.abrahamlincolnsclassroom.org/abraham-lincolns -contemporaries/abraham-lincoln-and-women/. The article notes that "his relationships with women were unsure and uneven, especially in his youth." See also, Rosa, Rafael. "Abraham Lincoln and Women: A Psychohistorical Analysis." PhD diss., Drew University, May 2017.

1. Framing Lincoln's Angel Mothers: Nancy Hanks and Sarah Bush Johnston

1. Shirley Temple Black, *Child Star* (New York, McGraw-Hill, 1988), 289.

2. Nancy Hanks Lincoln (February 5, 1789 [?]–October 5, 1819). She was twenty-five or twenty-six when she married Thomas Lincoln in 1806.

3. Sarah Lincoln (February 10, 1807–January 20, 1828).

4. Thomas Lincoln Jr. (born 1812 or 1813, died within three days).

5. Judith Waltzer Leavitt, "Under the Shadow of Maternity: American Women's Responses to Death and Debility Fears in Nineteenth-Century Childbirth," *Feminist Studies* 12, no. 1 (1986): 133.

6. Nancy Schrom Dye, "History of Childbirth in America," in "Women: Sex and Sexuality, Part 2," special issue, *Signs* 6, no. 1 (Autumn 1980): 97–108.

7. *Omnibus* was a high-minded television variety series underwritten by the Ford Foundation. It consisted of 152 episodes that ran from 1952 to 1961. The programs emphasized interviews with those in the creative arts as well as presenting original works of drama, music, and film.

8. Dialogue from Laurence Bergreen, *James Agee: A Life* (New York: Dutton, 1984), 371. The exchange in the final cut is a bit different; the midwife calls Nancy "sugar," not "honey."

9. Robert Barron, "Recovering the Strangeness of Easter," *Wall Street Journal*, April 2, 2021, https://www.wsj.com/articles/recovering-the-strangeness-of-easter-11617375562.

10. Michael Burlingame, *Abraham Lincoln: A Life*, 2 vols. (Baltimore, MD: Johns Hopkins University Press, 2008), vol. 1, 24.

11. Margaret Walsh, "Women's Place on the American Frontier," *Journal of American History* 29, no. 2 (August 1995): 244.

12. Ruth H. Block, "Feminine Ideals in Transition: The Rise of the Moral Mother, 1785–1815," *Feminist Studies* 4, no. 2 (June 1978): 108.

13. William Hughes, *James Agee, Omnibus, and "Mr. Lincoln": The Culture of Liberalism and the Challenge of Television, 1952–1953* (Lanham, MD: Scarecrow, 2004), 84.

14. James Agee and Walker Evans, *Let Us Now Praise Famous Men* (New York: Houghton Mifflin), 1941. With the text by Agee and photographs by Evans, it is an impressionistic, photojournalistic view of three Alabama sharecropper families during the Great Depression.

15. Lincoln was born on February 12, 1809. Based on a traditional air, the song did not appear until the late nineteenth century, reflecting the Scottish nationalist movement of the era.

16. Edwards took his inspiration for the title *The Better Angels* from Lincoln's first inaugural address: "The mystic chords of memory, stretching from every battlefield and patriot grave, to every heart and hearth-stone, all over this broad land, will yet swell the chorus of the Union, when again touched, as surely they will be, by the better angels of our nature."

17. Thomas McGregor, "Some New Facts about Abraham Lincoln's Parents," *Register of Kentucky State Historical Society* 2, no. 59 (May 1922): 217–18.

18. Lincoln quoted in Mark E. Neely Jr., *The Abraham Lincoln Encyclopedia* (New York: Mc-Graw Hill, 1982), s.v. "Nancy Hanks Lincoln."

19. David Herbert Donald, *Lincoln* (New York: Jonathan Cape, 1995), 20.

20. Catherine Clinton, "Abraham Lincoln: The Family That Made Him, the Family He Made," in *Our Lincoln: New Perspectives on Lincoln and His World,* ed. Eric Foner (New York: Norton, 2008), 252.

21. Burlingame, *Abraham Lincoln,* vol. 1, 19; Clinton, "Abraham Lincoln: The Family," 253.

22. Burlingame, *Abraham Lincoln,* vol. 1, 19.

23. William Herndon called upon his own memories and numerous other recollections by those who knew Lincoln as relatives and neighbors for an intimate biography. The reliability of Herndon's sources is the subject of considerable historiographical controversy. See the chapters below on Ann Rutledge and Mary Lincoln.

24. Herndon quoted in Burlingame, *Abraham Lincoln,* vol. 1, 14; emphasis in the original.

25. Burlingame, *Abraham Lincoln,* vol. 1, 13.

26. Clinton, "Abraham Lincoln: The Family," 253.

27. Donald, *Lincoln,* 23. The original source of the "angel mother" quotation can be found in Joshua F. Speed, *Reminiscences of Abraham Lincoln and Notes on a Visit to California: Two Lectures* (Louisville, KY: John P. Morton, 1884), 19.

28. Donald, *Lincoln,* 23. "Though our information is imperfect . . . both parents had characteristics suggestive of melancholy. Nearly all the descriptions of Nancy have her as sad" (Joshua Wolf Shenk, *Lincoln's Melancholia: How Depression Challenged a President and Fueled His Greatness* [New York: Houghton Mifflin, 2005], 12).

29. William Elery Curtis, *Abraham Lincoln* (Philadelphia: Lippincott, 1902), 31.

30. James Tackach, *Lincoln and the Environment* (Carbondale: Southern Illinois University Press, 2019), 11. See also Burlingame, *Abraham Lincoln,* vol. 1, 172.

31. Michael Green, *Lincoln and the Election of 1860* (Carbondale: University of Southern Illinois University Press, 2011), chap. 5, Kindle.

32. Burlingame, *Abraham Lincoln,* vol. 1, 11–15.

33. Walter J. Daly, "'The Slows': The Torment of Milk Sickness on the Midwest Frontier," *Indiana Magazine of History* 102, no. 1 (March 2006): 29–40. See also Burlingame, *Abraham Lincoln,* vol. 1, 25.

34. Burlingame, *Abraham Lincoln,* vol. 1, 25; William I. Christensen, "Milk Sickness: A Review of the Literature, *Economic Botany* 19, no. 3 (July-September 1965): 293–300.

35. Tackach, *Lincoln and the Environment,* 12.

36. William H. Herndon and Jesse W. Weik, *Herndon's Lincoln: The True Story of a Great Life* (Springfield, IL: Herndon's Lincoln Publishing Company, 1888), 27–28.

37. Quoted in Burlingame, *Abraham Lincoln,* vol. 1, 27.

38. Burlingame, *Abraham Lincoln,* vol. 1, 27; Clinton, "Abraham Lincoln: The Family," 256.

39. Clinton, "Abraham Lincoln: The Family," 256.

40. Burlingame, *Abraham Lincoln,* vol. 1, 19.

41. Ibid.

42. Tackach, *Lincoln and the Environment,* 50. See also Bruce Guernsey, "The Poetry of Abraham Lincoln," *Virginia Quarterly Review* 78, no. 2 (Spring 2002): 295–303.

43. Dialogue quoted in Donald, *Lincoln,* 271.

44. Carl Sandburg, *Abraham Lincoln: The Prairie Years,* 2 vols. (1926; New York: Charles Scribner's Sons, 1948), vol. 2, 417.

45. Frederick Trevor Hill, "Lincoln's Legacy to America: The Surroundings of Lincoln's Birth and Childhood," *New York Times,* February 1, 1909.

46. Austin Trunick, "Filmmaker A. J. Edwards Discusses "The Better Angels," *Under the Radar,* November 7, 2014, https://www.undertheradarmag.com/interviews/filmmaker_a.j._edwards _discusses_the_better_angels. In an online interview, A. J. Edwards commented on the sources for *The Better Angels:* "Some very seminal texts at the time would have been Benjamin Thomas's single-volume *Abraham Lincoln,* Carl Sandburg's *The Prairie Years,* Ida Tarbell's work, Eleanor Atkinson's now out-of-print texts, David Herbert Donald's *Lincoln.* Our historical consultant's book, *There I Grew Up* . . . he's the greatest living Lincoln scholar, named William Bartelt. Then Lincoln's own campaign autobiographies, which are fascinating to read."

47. Ibid.

48. Sundance 2014: "New Frontier Films," January 10, 2014, https://www.indiewire.com /2014/01/sundance-2014-new-frontier-films-31530.

49. Roger Ebert, review of *Badlands,* October 15, 1973, https://www.rogerebert.com/reviews /badlands-1973. Ebert's reflections on Malick's *Days of Heaven* (1978) apply to the *Better Angels* as well: "Nature is always deeply embedded in Malick's films. It occupies the stage and then humans edge tentatively onto it, uncertain of their roles. There is always much detail, of birds and small animals, of trees and skies, of empty fields and dense forest, of leaves and grain, and always too much space for the characters to fill. They are nudged here and there by events which they confuse with their destinies."

50. Lloyd Michaels, *Terrence Malick* (Champaign: University of Illinois Press, 2009), 40–41.

51. See *The Railsplitter. Abraham Lincoln: An Extraordinary Life* (exhibition), National Museum of American History, https://americanhistory.si.edu/lincoln/railsplitter.

52. William E. Bartelt, "The Making of *The Better Angels,*" *Journal of the Abraham Lincoln Association* 36, no. 2 (2015), https://quod.lib.umich.edu/j/jala/2629860.0036.205/—roundtable -the-better-%09angels?rgn=main;view=fulltext.

53. Marling quoted in "Brit Marling. Biography," IMDb, https://www.imdb.com/name /nm1779870/bio?ref_=nm_ov_bio_sm#quotes.

54. Todd McCarthy, "The Better Angels: Sundance Review," *Hollywood Reporter,* January 25, 2014, https://www.hollywoodreporter.com/news/general-news/better-angels-sundance -review-674057/.

55. Megan Kate Nelson, "Lincoln's Boyhood and Black and White," *Journal of the Abraham Lincoln Association* 36, no. 2 (2015), https://quod.lib.umich.edu/j/jala/2629860.0036.205 /—roundtable-the-better-%09angels?rgn=main;view=fulltext.

56. Jackie Hogan, "Searching for the 'Better Angels' of Historical Context," *Journal of the Abraham Lincoln Association,* 36, no. 2 (2015), https://quod.lib.umich.edu/j/jala/2629860.0036 .205/—roundtable-the-better-%09angels?rgn=main;view=fulltext.

57. Sandburg, *Abraham Lincoln: The Prairie Years,* vol. 1, 13.

58. Hill, "Lincoln's Legacy to America."

59. Donald H. Winkler, *Lincoln's Ladies: The Women in the Life of the Sixteenth President,* rev. and expanded ed. (Nashville, TN: Cumberland House, 2004), 15. For the books in Lincoln's life, see Robert Bray, "What Abraham Lincoln Read—An Evaluative and Annotated List," *Journal of the Abraham Lincoln Association* 28, no. 2 (Summer 2007), https://quod.lib.umich .edu/j/jala/2629860.0028.204/—what-abraham-lincoln-readan-evaluative-and-annotated -list?rgn=main;view=fulltext.

60. Peter Debruge, review of *The Better Angels,* Variety.com, November 7, 2014, https:// variety.com/2014/film/reviews/film-review-the-better-angels-1201350349/.

61. Bartelt, "The Making of *The Better Angels.*"

62. Glenn Kenny, review of *The Better Angels,* November 7, 2014, https://www.rogerebert .com/reviews/the-better-angels-2014.

63. Edwards quoted in John Stauffer, "The Christ-Haunted Lincoln," in "Roundtable: *The Better Angels," Journal of the Abraham Lincoln Association* 26, no. 2 (2015): 60, https://quod.lib .umich.edu/j/jala/2629860.0036.205/—roundtable-the-better-%09angels?rgn=main;view= fulltext.

64. Fonda quoted in Anne-Marie Paquet-Deyris, "From 'Plain Abe' to Mythical Mr. Lincoln: Constructing Various Representational Modes of a Screen Idol," *Idées d'Amériques* 7 (Spring 2016): 6.

2. The Romance of Ann Rutledge in Memory and Film

1. A brief biographical sketch of Wilma Frances Minor appears in "Noted Writer Aids in Star Annual Fiesta Edition with Clever Articles," *Chula Vista Star,* August 15, 1941, https://www .newspapers.com/clip/14250856/the_chula_vista_star/.

2. This summary of the Wilma Minor hoax draws on Don E. Fehrenbacher, *The Minor Affair: An Adventure in Forgery and Detection* (Fort Wayne, IN: Louis A Warren Lincoln Library and Museum, 1979). See also Don E. Fehrenbacher, "Lincoln's Lost Love Letters," *American Heritage* 32, no. 2 (February/March 1981), https://www.americanheritage.com/lincolns-lost-love-letters. See also Merrill D. Peterson, *Lincoln in American Memory* (New York: Oxford University Press, 1994), 257, 291–98.

3. The controversy surrounding Ann Rutledge began soon after William Herndon promoted the story of the love affair in 1866. Historians who to one degree or another support the story include Michael Burlingame, *Abraham Lincoln: A Life,* 2 vols. (Baltimore, MD: Johns Hopkins University Press, 2008), vol. 1; David Donald, *Lincoln* (New York: Simon & Schuster, 1995); H. Donald Winkler, *Lincoln's Ladies: The Women in the Life of the Sixteenth President, rev. and expanded ed.* (Nashville, TN: Cumberland House, 2004); John Y. Simon, "Abraham Lincoln and Ann Rutledge," *Journal of the Abraham Lincoln Association* 11 (1990): 13–33; and John Evangelist Walsh, *The Shadows Rise: Abraham Lincoln and the Ann Rutledge Legend* (Urbana: University of Illinois Press, 1993). Those denying its authenticity include Mark E. Neely Jr., *The Abraham Lincoln En-*

cyclopedia (New York: McGraw Hill, 1982), s.v. "Ann Rutledge"; James G. Randall, "Sifting the Anne Rutledge Evidence," in *Lincoln the President: Springfield to Gettysburg* (New York: Dodd, Mead, 1945); C. A. Tripp, *The Intimate World of Abraham Lincoln*, ed. Lewis Gannett (New York: Thunder Mouth, 2005); and Thomas F. Schwartz, "'Not Even Wrong': Herndon and His Informants," *Journal of the Abraham Lincoln Association* 35, no. 2 (2014): 37–54.

4. See Neely, *Lincoln Encyclopedia,* s.v. "William Eleazer Barton."

5. See Stewart Mitchell, "Worthington Chauncey Ford," *Proceedings of the Massachusetts Historical Society* 69 (1947): 407–11, http://www.jstor.org/stable/25080421.

6. See Judith A. Rice, "Ida M. Tarbell: A Progressive Look at Lincoln," *Journal of the Abraham Lincoln Association* 19, no. 1 (Winter 1998): 57–72.

7. Tarbell quoted in Fehrenbacher, *Minor Affair,* 14.

8. Tarbell quoted in Thomas, *Portrait for Posterity,* 195.

9. Wilma Frances Minor, "Lincoln the Lover. Part I: The Setting—New Salem," *Atlantic,* December 1928, https://www.theatlantic.com/magazine/archive/1928/12/lincoln-the-lover /304444/; "Lincoln the Lover. Part II: The Courtship," *Atlantic,* January 1929, https://www .theatlantic.com/magazine/archive/1929/01/lincoln-the-lover/304445/; "Lincoln the Lover. Part III: The Tragedy," *Atlantic,* February 1929, https://www.theatlantic.com/magazine/archive /1929/02/lincoln-the-lover/304442/.

10. Fehrenbacher, *Minor Affair,* 16.

11. Minor, "The Tragedy," https://www.theatlantic.com/magazine/archive/1929/02/lincoln -the-lover/304442/.

12. See Paul M. Angle, "The Minor Collection: A Criticism," *Atlantic Monthly,* April 1929.

13. Neely, *Lincoln Encyclopedia,* s.v. "Oliver Rogers Barrett." Barrett and Sandburg were connected. Barrett, a lawyer by profession, was well known among Lincoln scholars and buffs for his collection of Lincoln memorabilia. He wrote the introduction to Lincoln's *Last Speech in Springfield in the Campaign of 1858* (Chicago: University of Chicago Press, 1924). For his part, Sandburg wrote *Lincoln Collector: The Story of the Oliver R. Barrett Collection* (New York: Harcourt Brace, 1949).

14. Minor quoted in Peterson, *Lincoln in American Memory,* 291.

15. Minor quoted in Fehrenbacher, *Minor Affair,* 29.

16. Madelyn Kay Duhon, "Journalist and Hoaxer: William Francis Mannix and the Long History of Faked News" (master's thesis [no. 4415], LSU, 2017), https://digitalcommons.lsu.edu /gradschool_theses/4415.

17. Elizabeth Brown Pryor, *Six Encounters with Lincoln: A President Confronts Democracy and Its Demons* (New York: Penguin, 2018), 233.

18. Grace Kelly starred in *Ann Rutledge,* a 1950 television drama on NBC's Philco Television Playhouse. No copies appear to exist (see Mark S. Reinhart, *Abraham Lincoln on Screen: Fictional and Documentary Portrayals on Film and Television, 2nd ed.* [Jefferson, NC: McFarland, 2011], 48). A production still of Kelly can be found at Ask Me Anything, "The Blond at the Film," https://the blondeatthefilm.tumblr.com/post/142183992172/february-12-1950-actress-grace-kelly-as-ann.

19. Quoted in Lewis Gannett, "The Ann Rutledge Story: Case Closed?," *Journal of the Abraham Lincoln Association* 31, no. 2 (2011): 36. See also Burlingame, *Abraham Lincoln,* vol. 1, 331–32.

20. Audrey C. Peterson, "Brain Fever in Nineteenth-Century Literature Fact and Fiction," *Victorian Studies* 19, no. 4 (June 1976): 456.

21. Tripp, *Intimate World of Abraham Lincoln,* 74–75.

22. Carl Sandburg, *Abraham Lincoln: The Prairie Years,* 2 vols. (1926; New York: Charles Scribner's Sons, 1948), vol. 1, 189.

23. William B. Barringer, *Lincoln Day by Day: A Chronology, 1809–1865,* ed. Earl Schenck Miers, vol. 1: *1809–1848* (Dayton, OH: Morningside House, 1991), 50.

24. Tripp, *Intimate World of Abraham Lincoln,* 74–75.

25. Burlingame, *Abraham Lincoln,* vol. 1, 100.

26. Tripp, *Intimate World of Abraham Lincoln,* 75.

27. Daniel Scott Smith, "Differential Morality in the United States before 1900," *Journal of Interdisciplinary History* 13, no. 4 (Spring 1983): 735–36.

28. For the psychological impact on young Lincoln, see Burlingame, *Abraham Lincoln,* vol. 1, 26.

29. William Herndon, *Lincoln and Ann Rutledge: A Lecture by William H. Herndon* (Herrin, IL: Trovillion, 1945), 20.

30. James G. Randall, *Lincoln,* vol. 2, 328.

31. Charles B. Strozier, *Lincoln's Quest for Union: Public and Private Meanings* (New York: Basic, 1982), 35.

32. False memory is "a distorted recollection of an event or, most severely, recollection of an event that never actually happened. False memories are errors of commission, because details, facts, or events come to mind, often vividly, but the remembrances fail to correspond to prior events. Even when people are highly confident that they are remembering 'the truth' of the original situation, experimental evidence shows that they can be wrong. For example, one-quarter of adults in a particular experiment who were told an untrue story about being lost in a mall as a child—ostensibly obtained from their family members—adopted the story, sometimes embellishing it with vivid sensory detail" (American Psychological Association, https://dictionary.apa.org/false-memory).

33. Burlingame quoted in Joshua Wolf Shenk, *Lincoln's Melancholy: How Depression Challenged a President and Fueled His Greatness* (New York: Houghton Mifflin), 241.

34. Sandburg, *Abraham Lincoln: The Prairie Years,* vol. 1, 186.

35. Mary Lincoln to David Davis, March 4, 1867, in Justin G. Turner and Linda Levitt Turner, eds., *Mary Todd Lincoln: Her Life and Letters* (New York: Knopf, 1972), 415; emphasis in the original.

36. Dall quoted in Peterson, *Lincoln in American Memory,* 74.

37. Don E. Fehrenbacher and Virginia Fehrenbacher, eds., *Recollected Words of Abraham Lincoln* (Stanford, CA: Stanford University Press, 1996), 82, 257.

38. Sandburg was the source for Griffith's scene. In Sandburg's imagination, Lincoln visited Ann's grave: "A week after the burial of Ann Rutledge, Bill Green found him [Lincoln] rambling in the woods along the Sangamon River, mumbling sentences Bill could not understand. They watched him and tried to keep him safe among friend in New Salem. And he rambled darkly and idly past their circle to the burying ground seven miles away, where he lay with a arm across the one grave" (Sandburg, *Abraham Lincoln: The Prairie Years,* vol. 1, 190).

39. Shenk, *Lincoln's Melancholy,* 12.

40. David S. Reynolds, *Abe: Abraham Lincoln in His Times* (New York: Penguin, 2020), 157.

41. Library of Congress, Music for the Nation: American Sheet Music, ca. 1820–1839, 1830–1839, https://www.loc.gov/collections/american-sheet-music-1820-to-1860/articles-and-essays/greatest-hits-1820-60-variety-music-cavalcade/1830-to-1839.

42. Shenk, *Lincoln's Melancholy,* 191.

43. Benjamin P. Thomas, *Lincoln's New Salem* (1934; Victoria, British Columbia: Reading Essentials, n.d.), part 2, Kindle.

44. Shenk, *Lincoln's Melancholy,* 229.

45. Theodore Roosevelt, "Address of President Roosevelt on the Occasion of the Celebration of the Hundredth Anniversary of the Birth of Abraham Lincoln," Hodgenville, Ky., February 12, 1909, New York State Library, http://www.nysl.nysed.gov/mssc/tr/address.htm.

46. Theodore Roosevelt, "The Heirs of Abraham Lincoln," February 12, 1913, Document, Teaching American History, Ashbrook Center at Ashland University, https://teachingamerican history.org/library/document/the-heirs-of-abraham-lincoln.

47. Derek A. Webb, "The Natural Rights Liberalism of Franklin Delano Roosevelt: Economic Rights and the American Constitutional Tradition," *American Journal of Legal History* 55, no. 3 (2015): 322–30. See also Nina Silber, "Abraham Lincoln and the Political Culture of New Deal America," *Journal of the Civil War Era* 5, no. 3 (2015): 348–71.

48. Sandburg, *Abraham Lincoln: The Prairie Years,* vol. 1, 140–41.

49. Edmund Wilson, *Patriotic Gore: Studies in the Literature of the American Civil War* (New York: Oxford University Press, 1962), 116.

50. Sandburg, *Abraham Lincoln: The Prairie Years,* vol. 1, 189.

51. In response to criticism about his rendering of the affair, Sandburg downplayed the Rutledge story in a later edition of his Lincoln biography (see Wilson, *Patriotic Gore,* 116).

52. Peterson, *Lincoln in American Memory.*

53. Schwartz, "Not Even Wrong," 13.

54. Ibid., 26. Historian Melvyn Stokes divides the history of Lincoln in Hollywood into three distinct phases: Phase 1 (1903–1915); Phase 2 (1920–1930); and Phase 3 (after 1940). In the first period, filmmakers "portrayed Lincoln as "democratic and approachable, a 'man of the people' who was the merciful chief executive." From 1920 to 1940, he was the great unifier—the "focus of sectional reconciliation." After 1940, "Lincoln became less popular as a character in movies" as national attention turned national unity and reconciliation to civil rights and emancipation. Lincoln's views on race became suspect and "it became harder to represent Lincoln on screen" (Melvyn Stokes, "Abraham Lincoln and the Movies," *American Nineteenth Century History* 12, no. 2 [June 2011]: 223–24). Stokes's article, however, came out in June 2011, one year before Steven Spielberg's blockbuster film *Lincoln* premiered in November 2012. On a budget of $93 million, *Lincoln* grossed over $182 million domestically and $273 million worldwide. Daniel Day-Lewis won the Oscar for his portrayal of Lincoln as the Great Emancipator. Sally Field was nominated for best supporting actress as Mary Todd Lincoln. The prize, however, went to Anne Hathaway for her role as the suffering prostitute Fantine in *Las Misérables.* Despite the film's success, it did not signal a popular Lincoln revival. On the contrary, an anti-Lincoln sentiment among racial progressives beginning in 2020 called for the removal of his statues in public places and the erasing of his name on public school buildings (see, for example, Sidney Blumenthal and Harold Holzer, "Take Down Chicago's Lincoln Statues? It's Iconoclasm Gone Mad," *Chicago Tribune,* February 22, 2021).

55. Reinhart, *Abraham Lincoln on Screen,* 137–38. The online American Film Institute (AFI) Catalog also provides information on the background to the film and the producers' two years of biographical research that went into preparation for filming (see AFI Catalog, *Abraham Lincoln*

[1924], https://catalog.afi.com/Film/2-ABRAHAM-LINCOLN?sid=ca91f7a0-246e-4271-b75a
-df280232d76d&sr=17.111118&cp=1&pos=0).

56. Carl Sandburg, *"The Movies Are": Carl Sandburg's Film Reviews and Essays, 1920–1928,* ed.
Arnie Bernstein, introd. Roger Ebert (Chicago: Lake Claremont, 2000).

57. Ibid., 236–37.

58. Ibid., 240.

59. Ibid., 239.

60. Mark S Reinhart, *Abraham Lincoln on Screen: Fictional and Documentary Portrayals on
Film and Television,* 2nd ed. (Jefferson, NC: McFarland, 2011), 82–83.

61. Henry Fonda was one of the truly great American actors. His long career (1935–81) included many of Hollywood's classics. In 1939, he starred in two of Ford's greatest films, *Drums
along the Mohawk* (released November 3) and *Young Mr. Lincoln* (released May 30). In 1940,
Fonda starred in *The Grapes of Wrath,* another Ford masterpiece. Darryl F. Zanuck produced
the films for distribution by Twentieth Century–Fox. "Fonda found his most suitable director in John Ford. Fonda's statuesque gentleness, with politeness only reluctantly giving way
to anger, was very close to Ford's conception of a prairie Galahad." "As Lincoln, especially, he
captured a dreamy political calm, torn between peach and apple pie, but drawn to justice un-
failingly" (David Thomson, *The New Biographical Dictionary of Film* [New York: Knopf, 2002],
s.v. "Henry Fonda").

62. A. M. R. Wright, *The Dramatic Life of Abraham Lincoln: Illustrated with Scenes from the Photoplay. A First Nation Picture Presented by Al and Ray Rockett* (New York: Grosset & Dunlap, 1925).

63. Ibid., x.

64. Ibid., 12.

65. Ibid., 39.

66. Ibid., 71.

67. Gordon Berg, review of *Abraham Lincoln* (1930), https://www.historynet.com/acw-review
-abraham-lincoln-1930.

68. Iris Barry, *D. W. Griffith: American Film Master* (New York: Museum of Modern Art,
1940), 32.

69. The caustic film historian David Thomson wrote a denigrating, dismissive, and dis-
tasteful biographical entry for Joseph Schenck for his biographical dictionary: "You pronounce
the name 'Shenk' as in 'skunk,' and maybe that's all one needs to say." "Joe was a big slob, nearly
bald, rather Slavic looking [he was a Russian Jewish immigrant]: an actress he once chased
round the office . . . said he had a nose like a large boiled potato. He was effusive, sentimental,
affectionate, and grabby" (Thomson, *New Biographical Dictionary of Film* [New York: Knopf
2002], s.v, "Joesph M. Schenck and Nicholas Schenck"). The industry displayed more respect
for Joe Schenck. He was one of the founders of United Artists, Twentieth Century–Fox, as
well as the Academy of Motion Picture Arts and Sciences. The Academy awarded him a special
achievement Oscar in 1952. He also has a star on Hollywood's Walk of Fame.

70. Richard Schickel, *D. W. Griffith: An American Life* (New York: Simon & Schuster, 1984),
551–52.

71. Ibid.

72. The poem was later adapted for Broadway in 1953. Tyrone Power, Judith Anderson, and
Raymond Massey performed a dramatic reading directed by Charles Laughton.

73. Schickel, *D. W. Griffith,* 553.

74. Berg, review of *Abraham Lincoln.*

75. John W. Considine Jr. (1898–1961) produced forty-seven films between 1929 and 1943, including three in 1930: *One Romantic Night, Puttin' on the Ritz, Be Yourself,* and *The Bad One.* He received story and production advisory credits for *Abraham Lincoln* (IMDb, https://www .imdb.com/name/nm0175908/).

76. Schickel, *D. W. Griffith,* 556.

77. Walter Huston had a long and distinguished film career, including *The Birth of a Nation* (uncredited, 1915), *The Virginian* (1929), *Rain* (1932), *Gabriel over the White House* (1933), *Dragon Seed* (1944), *The North Star* (1944), and *The Treasure of Sierra Madre* (1948). He was the father of director Walter Huston and the grandfather of actress Angelica Huston. Huston portrayed Abraham Lincoln in D. W. Griffith's *Abraham Lincoln* (1930). He went to Hollywood in 1929, one of many stage actors invited after the advent of sound. For the next twenty years, he displayed his acting abilities in a wide range of roles ranging from Wyatt Earp (*Law and Order* 1932) to the film version of Sinclair Lewis's *Dodsworth* (1936), a role he first played on stage. He makes a brief but memorable appearance as the Captain Jacoby who delivers the Maltese Falcon to Sam Spade just before dying. His son, John Huston, directed *The Maltese Falcon* (1941). Walter Huston played an almost comic version of Sheriff Pat Garrett in the notorious Howard Hughes bullets-and-bras fiasco *The Outlaw* 1940/1946. Again working with his son, he received an Oscar for Best Supporting Actor for his unforgettable performance as the old miner in *The Treasure of Sierra Madre* (1947). According to David Thomson, Huston "made a big impact in *The Virginian* (29, Victor Fleming) and then showed his versatility in the title role of Abraham Lincoln (30, D. W. Griffith)" (Thomson, *New Biographical Dictionary of Film,* s.v., "Walter Huston").

78. Una Merkel has a long film and theater career (1923–68). Her film credits include *The Maltese Falcon* (1931), *42nd Street* (1933), *Broadway Melody of 1936* (1935), *Destry Rides Again* (1939), *The Bank Dick* (1940), and *Road to Zanzibar* (1941). "The blonde, blue-eyed Miss Merkel sometimes made as many as six movies a year, appearing as a supporting actress with such stars of the era as Jean Harlow, W. C. Fields, Harold Lloyd, and Marlene Dietrich. She was cast in much of her movie career as the typical wise-cracking comic foil, opposite a glamorous star, and she delivered her lines with a Southern drawl" (Alexander Reid, "Una Merkel Dies at Age of 82; From Silent Film to Tony," *New York Times,* January 5, 1982).

79. Rosemary Carr Benét (1898–1962), the wife of Stephen Vincent Benét, was a journalist, literary critic, and poet whose writings appeared in *Harper's Bazaar, Vogue,* and the *New Yorker.*

80. Harold Turney, *Film Guide to the 20th Century–Fox Picture, A Cosmopolitan Production, Young Mr. Lincoln: A Study Plan Prepared in Hollywood* (Hollywood, CA: Film Guide, 1939), n.p. Turney was the chair of the Department of Drama at Los Angeles City College. The film guide was part of a series of tie-ins that appeared as movies premiered.

81. Howard Movshovitz, "The Still Point: Women in the Westerns of John Ford," in "Women on the Western Frontier, special issue, *Frontiers: A Journal of Women Studies* 7, no. 3 (1984): 60–70.

82. Geoffrey O'Brien, "Young Mr. Lincoln: Hero in Waiting," *Current: An Online Magazine Covering Film Culture Past and Present,* Criterion Collection, February 13, 2006, https://www .criterion.com/current/posts/413-young-mr-lincoln-hero-in-waiting.

83. Derek Malcom, "John Ford: Young Mr. Lincoln, *Guardian,* June 24, 1999, https://www .theguardian.com/film/1999/jun/24/1.

84. Graham Greene, *The Pleasure Dome: The Collected Film Criticism, 1935–1940,* ed. John Russell Taylor (New York: Oxford University Press, 1980), 241.

85. Frank Nugent, "Twentieth Century-Fox's *Young Mr. Lincoln* Is a Human and Humorous Film of the Prairie Years," *New York Times,* June 2, 1939.

86. Sergei Eisenstein, "Mr. Lincoln by Mr. Ford," in *Film Essays and a Lecture, ed. Jay Layda* (Princeton, NJ: Princeton University Press, 1982), 149.

87. Massey, a Canadian, first appeared as Sherlock Holmes in *The Speckled Bird* (1931). He played Abraham Lincoln with much success on Broadway in Robert Sherwood's 1938 play. Massey again played Lincoln in the film version in 1939. Nominated for an Oscar for his role as Lincoln, his performance (though his voice was too deep and his interpretation characterized by more than a bit of overacting) represents one of the best Hollywood "Lincolns." He continued to work in film and, later, in television, including the successful *Dr. Kildare* series (NBC, 1961–66), in which he plays the wise senior physician. His performances in the 1940s and 1950s, according to David Thomson, may be his most memorable, for example in *The Fountainhead* (1949); *East of Eden* (1955); and *The Naked and the Dead* (1958). Earlier, he appeared as one of the scientists from Wings over the World (a technologically advanced organization of airmen) who are rebuilding a shattered planet in an adaptation of H. G. Wells's postapocalyptic *Things to Come* (1936); in John Ford's *The Hurricane* (1937); as John Brown in *Santa Fe Trail* (1940); in *Arsenic and Old Lace* (1944), doing a Boris Karloff imitation; in *Morning Becomes Electra* (1947); and as John Brown again in *Seven Angry Men* (1955) (see Thomson, *New Biographical Dictionary of Film,* s.v. "Raymond Massey").

88. Mary Howard (1914–2009) had a relatively short but successful career in Hollywood. Her credits included *Love Finds Andy Hardy* with Mickey Rooney (MGM, 1938); *Swamp Water* (Twentieth Century-Fox, 1941) with Walter Brennan and Walter Huston; and *Billy the Kid* (MGM, 1941) with Robert Taylor (see "Mary Howard," IMDb, https://www.imdb.com/name/nm0397486/).

89. Fehrenbacher and Fehrenbacher, *Recollected Words of Abraham Lincoln,* 111.

90. Isaiah 53:3.

91. Quoted in Robert Sherwood, *Abe Lincoln in Illinois: A Play in Twelve Scenes by Robert Sherwood,* with a foreword by Carl Sandburg (New York: Charles Scribner's and Son, 1937), 211.

92. James Naremore, "The Cinema According to James Agee," *New England Review* 35, no. 2 (2014).

93. Bergreen, *James Agee,* 369.

94. Joanne Woodward had a lengthy list of television and movie credits, including *The Three Faces of Eve* (Twentieth Century-Fox, 1957), for which she won an Oscar for best actress, and *Mr. and Mrs. Bridge* (Miramax, 1990), in which she co-starred with her husband, actor Paul Newman. "Few films have actually explained her reputation. Known as a wife and mother and as an articulate participant in radical, third-party politics, she is most striking on screen in slatternly roles that encourage her to exaggerate her Southern accent" (Thomson, *New Biographical Dictionary of Film,* s.v., "Joanne Woodward")

95. Brian J. Snee observes that the public reaction to *Mr. Lincoln* and the ensuing Nevins-Agee debate was "a clear sign that Americans were taking seriously the role of movies and miniseries in shaping their collective past" (Brian J. Snee, *Lincoln before Lincoln: Early Cinematic Adaptations of the Life of America's Greatest President* [Lexington: University Press of Kentucky, 2016], 109).

96. Nevins also served as the president of the American Historical Association in 1959. For a detailed description of the encounter between Agee and Nevins and its historiographical context, see William Hughes, *James Agee, Omnibus, and Mr. Lincoln: The Culture of Liberalism and the Challenge of Television, 1952–1953* (Lanham, MD: Scarecrow, 2004), 103–5, 136.

97. Agee quoted in Jeffery Couchman, "James Agee's Experimentally Traditional Mr. Lincoln," in *Agee at 100: Centennial Essays of the Works of James Agee,* ed. Michael A. Lofaro (Knoxville: University of Tennessee Press, 2012), 244; emphasis in the original.

3. Hollywood Interprets the Troubled Courtship
of Miss Owens and Mr. Lincoln

1. Abraham Lincoln to Mary S. Owens, December 13, 1836, Sotheby's Auctions, https://www.sothebys.com/en/auctions/ecatalogue/2015/fine-books-manuscripts-americana-n09435/lot.71.html?locale=en. See also Gerald McMurtry, appendix to Olive Carruthers, *Lincoln's Other Mary* (Chicago: Ziff-Davis, 1945), 196. According to Mark E. Neely, "There is no better account" of the Lincoln-Owens affair than McMurtry's. It is "the last word on the romance" (Mark E. Neely Jr., *The Abraham Lincoln Encyclopedia* [New York: McGraw Hill, 1982], s.v. "Mary Owens").

2. Neely, *Lincoln Encyclopedia,* s.v. "Mary Owens."

3. Quoted in McMurtry, appendix to Carruthers, *Lincoln's Other Mary,* 201; emphasis in the original.

4. Harold Holzer, "Lincoln—The Unlikely Celebrity," in *Lincoln: A President for the Ages,* ed. Karl Weber (New York: Public Affairs, 2012), 241–42; emphasis added.

5. Quoted in McMurtry, appendix to Carruthers, *Lincoln's Other Mary,* 196.

6. Carl Sandburg, *Abraham Lincoln: The Prairie Years, 2 vols.* (1926; New York: Charles Scribner's Sons), vol. 1, 201.

7. Nominated for an Academy Award for Best Supporting Actress in *Last Summer* (1971), Catherine Burns was a film and television actress and screenwriter whose career lasted from 1967 to 1984. Hollywood columnist Dick Kleiner observed that at 5-foot-1 and freckled, she was not Hollywood's idea of a starlet." Film critic Gene Siskel called her homely but talented (Scott Feinberg and Scott Johnson, "Catherine Burns: The Vanishing of an Oscar Nominated Actress," *Hollywood Reporter,* February 3, 2020, https://www.hollywoodreporter.com/movies/movie-features/catherine-burns-inside-50-year-disappearance-an-oscar-nominee-1275646). Her interpretation of the character of Mary Owens was close to what we know of her intelligence.

8. Quoted in Michael Burlingame, *Abraham Lincoln: A Life, 2 vols.* (Baltimore, MD: Johns Hopkins University Press, 2008), vol. 1, 168–69; emphasis added.

9. Papers of the Abraham Lincoln Digital Library, https://papersofabrahamlincoln.org/persons/OW47299.

10. Burlingame, *Abraham Lincoln,* vol. 1, 142.

11. William Eldon Baringer, *Lincoln's Vandalia: A Pioneer Portrait* (New Brunswick, NJ: Rutgers University Press, 1949), 90.

12. Abraham Lincoln to Mrs. Orville H. Browning, April 1, 1838, in *The Collected Works of Abraham Lincoln,* vol. 1, ed. Roy P. Basler, Marion Dolores Pratt, and Lloyd A. Dunlap (New Brunswick, NJ, Rutgers University Press, 1953). Fred Kaplan, in *Lincoln: The Biography of a Writer* (New York: HarperCollins, 2008), provides this exegesis of Lincoln's description of Mary Owens: "The coda is Lincoln's self-serving, partly-deflating, semi-fictional account of the af-

fair, the facts are transformed into a more useful retelling of the story, an instance in which the master storyteller invents a narrative superior, for his purposes, to what reality provided. It is partly a self-exculpatory lie. It is also self-consciously literary, a Shakespearean comedy of exaggeration in regard to Mary's appearance and Lincoln's dialectic between honor and language, values and words" (88).

13. Mary Owens quoted in McMurtry, appendix to Olive Carruthers, *Lincoln's Other Mary*, 204.

14. There are two grave markers at the site. The original reads: "Sacred to the Memory of Our Mother Mary S. Vineyard. Born September 29, 1808. Passed to a better land, July 4, 1877." The website Find a Grave states: "Lincoln's first love. She met Lincoln in 1833. In 1836 at New Salem, Illinois, Lincoln proposed marriage to her. She declined. She married Jesse Vineyard about 1842. Jesse founded the Pleasant Ridge College, and later died in the Civil War. Their sons joined the confederacy. Her home stands near Walnut and Main in Weston. Mary and Jesse lived on a farm about two miles from Weston, MO. When Jesse died during the Civil War, Mary, now a widow, moved into the home in Weston on Walnut Street between Welt and Main Streets. The country place became known as the Cunningham Farm because Mary's and Jesse's daughter Katie married a Cunningham and together they lived there. (A side note: that farm was registered with the state as 'Breezy Park.') That property remained in the family until the early 1990s. A newer Monument was added to her gravesite for $1,097 by Robert Bloch of the Henry W. and Marion H. Bloch Foundation" (https://www.findagrave.com /memorial/8456521/mary-smith-vineyard). The *Kansas City Star* (August 3, 2018) reported that the foundation added the "Lincoln's Other Mary" headstone in 1999 and that "Somewhere, Mary Todd Lincoln is furious." From the "The Papers of Abraham Lincoln," https://papers ofabrahamlincoln.org/persons/OW39688): Mary judged Lincoln as "deficient in those little links which make up the great chain of woman's happiness not that I believed it proceeded from a lack of goodness of heart, but his training had been different from mine."

4. When Abe Met Mary: The Courtship and Marriage of Mary Todd and Abraham Lincoln on Film

1. Stacy Pratt McDermott, *Mary Lincoln: Southern Girl, Northern Woman* (New York: Routledge, 2015), 6.

2. Mary Lincoln to Sally Orne, December 16, 1869, in *Mary Todd Lincoln: Her Life and Letters, ed.* Justin G. Turner and Linda Levitt Turner (New York: Knopf, 1972), 183; emphasis in the original.

3. "Like Lincoln she embraced a southern political and cultural tradition that vehemently opposed slavery" (Orville Vernon Burton, *The Age of Lincoln* [New York: Hill and Wang, 2007], 109).

4. According to Turner and Turner, she was "as free of racial prejudice and condensation as was possible in that day" (Turner and Turner, *Mary Todd Lincoln,* 471).

5. Quoted in Michael Burlingame, *Abraham Lincoln: A Life,* 2 vols. (Baltimore, MD: Johns Hopkins University Press, 2008), vol. 1, 521–22.

6. Carl Sandburg, *Mary Lincoln: Wife and Widow* (New York: Harcourt, Brace, 1932), 16.

7. Lauren MacIvor Thompson, "'I Wish I Could Forget Myself . . .': Mary Todd Lincoln and the Pursuit of True Womanhood," *Annual Journal,* Corcoran Department of History, University of Virginia, 44 (2011): 21.

8. Erika Holst, *Courtship and Weddings in Abraham Lincoln's Springfield* (n.p., n.d.), "Why They Courted," Kindle. Holst is the curator of history, Illinois State Museum, Springfield.

9. The Bad Mary school of interpretation includes Michael Burlingame, *Abraham Lincoln: A Life* and "Mary Todd Lincoln's Unethical Conduct," in *At Lincoln's Side: John Hay's Civil War Correspondence and Selected Writings,* ed. Burlingame (Carbondale: Southern Illinois University Press, 2000), 185–203; William H. Herndon and Jesse W. Weik, *Lincoln: The True Story of a Great Life,* 3 vols. (New York: Belford, Clarke, 1899); and Ward Hill Lamon, *The Life of Abraham Lincoln: From His Birth to His Inauguration* (Boston: James R. Osgood, 1872).

10. Michael Burlingame, "The Mary Lincoln Enigma: Historians on America's Most Controversial First Lady," *Civil War Book Review* 15, no. 2 (2013), https://digitalcommons.lsu.edu/cgi/viewcontent.cgi?article=2584&context=cwbr. Two chapters in Burlingame's *Abraham Lincoln: A Life* provide in-depth criticisms of the marriage and Mary Lincoln: vol. 1, 168–212; and vol. 2, 249–84. See also Burlingame's *The Inner World of Abraham Lincoln* (Urbana: University of Illinois Press, 1994).

11. Burlingame, "Author Interview: Abraham Lincoln: A Life," 2009, Abraham Lincoln Online, http://www.abrahamlincolnonline.org/lincoln/books/burlingame.htm.

12. Burlingame, "The Mary Lincoln Enigma." Biographies by Mary's "apologists" include Ruth Painter Randall, *Mary Lincoln: Biography of a Marriage* (Boston: Little, Brown, 1956); Jean H. Baker, *Mary Todd Lincoln: A Biography* (New York: Norton, 1987); and Catherine Clinton, *Mrs. Lincoln: A Life* (New York: HarperCollins, 2009). For the most recent biography, see Stacy Pratt McDermott, *Mary Lincoln: Southern Girl, Northern Woman* (New York: Routledge/Taylor & Francis Group, 2015). Jason Emerson, *Mary Lincoln for the Ages* (Carbondale: Southern Illinois University Press, 2019), provides an authoritative and comprehensive annotative bibliography that includes references to biographical studies, newspaper articles, online articles, stage dramas, and poetry. While recognizing the value of feminist insights into Mary's life, like Burlingame, Emerson is equally critical: "In the case of Mary Lincoln, the feminist revisionists ignore or excuse all of Mary's faults and bad behaviors, calling her simply a victim of male chauvinism, or they make her into some sort of superhero at the expense of her husband, i.e., that she was the real president, the brains behind the bumpkin Lincoln . . . and turn her into someone she never was, and someone she would never recognize" (Emerson, *Mary Lincoln for the Ages,* 186). A six-hour PBS television documentary *Abraham and Mary Lincoln: A House Divided* (prod. David Grubin, David Grubin Productions, 2001, 360 min.) surveys the marriage. The authoritative "talking-heads" in the episodes include Jean Baker, Linda Levitt Turner, Mary Genevieve Murphy, David Donald, Charles B. Strozier, Douglas Wilson, David E. Long, Donald Miller, Frank J. Williams, Margaret Washington, Mark Neely Jr., James McPherson, and John Hope Franklin. Unfortunately, the film does not include the opinions of Michael Burlingame. The documentary reflects the Ken Burns effect—a "voice-of-God" narration followed by voice actors reading contemporary letters and accounts. David McCulloch narrates the episodes. David Morse reads the words of Abraham, and Holly Hunter gives voice to Mary Lincoln. Historian Scott A. Sandage asks in a review of the program: "How is this for a story? A poor southern boy who never wanted to be anything but president gets his wish. . . . Aiding his rise is a smart, ambitious wife who sees herself his equal partner and chief adviser but who is slandered as a hellcat who meddles in official business and commits financial improprieties." He concludes, "This film's strengths are its dual perspective. Toggling between husband and wife," the film depicts Lincoln's "life from cabin to pantheon and hers from the manse to the

asylum" (Sandage, review of *Abraham and Mary Lincoln: A House Divided, Journal of American History* 88, no. 3 [December 2001]: 1184–86). "The overall theme (repeated a bit too often)," according to citric Megan Rosenfield, "is that suffering and hardship made Lincoln a stronger and more spiritual person, while Mary crumbled under the weight of grief and difficulty" (Megan Rosenfield, "Abe and Mary, A First Couple Apart," *Washington Post,* February 19, 2001).

13. Burlingame, *An American Marriage: The Untold Story of Abraham Lincoln and Mary Todd* (New York: Pegasus, 2021), appendix, Kindle.

14. Baker quoted in McDermott, *Mary Lincoln,* 5.

15. Jean H. Baker, "Mary and Abraham: A Marriage," in *The Lincoln Enigma: The Changing Faces of an American Icon,* ed. Gabor Boritt (New York: Oxford University Press, 2001), 37.

16. Jean H. Baker, *Mary Lincoln: A Biography* (New York: Norton, 2008), preface, Kindle.

17. Jean H. Baker, *The Lincoln Marriage: Beyond the Battle of Quotations,* 38th Annual Robert Fortenbaugh Memorial Lecture (Gettysburg, PA: Civil War Institute, Gettysburg College, 1999), 27.

18. John Dean, "The Social and Cultural Construction of Abraham Lincoln in U.S. Movies and on U.S. Television," *American Studies Journal* 53 (2009): n.p., http://www.asjournal.org /53-2009/social-and-cultural-construction-of-lincoln-in-movies-and-on-tv/.

19. Barbara Welter, "The Cult of True Womanhood: 1820–1860," *American Quarterly* 18, no. 2 (1966): 151–74. See also Thompson, "I Wish I Could Forget Myself."

20. McDermott, *Mary Lincoln,* 8.

21. Stacy Pratt McDermott, "A Tale of Two Marys," review of Spielberg's *Lincoln,* Civil War Pop, November 16, 2012, https://civilwarpop.com/2015/04/07/entry-9-a-tale-of-two-marys.

22. Cecil B. DeMille, *The Autobiography of Cecil B. DeMille* (New York: Prentice-Hall), 125.

23. Agee quoted in James Naremore, "The Cinema According to James Agee," *New England Review* 35, no. 2 (2014): 106.

24. David Thomson, *The New Biographical Dictionary of Film* (New York: Knopf, 2002), s.v. "D. W. Griffith."

25. Fitzgerald quoted in Angelica Jade Bastien, "The Feminine Grotesque: On the Warped Image of Joan Crawford," May 14, 2006, https://www.rogerebert.com/features/the-feminine -grotesque-on-the-warped-legacy-of-joan-crawford.

26. Quoted in Samuel A. Schreiner Jr., *The Trials of Mrs. Lincoln* (New York: Donald I. Fine, 1987), 139.

27. Louis Bayard, *Courting Mr. Lincoln* (Chapel Hill, NC: Algonquin, 2020), 12.

28. Carl Sandburg, *Abraham Lincoln: The Prairie Years, 2 vols. (1926; New York: Charles Scrib- ner's Sons, 1948),* vol. 1, 257.

29. Abraham Lincoln quoted in McDermott, *Mary Lincoln,* 93.

30. Though economically unsuccessful and virtually illiterate, Thomas Lincoln was a re- spectable man, a skilled carpenter, well-liked by his neighbors, who had a talent for storytelling that he passed on to his son. Lincoln was, however, alienated from his father (see Mark E. Neely Jr., *The Abraham Lincoln Encyclopedia* [New York: McGraw-Hill, 1982], s.v. "Thomas Lincoln").

31. American actress Kay Hammond (1901–1982) had a career of eleven film parts, three of them uncredited. She is often confused with the prominent English actress of the same name who is often incorrectly credited with the role of Mary Todd in Griffith's film.

32. Roger Ebert, review of *Body Heat* (Warner Brothers, 1981), https://www.rogerebert .com/reviews/great-movie-body-heat-1981.

33. George F. Custen, *Bio/Pics: How Hollywood Constructed Public History* (New Brunswick, NJ: Rutgers University Press, 1922), 135.

34. Zanuck quoted in Mark A. Vieira, *Majestic Hollywood: The Greatest Films of 1939* (Philadelphia: Running Press, 2013), 82.

35. Lamar Trotti, *Young Mr. Lincoln: Original Story and Screenplay,* rev. final script, n.p., February 27, 1939.

36. Ford quoted in Peter Bogdanovich, *John Ford* (Berkeley: University of California Press, 1978), 72.

37. Pauline Kael, *The Age of Movies: Selected Writings of Pauline Kael,* ed. Sanford Schwarts (New York: Library of America, 2011), 171.

38. David Meuel, *Women in the Films of John Ford* (Jefferson, NC: MacFarland, 2014), 175.

39. Ibid., 136.

40. Andrew Sarris, *The John Ford Movie Mystery* (Bloomington: Indiana University Press, 1975), 30.

41. Meuel, *Women in the Films of John Ford,* 179.

42. Trotti, *Young Mr. Lincoln: Original Story and Screenplay.*

43. Sandburg, *Abraham Lincoln: The Prairie Years,* vol. 1, 255.

44. Turner and Turner, *Mary Todd Lincoln,* 11.

45. Smyth, *Reconstructing American Historical Cinema,* chap. 6, Kindle.

46. David Thomson, *The New Biographical Dictionary of Film* (New York: Knopf, 2002), s.v. "Ruth Gordon."

47. Various sources describe Mary's hair as light brown, dark brown, or chestnut with hints of bronze, not black. The director, apparently, chose the black "Chinese" wig to emphasize Mary's abrasive character.

48. Joshua Wolf Shenk, *Lincoln's Melancholy: How Depression Challenged a President and Fueled His Greatness* (New York: Houghton Mifflin, 2006), 47.

49. Lincoln had three law partners in Springfield: John Todd Stuart (1837–41); Stephen T. Logan (1841–44); and William H. Herndon (1844–61). Lincoln imagined returning to Springfield after his presidency to continue practicing law with Herndon, whom Mary Lincoln loathed.

50. Michael J. Gerhart, *Lincoln's Mentors: The Education of a Leader* (New York: Custom House, 2021), 85.

5. Mrs. Lincoln Goes to Washington: The White House Years

1. Mary Todd quoted in Jean Baker, *Mary Todd Lincoln: A Biography* (New York: Norton, 1987), 85.

2. Mary Todd Lincoln (Leila McIntyre) to Abraham Lincoln (Frank McGlynn Jr.) in *The Plainsman* (1936).

3. Frank S. Nugent, "The Screen in Review; The Music Hall Celebrates Washington's Birthday with a Brilliant Edition of Sherwood's 'Abe Lincoln in Illinois,' with Raymond Massey and Ruth Gordon," *New York Times,* February 23, 1940.

4. Thomas S. Hischak, *100 Greatest American Plays* (New York: Rowman & Littlefield, 2017), 3.

5. Mark E. Neely Jr., "The Young Mr. Lincoln: Two Films," in *Past Imperfect: History According to the Movies,* ed. Ted Mico, John Miller-Monzon, and David Rubel (New York: Henry Holt, 1995), 126.

6. Lincoln quoted in Ward Hill Lamon, *The Life of Abraham Lincoln: From His Birth to His Inauguration* (Boston: James R. Osgood, 1872), 135.

7. J. E. Smyth, *Reconstructing American Historical Cinema* (Lexington: University of Kentucky Press, 2006), chap. 6, Kindle.

8. "In seeking the presidency—and let there be no doubt, Lincoln sought it—he demonstrated great political and managerial acumen" (Michael S. Green, *Lincoln and the Election of 1860* [Carbondale: Southern Illinois University Press, 2011], preface, Kindle.)

9. Ibid.

10. Robert Sherwood, *Abe Lincoln in Illinois: A Play by Robert Emmet Sherwood* (New York: Charles Scribner's Sons, 1939), 244.

11. Ibid.

12. Nugent, "The Screen in Review; The Music Hall Celebrates Washington's Birthday with a Brilliant Edition of Sherwood's 'Abe Lincoln in Illinois.'"

13. Winifred L. Dusenbury, *The Theme of Loneliness in Modern American Drama* (Gainesville: University of Florida Press, 1960), 182.

14. Ibid., 182–83.

15. Ibid., 182.

16. Child quoted in Michael Burlingame, *Abraham Lincoln: A Life, 2 vols. (Baltimore, MD: Johns Hopkins University Press, 2008)*, vol. 2, 2775.

17. Dana quoted ibid., vol. 2, 2733.

18. Quoted in Burlingame, *Abraham Lincoln,* vol. 2, 2773.

19. Quoted ibid.

20. Quoted ibid., vol. 2, 2774.

21. Adam Gopnik, "Why We Keep Inventing Abraham Lincoln," *New Yorker,* September 28, 2020, https://www.newyorker.com/magazine/2020/09/28/why-we-keep-reinventing-abraham-lincoln.

22. David Donald, *Lincoln Reconsidered: Essays on the Civil War Era* (New York: Vintage, 1956), 56. See also chapter 3, "Herndon and Mrs. Lincoln," 36–56.

23. Burlingame, *Abraham Lincoln,* vol. 2, 2773.

24. Margaret Leech, *Reveille in Washington, 1860–1865* (New York: Harper & Brothers, 1941), 9.

25. Gary L. Bunker, "The *Comic News,* Lincoln, and the Civil War," *Journal of the Abraham Lincoln Association* 17, no. 1 (1996): 53–87.

26. Mary Lincoln quoted in *Mary Todd Lincoln: Her Life and Letters, ed.* Justin G. Turner and Linda Levitt Turner (New York: Knopf, 1972), 156.

27. "Mrs. Lincoln," *New York Times,* July 18, 1882.

28. Bancroft quoted in Burlingame, *Abraham Lincoln,* vol. 2, 2733.

29. *New York Evening Post* quoted in Doris Kearns Goodwin, *Team of Rivals* (New York: Simon & Schuster, 2005), 295.

30. Mary Clemmer Ames, *Ten Years in Washington or, Inside Life and Scenes in Our National Capital as a Woman Sees Them* (Hartford, CT: Hartford Publishing, 1882), 242.

31. Martin A. Jackson, "Abraham Lincoln," in *The Columbia Companion to American History on Film: How the Movies Have Portrayed the American Past, ed. Peter Robbins* (New York: Columbia University Press, 2003), 176.

32. Gore Vidal, *Screening History* (Cambridge, MA: Harvard University Press, 1992), 67.

33. Roy Basler Jr., "Lincoln and American Writers," *Journal of the Abraham Lincoln Association* 7, no. 1 (1985), https://quod.lib.umich.edu/j/jala/2629860.0007.103/—lincoln-and-american-writers?rgn=main;view=fulltext.

34. Gore Vidal, *United States: Essays, 1952–1992* (New York: Broadway, 1993), chap. 62, Kindle.

35. Gore Vidal, *I Told You So: Gore Vidal Talks Politics: Interviews with Jon Wiener* (Berkeley, CA: Counterpoint, 2012), 107.

36. Vidal, *Lincoln,* 413. For an in-depth analysis of the issue, see John G. Soto, MD, *The Physical Lincoln Complete* (Mt. Vernon, VA: Mt. Vernon Book Systems, 2008), 390–400. Soto concludes that although the evidence is at best fragmentary and inconclusive, Lincoln possibly had contracted venereal disease. It was common in his time. Nonetheless, the case rests primarily on the disputed provenance of Herndon's letter.

37. Gore Vidal, *Lincoln: A Novel. First International Edition* (1984; New York: Random House, 2000), chap. 10, Kindle.

38. The feminist movement progressed through in three phases: first wave (1848–1920); second wave (1963–80); and third wave (1991–present). Other than the advancement of the social, economic, political, and economic liberation of women, what the three stages have in common is arguable.

39. "The Nuptials of Miss Kate Chase and Ex-Gov. Sprague: Scenes and Incidents," *New York Times,* November 15, 1860.

40. Ishbel Ross, *Proud Kate: Portrait of an Ambitious Woman* (New York: Harper & Brothers, 1953), 290.

41. Chase's maneuverings were not entirely out of order. "He was Lincoln's one serious rival within the Republican Party for the 1864 presidential nomination, something that now seems odd and outrageous but seemed less so at the time, when presidents generally served only a single term and were often succeeded by their senior Cabinet members." Once Lincoln secured the nomination, Chase withdrew from the race, remained loyal, and campaigned for Lincoln (Walter Stahr, *Salmon P. Chase: Lincoln's Vital Rival* [New York: Simon & Schuster, 2021]. 5).

42. "Kate Chase Sprague Dead: The Once Beautiful Daughter of Salmon P. Chase Ended in Washington," *New York Times,* August 1, 1899.

43. Charles Alfred Townsend, "Mrs. Kate Chase Sprague: She Was One of the Most Romantic Characters at the Capital: Beautiful and Ambitious to Make Her Father President and Then to Rule through Him," *New York Times,* August 27, 1899.

44. Vidal, *United States: Essays, 1952–1992* (New York: Random House, 1993), chap. 18, Kindle.

45. Near destitute by the 1890s, "she kept chickens and ran a dairy for a time, with a man to help milk the cows. She opened a little shop in a suburb of Washington and sold milk and eggs" until the little enterprise failed. There were other humiliations: "Once she had bought her gloves six dozen pairs at a time and had been outdone in this respect only by Mary Lincoln, who was known to have ordered three hundred pairs in four months. Kate still had a few, soiled, but of the finest quality. She donned them to cover her coarsened hands, perhaps to remind her that eggs could be peddled with style" (Ross, *Proud Kate,* 274).

46. "Overlooked: Amisha Padnami," *New York Times,* January 19, 2019.

47. Elizabeth spelled her last name "Keckly." Until recently, most sources spelled it as "Keckley." Her name is rendered "Keckley" in the screenplays for *Gore Vidal's Lincoln* (1988) and in Spielberg's *Lincoln* (2012).

48. "New Publication," *New York Times,* April 19, 1868.

49. Dolen Perkins-Valdez, introduction to *Behind the Scenes or Thirty Years a Slave, and Four Years in the White House,* by Elizabeth Keckley (originally published by G.W. Carleton & Co., 1868; Eno Publishers, 2016), Kindle.

50. Ibid.

51. Ibid.

52. Alan Bunce, "Books Inspire Two Historical Miniseries: Vidal's '*Lincoln'* Says 'Here's How It Might Have Been,'" *Christian Science Monitor,* https://www.csmonitor.com/1988/0324/llinc .html.

53. Vidal, *Lincoln,* 662.

54. The Turner story also appears in Robert Penn Warren's novel *All the King's Men* (1946). Jack Burden, the would-be history PhD and the book's narrator, finds during his uncompleted dissertation research the account of the Turner affair in the private journal of his Civil War ancestor, Cass Mastern. The Turner affair does not appear in the 1949 film adaptation of the novel.

55 Petition 20784112, "To the Hon. The Judge of Fayette Court of Chancery," Filing Date, July 6, 1841, Ending Date, March 1843, Race and Slavery Petition Project, University of North Carolina, Greensboro, http://library.uncg.edu/slavery/petitons/details.aspx?=6313.

56. John E. Washington, *They Knew Lincoln* (New York: Oxford University Press, 2018), 244.

57. The assassination attempt actually occurred. Nine months before John Wilkes Booth murdered the president, Lincoln was on horseback on his way to the Old Soldiers' Home when someone took a shot at him and missed. The bullet went through his tall hat. In the Vidal script, a bodyguard arrives at the door and interrupts the séance to tell him that the hat (lost as Lincoln galloped off after the shot was fired) has been recovered. It missed his head, he is informed, by only four inches.

58. Jay Monaghan, "Was Abraham Lincoln a Spiritualist?," *Journal of the Illinois State Historical Society* 34, no. 2 (June 1941): 209–32.

59. Nancy Gray Schoonmaker, "Mystery and Possibility: Spiritualist in the Nineteenth-Century South" (PhD diss., University of North Carolina, Chapel Hill, 2010), 430.

60. A Canadian actress, Gloria Elizabeth Reuben is best known for playing a recurring character, Jeanie Boulet, in the television medical drama *ER* (NBC, 1994–2009), for which she received two Emmy nominations.

61. *Lincoln: A Cinematic and Historical Companion,* 178.

62. Cory Rosenberg, "Spielberg's Lincoln: An Ambitious Pastiche," *Pennsylvania History: A Journal of Mid-Atlantic Studies* 80, no. 2 (Spring 2013): 331.

63. Smith quoted in David Know, "Vale: Sada Thompson," https://tvtonight.com .au/2011/05/vale-sada-thompson.html.

64. Serafina Bathrick, "The Mary Tyler Moore Show: Women at Home and at Work," in *MTM: Quality Television,* ed. Jane Feuer, Paul Kerr, and Tise Vahimagi, 99–131 (London: British Film Institute, 1984).

65. Mark S. Reinhart, *Abraham Lincoln on Screen: Fictional and Documentary Portrayals on Film and Television, 2nd ed.* (Jefferson, NC: McFarland, 2009), 99.

66. F. R. Carpenter, *The Inner Life of Abraham Lincoln: Six Months at the White House* (New York: Hurd and Houghton, 1872), chap. 74, Kindle; emphasis in the original.

67. Vidal, *Lincoln,* 662.

68. Steven Spielberg, foreword to *Lincoln: A Cinematic and Historical Companion, by David Rubel* (New York: A Welcome Book, Disney Editions, 2012), 7.

69. William H. Epstein and R. Barton Palmer, eds., *Invented Lives, Imagined Communities: The Biopic and American National Identity* (Albany: State University of New York, 2016), 288–89.

70. Andrea Foroughi, "'Your Household Accounts Have Always Been So Interesting': Family, Relations and Gender Politics in Lincoln's Two Houses," *Rethinking History* 19, no. 2 (2019): 521.

71. Tony Kushner (b. 1956) is best known for his two-part epic play *Angels in America: A Gay Fantasia on National Themes* (1993). He also wrote the screenplay for Spielberg's *Munich* (2005), among his extensive body of work.

72. Rubel, *Lincoln: A Cinematic and Historical Companion,* 219.

73. Steven Spielberg, interview by Mike Fleming, *Oprah Magazine,* December 6, 2012; "Mike Fleming's Q&A with Steven Spielberg: Why It Took 12 Years to Find 'Lincoln,'" https://deadline .com/2012/12/steven-spielberg-lincoln-making-of-interview-exclusive-383861.

74. Doris Kearns Goodwin, *Team of Rivals: The Political Genius of Abraham Lincoln* (New York: Simon & Schuster, 2005).

75. Timothy Noah, "Tony Kushner's Real Source for Lincoln," *New Republic,* January 9, 2013, https://newrepublic.com/article/111810/tony-kushners-real-source-lincoln. See also Michael Vorenberg, *Final Freedom: The Civil War, the Abolition of Slavery, and the Thirteenth Amendment* (New York: Cambridge University Press, 2001).

76. Timothy Noah, "Kushner Replies about Sources," *New Republic,* January 10, 2013, https://newrepublic.com/article/111833/kushner-replies-about-sources.

77. Rubel, *Lincoln: A Cinematic and Historical Companion.*

78. Ibid., 151–52.

79. Ibid., 191–92.

80. Rosenberg, "Spielberg's Lincoln," 330.

81. The word "bottleneck" dates from 1896 and was not in use in 1865.

82. Quoted in Rubel, *Lincoln: A Cinematic and Historical Companion,* 182. Commenting on her role as Mary Lincoln in *Abraham Lincoln: Vampire Hunter,* actress Mary Elizabeth Winstead says, "When I first signed up to play the role everybody was like, 'Oh, you're the crazy lady.' 'Oh, you're playing the one who ended up in a mental institution.' And that kinda became her legacy. In a lot of ways is what we remember about her is what her life ends up as. And when I read about her I realized that she actually was so complex and so smart and well educated and well-liked and outspoken and opinionated and just really grew to love her so much that the more I read about her and the fact that she was all those things in a time when it was not cool for a woman to be those things. So, I was really excited to portray her" (Mary Elizabeth Winstead, interview by Ezequiel Gutierrez, HeyUGuys, June 19, 2012, https://www.youtube .com/watch?v=15VEFbkTziQ).

6. Redux: *The Last of Mrs. Lincoln*

1. Michael Holroyd, "History and Biography," *Salmagundi,* no. 46 (1979): 17.

2. "Mrs. Lincoln," *New York Times,* July 18, 1882.

3. James S. Burst, MD, "A Psychiatrist Looks at Mary Lincoln," in *The Mary Lincoln Enigma: Historians on America's Most Controversial First Lady,* ed. Frank J. Williams and Michael Burkhimer

(Carbondale: Southern Illinois University Press, 2012). See also Helmer Pritchard, *The Dark Days of Abraham Lincoln's Widow as Revealed by Her Own Letters,* ed. Jason Emerson (Carbondale: Southern Illinois University Press, 2012). Emerson is the leading authority on Mary Lincoln historiography.

4. Quoted in W. A. Evans, *Mrs. Abraham Lincoln* (New York: Knopf, 1932), 242.

5. Despite chronic poor health, real or imagined, Mary lived to be sixty-three. The average life expectancy in the 1880s was 39 to 41.2 years. For an in-depth study of Mary's medical history, see John G. Soto, MD, *The Mary Lincoln Mind-Body Sourcebook: Including a Unifying Diagnosis to Explain Her Public Decay, Manifest Insanity, and Slow Death* (Mt. Vernon, VA: Mt. Vernon Book Systems, 2017).

6. Dennis Bingham, *Whose Lives Are They Anyway? The Biopic as Contemporary Film Genre* (New Brunswick, NJ: Rutgers University Press, 2010).

7. See Jason Emerson, *The Madness of Mary Lincoln* (Carbondale: Southern Illinois University Press, 2007). Emerson argues that Mary was in fact bipolar and that her son Robert was justified in having her committed.

8. Woodrow quoted in Glenna R. Schroeder-Lein, *Lincoln and Medicine* (Carbondale: Southern Illinois University Press, 2012), chap. 2, Kindle. Margaret Woodrow was one of Herndon's "informants."

9. Mary Lincoln to Sally Orne, December 12, 1869, in *Mary Todd Lincoln: Her Life and Letters,* ed. Justin G. Turner and Linda Levitt Turner (New York: Knopf, 1972), 534; emphasis in the original.

10. Mary Lincoln to Sally Orne, January 2, 1870, in *Mary Todd Lincoln,* ed. Turner and Turner, 539.

11. Jean H. Baker, *Mary Todd Lincoln: A Biography* (New York: Norton, 1987), 311.

12. Peter Manseau, *The Apparitionists: A Tale of Phantoms, Fraud, Photography, and the Man Who Captured Lincoln's Ghost* (New York: Houghton, Mifflin, Harcourt, 2017), 309.

13. Quoted in Evans, *Mrs. Abraham Lincoln,* 279.

14. Vidal quoted in Jay Parini and Gore Vidal, "An Interview with Gore Vidal," *New England Review* 14, no. 1 (Fall 1991): 97.

15. Johnson Laurie, "Julie Harris Styles Mrs. Lincoln from the Heart Out," *New York Times,* December 22, 1972.

16. Mary's post-assassination story also appears in *Look Away: A Drama in Two Acts,* by Jerome Kelly. The action takes place on the evening of June 14, 1875, during her last night of incarceration in the Bellevue Hospital for Insane Persons, in Batavia, Illinois. Theater critic Clive Barnes (*New York Times,* January 8, 1973) describes Mary as a "foolish woman, but a woman much plagued by events and troubled by circumstances." Rip Torn directed. Geraldine Page plays Mary as "slightly bitter, very faded, and with a sadness that erodes the soul." Poet and actress Maya Angelou is Elizabeth Keckley as a woman of "strength and coolness." Barnes notes the contrast between "Miss Page's Mrs. Lincoln . . . with the paler yet more heroic approach taken by Julie Harris." *The Last of Mrs. Lincoln* opened on December 12, 1972, and *Look Away* on January 7, 1973.

17. John J. O'Connor, "'The Last of Mrs. Lincoln' with Julie Harris Is a Sensitive and Detailed Drama," *New York Times,* September 16, 1976.

7. Coda: Shirley Temple and Marilyn Monroe in Lincoln's Legacy

1. Frank S. Nugent, "Fantasy Comes a Trip in Miss Temple's 'Blue Bird' at the Hollywood," *New York Times,* January 20, 1940, https://www.nytimes.com/1940/01/20/archives/the-screen -fantasy-comes-a-trip-in-miss-temples-blue-bird-at-the.html.

2. Mark A. Vieira, *Majestic Hollywood: The Greatest Films of 1939* (Philadelphia: Running Press, 2013), 39.

3. Andre Sennwald, "Shirley Temple and Bill Robinson in 'The Littlest Rebel,' the Christmas Film at the Music Hall," *New York Times,* December 20, 1935, https://www.nytimes.com/1935 /12/20/archives/the-screen-shirley-temple-and-bill-robinson-in-the-littlest-rebel.html.

4. David Thomson, *The New Biographical Dictionary of Film* (New York: Knopf, 2002), s.v. "Shirley Temple."

5. Charles Eckert, "Shirley Temple and the House of Rockefeller," *Jump Cut: A Review of Contemporary Media* 2 (1974): 1, 17–20.

6. Shirley Temple Black, *Child Star: An Autobiography* (New York: McGraw-Hill, 1988), 15.

7. Ibid., 23

8. Ibid., 21.

9. Ibid., 184.

10. Graham Greene, *The Graham Greene Film Reader: Reviews, Essays, Interviews & Film Stories,* ed. David Parkinson (New York: Applause Theatre Book Publishers, 1994), 128.

11. "The story," Greene states, "—about an Afghan robber converted by Wee Willie Winkie to the British Raj—is a long way from Kipling" (ibid., 233–34). True, but right in line with the continual theme(s) of Temple's films, namely the gritty little kid facing great odds, changing the bad into the good, which is a metaphor for the American nation as well as the British Empire.

12. Ibid., 234.

13. Graham Greene, *The Pleasure Dome: The Collected Film Criticism, 1935–1940,* ed. John Russell Taylor (New York: Oxford University Press, 1980), 2.

14. Ann DuCille, "The Shirley Temple of My Familiar," *Transition,* no. 73 (1997): 15.

15. Greene quoted in Temple Black, *Child Star,* 186.

16. Greene, *The Pleasure Dome,* 78.

17. Temple Black, *Child Star,* 186–87.

18. DuCille, "The Shirley Temple of My Familiar," 15. An even more lascivious suggestion occurs in *Little Miss Marker* (1938). DuCille comments, "Temple plays Martha Jane, a fetching five-year-old whose father leaves her with bookies as collateral for a twenty-dollar bet. [Adolphe] Menjou's character, Sorrowful Jones, does not accept markers but *after picking up the child and gazing into her brown eyes, the smitten boss tells his stunned underling to take the kid in lieu of cash: 'Little doll like that's worth twenty bucks any way you look at it.'*" The father commits suicide when his horse loses and Martha, now nicknamed "Little Miss Marker," becomes Sorrowful's property, "his ownership confirmed by the manly way he scoops her up under one arm and carries her off, exposing her bare legs and bottom to the camera." For a deep dive into the topic, see Ara Osterwell, "Reconstructing Shirley: Pedophilia and Interracial Romance in Hollywood's Age of Innocence," *Camera Obscura* (72), vol. 24, no. 3 (2009): 1–39.

19. Temple Black, *Child Star,* 232–33.

20. "Shirley Temple," Celebrity Net Worth, https://www.celebritynetworth.com/richest -celebrities/actors/shirley-temple-net-worth.

21. John F. Kasson, *The Little Girl Who Fought the Great Depression: Shirley Temple and 1930s America* (New York: Norton, 2014), 60.

22. Thomson, *New Biographical Dictionary of Film, s.v. "Shirley Temple."*

23. "Shirley: Origin and Meaning," Nameberry.com, https://nameberry.com/babyname/Shirley.

24. Champ Clark, "Merry Christmas, Shirley Temple," December 21, 2018, RogerEbert.com, https://www.rogerebert.com/features/merry-christmas-shirley-temple.

25. Martha Sherrill, "Dimply the Best: Shirley Temple Charmed a Depressed Nation, and It Wasn't Just Another Song and Dance," *Washington Post,* July 16, 1995, https://www.washingtonpost.com/lifestyle/style/dimply-the-best-shirley-temple-charmed-a-depressed-nation-and-it-wasnt-just-another-song-and-dance/2014/02/11/dc62e4f0-933b-11e3-83b9-1f024193bb84_story.html.

26. Joseph Henabery (1888–1976) acted in twenty-four films between 1914 and 1916. Between 1916 and 1948, he also directed an astonishing 208 films.

27. Frank S. Nugent, "Miss Temple Plats Little Eva in Dimples, at the Roxy," *New York Times,* October 10, 1936, https://www.nytimes.com/1936/10/10/archives/miss-temple-plays-little-eva-in-dimples-at-the-roxy-the-rialto.html.

28. Bill "Bojangles" Robinson (1878–1949) also danced with Temple in *The Little Colonel* (1935), which featured the first interracial dance in American film. The studio cut the scene for theaters in the South. It was too controversial. Robinson also appeared with Temple in *Rebecca of Sunnybrook* (1938) and *Just around the Corner* (1938). Three other African American actors had small roles in *The Littlest Rebel.* They represented Hollywood's racist stereotypes: "Mammy" (Bessie Lyle); "James Henry," a slow-talking comic character (Willie Best); and a "pickaninny" (Hannah Washington).

29. Frank McGlynn Sr. (1866–1951) acted in 139 films. He played Lincoln several times starting in 1915 in a short titled *The Life of Abraham Lincoln* and in another short in 1924 titled *Abraham Lincoln.* After his "Great Heart" appearance in 1935, he continued to play Lincoln in such films as John Ford's *Prisoner of Shark Island* (1936); *Hearts in Bondage* (1936); *The Plainsman* (1936); *Western Gold* (1937); *Wells Fargo* (1937); *The Lone Ranger—Episode 1* (1938); and *The Mad Empress* (1939). He also appeared as Lincoln in shorts from 1938, 1939, 1942, and 1950.

30. Kasson, *The Little Girl Who Fought the Great Depression,* 107.

31. Ibid., 108.

32. Ibid., 112.

33. Quoted in Silber, "Abraham Lincoln and the Political Culture of New Deal America," 198n4.

34. Some twenty-three actors have played Lincoln on screen, including Frank McGlynn Sr.; Joseph Henabery; Walter Huston; Raymond Massey; John Carradine; Henry Fonda; Hal Holbrook; John Anderson; Gregory Peck; Robert V. Barron; Brendan Fraser; Jason Robards; Michael Krebs; Lance Henriksen; Kris Kristofferson; Benjamin Walker; Gerald Bestrom; Kevin Sorbo; Bill Oberst Jr.; Billy Campbell; Tom Amandes; Arlo Kasper; Kevin McKinney; Royal Dano; and Daniel Day-Lewis.

35. Edward Peple, *The Littlest Rebel* (New York: Grosset & Dunlap, 1914). The book has little in common with the Temple movie; Lincoln does not even appear in the novel. In the Broadway play inspired by the Peple's book, General Grant rather than the president issues the pardon.

36. Barry Schwartz, *Abraham Lincoln in the Post-Heroic World: History and Memory in Late Twentieth-Century America* (Chicago: University of Chicago Press, 2008), 272.

37. Shirley Temple quoted in Anne Edwards, *Shirley Temple: American Princess* (Gilford, CT: Globe Pequot, 2017), chap. 12, Kindle.

38. Kasson, *The Little Girl Who Fought the Great Depression,* 108.

39. Griffith quoted ibid.

40. Sennwald, "Shirley Temple and Bill Robinson."

41. Edward Peple (1869–1924) was a Virginia-born playwright whose work included *The Prince Chap* and *A Pair of Sixes.* His Broadway musical *Queen High* became a Paramount pre-Code movie in 1930 starring Charlie Ruggles, Frank Morgan, and Ginger Rogers.

42. Variety Staff, review of *The Littlest Rebel, Variety,* December 31, 1934, https://variety.com/1934/film/reviews/the-littlest-rebel-1200410951.

43. Temple Black, *Child Star,* 223–33.

44. Roosevelt quoted in Anne Edwards, *Shirley Temple: American Princess* (Gilford, CT: Globe Pequot, 1988), foreword, Kindle.

45. Marilyn's birth name was Norma Jeane Mortenson. Her baptismal name: Norma Jeane Baker. School records list her as Norma Jeane Baker or Norma Jean Baker (Adam Victor, *The Marilyn Monroe Encyclopedia* [Woodstock, NY: Overlook, 1999], s.v., "Names"). Both spellings, Jeane and Jean, appear in the sources.

46. Maurice Zolotow, *Marilyn Monroe,* rev. ed. (New York: Perennial Library, 1990), 34.

47. Lois Banner, *Marilyn: The Passion and the Paradox* (New York: Bloomsbury, 2012), 75.

48. Elizabeth Winder, *Marilyn in Manhattan: Her Year of Joy* (New York: Flatiron, 2017), 27.

49. Joyce Carol Oates, *Blonde: A Novel* (New York: HarperCollins, 2000), chap. 2, Kindle.

50. Marilyn Monroe, *My Story: Illustrated Edition, with Ben Hecht,* with a foreword by Joshua Greene (New York: First Taylor Trade Publication, 2007), 37.

51. Nina Silber, *This War Ain't Over: Fighting the Civil War in New Deal America* (Chapel Hill: University of North Carolina Press, 2018), 102.

52. Ibid., 103. *Abraham Lincoln: The Prairie Years* appeared in two volumes in 1926. *Abraham Lincoln: The War Years* appeared in four volumes in 1939. His account of Lincoln's Civil War won the Pulitzer Prize in 1940. Both series were enormously influential in creating the popular image of Lincoln. Later years brought multiple attacks on Sandburg and his approach to history and biography (see David Donald, "Getting Right with Lincoln," *Harper's,* April 1, 1951, 74–80).

53. Walter Moss, "Carl Sandburg, Hollywood, Media, and Marilyn Monroe," *Hollywood Progressive,* January 12, 2012. Sandburg was the main film critic for the *Chicago Daily News* between 1920 and 1928; including all his reviews, he wrote more than two thousand columns dealing with films. Many of the pieces are available in *The Movies Are: Carl Sandburg's Film Reviews and Essays, 1920–1928.*

54. George Sanders, *Memoirs of a Professional Cad* (New York: Avon, 1960), 70.

55. Quoted also in Donald Soto, *Marilyn Monroe: The Biography* (New York: Cooper Union, 1993), 186.

56. Anthony Summers, *Goddess: The Secret Life of Marilyn Monroe* (New York: Open Road Integrated Media, 1985), 235.

57. Quoted in Jeanine Basinger, *The Star Machine* (New York: Knopf, 2007), 599.

58. Quoted in Summers, *Goddess,* 205.

59. Ibid.

60. Mark B. Pollad, "Harriett Monroe's Abraham Lincoln," *Journal of the Abraham Lincoln Association* 37, no. 2 (Summer 2016). Literary scholar Harriett Monroe (no relation to the actress) "was instrumental in the creation of the modern literary treatment of Abraham Lincoln" (33). She wrote in 1926: Sandburg "rose from the same soil, and met in his youth some of the same problems. One feels that he knows the man, that he has a fist big enough to shake Lincoln's hand, a figure tall enough to look him in the eye, and a style strong enough to give us the whole story, without exaggeration or eloquence" (quoted ibid.).

61. John Harbin, "A Closer Look at the Carl Sandburg Home," *Burlington (NC) Times-News,* April 19, 2011.

62. The photograph of Lincoln was from a solio print (a paper print process introduced by Eastman Kodak in 1888) of the original ambrotype (a process using glass coated in certain chemicals) (James Mellon, ed., *The Face of Lincoln* [New York: Bonanza, 1979], 31).

63. Ibid., 191.

64. Norman Mailer, *Of Women and Their Elegance, with photographs by Milton H. Greene* (New York: Simon & Schuster, 1980), 46.

65. Maurice Zolotow, *Marilyn Monroe, updated and expanded ed.* (New York: Perennial Library, 1990). The caption reads, "John Dougherty, in 1953, standing in front of the bungalow he and Norma Jean occupied in Van Nuys, California."

66. Adam Victor, *The Marilyn Encyclopedia* (Woodstock, NY: Overlook, 1999), s.v., "Abraham Lincoln."

67. Gloria Steinem, *Marilyn: Norma Jean* (New York: Henry Holt, 1988), chap. 3, Kindle.

68. Zolotow, *Marilyn Monroe,* 262.

69. Sean Crawford, "A Bombshell Dropped (in Bement) 60 Years Ago," Illinois Public Radio, August 7, 2015, https://will.illinois.edu/news/story/a-bombshell-dropped-in-bement-60-years -ago. See also Tony Reid, "Bement's Star Shines Again with Marilyn Monroe, August 6, 2015, https://herald-review.com/news/local/state-and-regional/bements-star-shines-again-with -marilyn-monroe/article_93b1e0ad-9517-5f71-80cd-cc8c34381407.html.

70. Bosley Crowther, "Marilyn Monroe Arrives: Glitters as Floozie in 'Bus Stop' at the Roxy," *New York Times,* September 1, 1956, https://www.nytimes.com/1956/09/01/archives/the-screen -marilyn-monroe-arrives-glitters-as-floozie-in-bus-stop.html.

71. Sixty-three years later, on April 26, 2019, *Business Standard* published an interview with eighty-nine-year-old Don Murray. He spoke of his experience filming *Bus Stop* with Monroe, recalling her crippling anxiety every time she had to shoot a scene: "She was very insecure, very frightened of acting in front of the camera, which is amazing. . . . Being such a big star, she had done so many films, and yet, she was so frightened. But she took the part very seriously, listened to Josh Logan and took his directions" (Business Standard, "Don Murray Opens up about Marilyn Monroe's Anxiety on 'Bus Stop' Set," https://www.business-standard.com /article/news-ani/don-murray-opens-up-about-marilyn-monroe-s-anxiety-on-bus-stop-set -119042601378_1.html).

72. Summers, *Goddess,* 45.

73. Lincoln shows up in an even odder corner of Marilyn's life in Stuart P. Coates's science fiction novel *Norma Jeane's Wishes in Time: A Four-Part Adventure* (New York: IUniverse, Inc., 2008). In the book, a "Time Bubble" whisks Marilyn back to April 14, 1865. She had already met Lincoln at a White House reception in 1862. After stopping John Wilkes Booth from killing Lin-

coln, she realizes, back in her own time, that the fallout from stopping the assassination would prevent her from even being born. (Changing history can result in unintended personal consequences; apparently, it is one of the quirks in time-travel science.) So, Marilyn hurries back to the fateful night. And *this second Marilyn* prevents *that first Marilyn* from stopping Booth. At one point in the plot, the *first* Marilyn says to the president and his wife, "Mr. Lincoln, Mrs. Lincoln . . . Abraham . . . Mary, I know this is terribly rude of me, but I have to go back to my own time . . . immediately!" (224–25, 237–44, 255–57).

74. Ray Long, "Lincoln Foundation Puts Marilyn Monroe Dress on the Block to Save Presidential Memorabilia from Same Fate," *Chicago Tribune,* June 25, 2018. https://www.chicago tribune.com/politics/ct-met-illinois-lincoln-foundation-marilyn-monroe-auction-20180511 -story.html.

75. Stevenson quoted in Donald Spoto, *Marilyn Monroe: The Biography,* chap. 20, Kindle.

76. James Patterson, *The House of Kennedy* (New York: Hachette Book Group, Little, Brown, 2020), chap. 22, Kindle.

77. Summers, *Goddess,* 393.

78. Other sources credit comedian Jack Benny as the evening's host.

79. Adams, *Marilyn Encyclopedia, s.v.* "John Fitzgerald Kennedy." See also Soto, *Marilyn Monroe,* 519–20.

80. Robert W. Welkos, "Marilyn's Secret Tapes," *Los Angeles Times,* September 15, 2014, https://www.latimes.com/news/la-et-marilyn5aug05-story.html. The newspaper obtained the tapes of Monroe's sessions with her psychiatrist, Ralph Greenson, in 1962.

81. Rose Kennedy quoted in Patterson, *The House of Kennedy, chap. 22,* Kindle.

82. S. Paige Baty, *American Monroe: The Making of a Body Politic* (Berkeley: University of California Press, 1995), chap. 3, Kindle.

83. Ibid.

84. Soto, *Marilyn Monroe,* 521.

85. John Louis quoted in J. Randy Taraborrelli, *The Secret Life of Marilyn Monroe* (New York: Rose Books/Hachette Book Group, 2009), part 6, Kindle.

86. Banner, *Marilyn,* 376.

87. Summers, *Goddess,* 394. In feminist theory, Kennedy was exhibiting the "male gaze." According to Robert Schultz: "Sexual anxiety drives the gaze. A man's pleasure in watching Marlene Dietrich, Marilyn Monroe, or Sharon Stone on the screen [or in person that night at Madison Square Garden] is artfully wrought out of the deep misgivings she stirs. Her difference and mystery arouse an anxiety that is sexual and, usually, subliminal. In psychoanalytic terms, a man, confronted by the biological difference of a woman, suffers castration anxiety—for Freud the origin of the entire symbol-making enterprise. According to male gaze theory, films deal with this intolerable anxiety in two ways. One strategy Mulvey describes is voyeurism, in which the disturbing woman is relentlessly investigated in an effort to demystify her. In the process she is often found in some way guilty, in need of punishment or saving. Either way, she comes under male judgment and control" (Robert Schultz, "When Men Look at Women: Sex in an Age of Theory," *Hudson Review* 48, no. 3 [1995]: 368).

88. Quoted in Summers, *Goddess,* 394.

89. Quoted in Marilyn Facts, http://www.marilynmonroe.ca/camera/about/facts/voice .html.

90. Quoted in Maryrose Lane Grossman, "Happy Birthday, Mr. President," The JFK Library Archives: An Inside Look (May 21, 2022), https://jfk.blogs.archives.gov/2020/05/21/happy-birthday-mr-president.

91. Taraborrelli, *The Secret Life of Marilyn Monroe,* part 6, Kindle.

92. For a chronological list of her ailments, see Randall Riese and Neal Hitchens, *The Unabridged Marilyn: Her Life from A to Z* (New York: Bonanza, 1987), 229.

93. Alanna Bennett, "Shirley and Marilyn Monroe Were Very Similar," February 11, 2014, https://www.bustle.com/articles/15317-shirley-temple-marilyn-monroe-had-something-very-interesting-in-common.

94. Gore Vidal, *United States: Essays, 1952–1992* (New York: Random House, 1993), chap. 61, Kindle.

Conclusion: Fade Out

1. George McDonald Fraser, *The Hollywood History of the World: From One Million B.C. to Apocalypse Now* (New York: Beech Tree Books, William Morrow, 1988), xii. Frazer wrote the "Flashman Papers"—a series of eleven novels based on the fictitious memoirs of a nineteenth-century rogue, one Harry Flashman. In *Flash for Freedom* (London: Barrie & Jenkins, 1971), the antihero meets a junior congressman from Illinois, Abraham Lincoln. Frazer worked on ten film scripts, including *The Three Musketeers* (1972), *The Four Musketeers* (1974), and *Royal Flash* (1975). He later contributed to the James Bond film *Octopussy* (1983), among other projects.

2. Harold Holzer, "History through a Poet's Eyes," *Wall Street Journal,* February 14, 2020.

BIBLIOGRAPHY

Books

Agee, James, and Walker Evans. *Let Us Now Praise Famous Men.* New York: Houghton-Mifflin, 1941.

Ames, Mary Clemmer. *Ten Years in Washington or, Inside Life and Scenes in Our National Capital as a Woman Sees Them.* Hartford, CT: Hartford Publishing, 1882.

Baker, Jean H. *Mary Todd Lincoln: A Biography.* New York: Norton, 1987. Kindle.

Banner, Lois. *Marilyn: The Passion and the Paradox.* New York: Bloomsbury, 2012.

Baringer, William Eldon. *Lincoln's Vandalia: A Pioneer Portrait.* New Brunswick, NJ: Rutgers University Press, 1949.

Barr, John McKee. *Loathing Lincoln: An American Tradition from the Civil War to the Present.* Baton Rouge: Louisiana State University Press, 2014.

Barrett, Oliver. *Lincoln's Last Speech in Springfield in the Campaign of 1858.* Chicago: University of Chicago Press, 1924.

Barringer, William B. *Lincoln Day by Day: A Chronology, 1809–1865.* Dayton, OH: Morningside House, 1991.

Barry, Iris. *D. W. Griffith: American Film Master.* New York: Museum of Modern Art, 1940.

Basinger, Jeanine. *The Star Machine.* New York: Knopf, 2007.

Baty, S. Paige. *American Monroe: The Making of a Body Politic.* Berkeley: University of California Press, 1995.

Bayard, Louis. *Courting Mr. Lincoln.* Chapel Hill, NC: Algonquin, 2020.

Bergreen, Laurence. *James Agee: A Life.* New York: Dutton, 1984.

Bingham, Dennis. *Whose Lives Are They Anyway? The Biopic as Contemporary Film Genre.* New Brunswick, NJ: Rutgers University Press, 2010.

Black, Shirley Temple. *Child Star: An Autobiography.* New York: McGraw-Hill, 1988.

Bogdanovich, Peter. *John Ford.* Berkeley: University of California Press, 1978.

Boritt, Gabor, ed. *The Lincoln Enigma: The Changing Face of an American Icon.* New York: Oxford University Press, 2001.

Burlingame, Michael. *Abraham Lincoln: A Life.* 2 vols. Baltimore, MD: Johns Hopkins University Press, 2008.

———. *An American Marriage: The Untold Story of Abraham Lincoln and Mary Todd.* New York: Pegasus, 2021.

———. *The Inner World of Abraham Lincoln.* Urbana: University of Illinois Press, 1994.

Carnes, Mark, Ted Mico, John Miller-Monzon, and David Rubel, eds. *Past Imperfect: History According to the Movies.* New York: Henry Holt, 1995.

Carpenter, F. R. *The Inner Life of Abraham Lincoln: Six Months at the White House.* New York: Hurd and Houghton, 1872.

Carruthers, Olive. *Lincoln's Other Mary: The Courtship of Mary Owens.* Chicago: Ziff-Davis, 1945.

Clinton, Catherine. *Mrs. Lincoln: A Life.* New York: HarperCollins, 2009.

Coates, Stuart P. *Norma Jeane's Wishes in Time: A Four-Part Adventure.* New York: IUniverse, Inc., 2008.

Curtis, William Elery. *Abraham Lincoln.* Philadelphia: Lippincott, 1902.

Custen, George F. *Bio/Pics: How Hollywood Constructed Public History.* New Brunswick, NJ: Rutgers University Press, 1922.

DeMille, Cecil B. *The Autobiography of Cecil B. DeMille.* New York: Prentice Hall, 1959.

Donald, David Herbert. *Lincoln.* New York: Simon & Schuster, 1995.

———, ed. *Lincoln Reconsidered: Essays on the Civil War Era. 2nd ed.* New York: Vintage, 1956.

Dusenbury, Winifred. *The Theme of Loneliness in Modern American Drama.* Gainesville: University of Florida Press, 1960.

Edwards, Anne. *Shirley Temple: American Princess. 2nd ed.* Gilford, CT: Globe Pequot, 1988. Kindle.

Emerson, Jason. *Mary Lincoln for the Ages.* Carbondale: Southern Illinois University Press, 2019.

Epstein, William H., and R. Barton Palmer, eds. *Invented Lives, Imagined Communities: The Biopic and American National Identity.* Albany: State University of New York Press, 2016.

Evans, W. A. *Mrs. Abraham Lincoln.* New York: Knopf, 1932.

Fehrenbacher, Don E. *The Minor Affair: An Adventure in Forgery and Detection.* Fort Wayne, IN: Louis A. Warren Lincoln Library and Museum, 1979.

Fehrenbacher, Don E., and Virginia Fehrenbacher, eds. *Recollected Words of Abraham Lincoln.* Stanford, CA: Stanford University Press, 1996.

Foner, Eric, ed. *Our Lincoln: New Perspectives on Lincoln and His World.* New York: Norton, 2008.

Fraser, George McDonald. *The Hollywood History of the World: From One Million B.C. to Apocalypse Now.* New York: Beech Tree Books, William Morrow, 1988.

Gerhart, Michael J. *Lincoln's Mentors: The Education of a Leader.* New York: Custom House, 2021.

Goodwin, Doris Kearns. *Team of Rivals: The Political Genius of Abraham Lincoln.* New York: Simon & Schuster, 2005.

Green, Michael S. *Lincoln and the Election of 1860.* Carbondale: Southern Illinois University Press, 2011. Kindle.

Greene, Graham. *The Graham Greene Reader: Reviews, Essays, Interviews & Film Stories.* New York: Applause Theater Book Publishers, 1994.

———. *The Pleasure Dome: The Collected Film Criticism, 1935–1940.* Edited by John Russell Taylor. New York: Oxford University Press, 1980.

Hay, John. *At Lincoln's Side: John Hay's Civil War Correspondence and Selected Writings.* Edited by Michael Burlingame. Carbondale: Southern Illinois University Press, 2000.

Herndon, William H. *Lincoln and Ann Rutledge: A Lecture.* Herrin, IL: Trovillion, 1945.

Herndon, William W., and Jesse W. Weik. *Herndon's Lincoln: The True Story of a Great Life.* Springfield, IL: Herndon's Lincoln Publishing Company, 1888.

Holst, Erika. *Courtship and Weddings in Abraham Lincoln's Springfield.* N.p., n.d. Kindle.

Hughes, William. *James Agee, Omnibus, and Mr. Lincoln: The Culture of Liberalism and the Challenge of Television, 1952–1953.* Lanham, MD: Scarecrow, 2004.

Kael, Pauline. *The Age of Movies: Selected Writings of Pauline Kael.* Edited by Sanford Schwarts. New York: Library of America, 2011.

Kaplan, Fred. *Lincoln: The Biography of a Writer.* New York: HarperCollins, 2008.

Kasson, John F. *The Little Girl Who Fought the Great Depression: Shirley Temple and 1930s America.* New York: Norton, 2014.

Kushner, Tony. *Lincoln: The Screenplay.* Foreword by Doris Kearns Goodwin. New York: Theater Communications Group, 2012.

Lamon, Ward Hill. *The Life of Abraham Lincoln: From His Birth to His Inauguration.* Boston: James R. Osgood, 1872.

Layda, Jay, ed. *Film Essays and a Lecture.* Princeton, NJ: Princeton University Press, 1982.

Leech, Margaret. *Reveille in Washington, 1860–1865.* New York: Harper & Brothers, 1941.

Mailer, Norman. *Of Women and Their Elegance.* Photographs by Milton H. Greene. New York: Simon & Schuster, 1980.

Manseau, Peter. *The Apparitionists: A Tale of Phantoms, Fraud, Photography, and the Man Who Captured Lincoln's Ghost.* New York: Houghton, Mifflin, Harcourt, 2017.

McDermott, Stacy Pratt. *Mary Lincoln: Southern Girl, Northern Woman.* New York: Routledge/Taylor & Francis Group, 2015.

McMurtry, Gerald. Appendix to *Lincoln's Other Mary: The Courtship of Mary Owens,*
    by Olive Carruthers. Chicago: Ziff-Davis, 1945.

Mellon, James, ed. *The Face of Lincoln.* New York: Bonanza, 1979.

Meuel, David. *Women in the Films of John Ford.* Jefferson, NC: MacFarland, 2014.

Michaels, Lloyd. *Terence Malick.* Champaign: University of Illinois Press, 2009.

Monroe, Marilyn. *My Story: Illustrated Edition.* With Ben Hecht. New York: First
    Taylor Trade Publication, 2007.

Oates, Joyce Carol. *Blonde: A Novel.* HarperCollins, 2000. Kindle.

Patterson, James. *The House of Kennedy.* New York: Hachette/Little, Brown, 2020.

Peple, Edward. *The Littlest Rebel.* New York: Grosset & Dunlap, 1914.

Peterson, Merrill D. *Lincoln in American Memory.* New York: Oxford University
    Press, 1994.

Pritchard, Helmer. *The Dark Days of Abraham Lincoln's Widow as Revealed by Her
    Own Letters.* Carbondale: Southern Illinois University Press, 2012.

Pryor, Elizabeth Brown. *Six Encounters with Lincoln: A President Confronts Democracy
    and Its Demons.* New York: Penguin, 2018.

Randall, J. G. *Lincoln the President: Springfield to Gettysburg.* New York: Dodd, Mead,
    1945.

Randall, Ruth Painter. *Mary Lincoln: Biography of a Marriage.* Boston: Little, Brown, 1956.

Reinhart, Mark S. *Abraham Lincoln on Screen: Fictional and Documentary Portrayals
    on Film and Television.* 2nd ed. Jefferson, NC: McFarland, 2011.

Reynolds, David S. *Abe: Abraham Lincoln in His Times.* New York: Penguin, 2020.

Ross, Ishbel. *Proud Kate: Portrait of an Ambitious Woman.* New York: Harper & Brothers,
    1953.

Rubel, David. *Lincoln: A Cinematic and Historical Companion.* New York: Disney
    Editions, 2012.

Sandburg, Carl. *Abraham Lincoln: The Prairie Years.* 2 vols. 1926. New York: Charles
    Scribner's Sons, 1948.

———. *Lincoln Collector: The Story of the Oliver R. Barrett Collection.* New York: Har-
    court Brace, 1949.

———. *Mary Lincoln: Wife and Widow.* New York: Harcourt, Brace, 1932.

———. *"The Movies Are": Carl Sandburg's Film Reviews and Essays, 1920–1928.* Edited
    by Arnie Bernstein. Introduced by Roger Ebert. Chicago: Lake Claremont, 2000.

Sanders, George. *Memoirs of a Professional Cad.* New York: Avon, 1960.

Sarris, Andrew. *The John Ford Movie Mystery.* Bloomington: Indiana University Press,
    1975.

Schickel, Richard. *D. W. Griffith: An American Life.* New York: Simon & Schuster,
    1984.

Schreiner, Samuel A., Jr. *The Trials of Mrs. Lincoln.* New York: Donald I. Fine, 1987.

Schroeder-Lein, Glenna R. *Lincoln and Medicine.* Carbondale: Southern Illinois Uni-
    versity Press, 2012.

Schwartz, Barry. *Abraham Lincoln in the Post-Heroic World: History and Memory in Late Twentieth-Century America.* Chicago: University of Chicago Press, 2008.

Shenk, Joshua Wolf. *Lincoln's Melancholy: How Depression Challenged a President and Fueled His Greatness.* New York: Houghton Mifflin, 2006.

Sherwood, Robert. *Abe Lincoln in Illinois: A Play.* New York: Charles Scribner, 1939.

Silber, Nina. *This War Ain't Over: Fighting the Civil War in New Deal America.* Chapel Hill: University of North Carolina Press, 2018.

Smyth, J. E. *Reconstructing American Historical Cinema.* Lexington: University of Kentucky Press, 2006. Kindle.

Snee, Brian J. *Lincoln before Lincoln: Early Cinematic Adaptations of the Life of America's Greatest President.* Lexington: University of Kentucky Press, 2016.

Soto, Donald. *Marilyn Monroe: The Biography.* New York: Cooper Union, 1993.

Soto, John G., MD. *The Mary Lincoln Mind-Body Sourcebook: Including a Unifying Diagnosis to Explain Her Public Decay, Manifest Insanity, and Slow Death.* Mt. Vernon, VA: Mt. Vernon Book Systems, 2017.

Speed, Joshua F. *Reminiscences of Abraham Lincoln and Notes on a Visit to California: Two Lectures.* Louisville, KY: John P. Morton, 1884.

Spoto, Donald, *Marilyn Monroe: The Biography.* 2014. Kindle.

Stahr, Walter. *Salmon P. Chase: Lincoln's Vital Rival.* New York: Simon & Schuster, 2021. Kindle.

Steers, Edward, Jr. *Lincoln Legends: Myths, Hoaxes, and Confabulations Associated with our Greatest President.* Lexington: University of Kentucky Press, 2007.

Steinem, Gloria. *Marilyn: Norma Jean.* New York: Henry Holt, 1988. Kindle.

Strozier, Charles B. *Lincoln's Quest for Union: Public and Private Meanings,* New York: Basic, 1982.

Summers, Anthony. *Goddess: The Secret Life of Marilyn Monroe.* New York: Open Road Integrated Media, 1985.

Tackach, James. *Lincoln and the Environment.* Carbondale: Southern Illinois University Press, 2019.

Taraborrelli, J. Randy. *The Secret Life of Marilyn Monroe.* New York: Rose Books/Hachette Book Group, 2009. Kindle.

Thomas, Benjamin P. *Lincoln's New Salem.* Victoria, British Columbia: Reading Essentials, 1934. Kindle.

———. *Portrait for Posterity: Lincoln and His Biographers.* New Brunswick, NJ: Rutgers University Press, 1947.

Tripp, C. A. *The Intimate World of Abraham Lincoln.* New York: Thunder Mouth, 2005.

Turner, Justin G., and Linda Levitt Turner, eds. *Mary Todd Lincoln: Her Life and Letters.* New York: Knopf, 1972.

Turney, Harold. *Film Guide to the 20th Century–Fox Picture, A Cosmopolitan Production, Young Mr. Lincoln: A Study Plan Prepared in Hollywood.* Hollywood, CA: Film Guide, 1939.

Vidal, Gore. *I Told You So: Gore Vidal Talks Politics: Interviews with Jon Wiener.* Berkeley, CA: Counterpoint, 2012.

———. *Lincoln: A Novel.* 1984. First International Edition. New York: Random House, 2000. Kindle.

———. *Screening History.* Cambridge, MA: Harvard University Press, 1992.

———. *United States: Essays, 1952–1992.* New York: Broadway, 1993. Kindle.

Vieira, Mark A. *Majestic Hollywood: The Greatest Films of 1939.* Philadelphia: Running Press, 2013.

Vorenburg, Michael. *Final Freedom: The Civil War, the Abolition of Slavery, and the Thirteenth Amendment.* New York: Cambridge University Press, 2001.

Walsh, John Evangelist. *The Shadow's Rise: Abraham Lincoln and Ann Rutledge Legend.* Urbana: University of Illinois Press, 1993.

Washington, John E. *They Knew Lincoln.* New York: Oxford University Press, 2018.

Weber, Karl, ed. *Lincoln: A President for the Ages.* New York: Public Affairs, 2012.

Williams, Frank J., and Michael Burkhimer, eds. *The Mary Lincoln Enigma: Historians on America's Most Controversial First Lady.* Carbondale: Southern Illinois University Press, 2012.

Wilson, Edmund. *Patriotic Gore: Studies in the Literature of the American Civil War.* New York: Oxford University Press, 1962.

Winder, Elizabeth. *Marilyn in Manhattan: Her Year of Joy.* New York: Flatiron, 2017.

Winkler, H. Donald. *Lincoln's Ladies: The Women in the Life of the Sixteenth President.* Rev. and expanded ed. Nashville, TN: Cumberland House, 2004.

Wright, A. M. R. *The Dramatic Life of Abraham Lincoln: Illustrated with Scenes from the Photoplay. A First Nation Picture Presented by Al and Ray Rockett.* New York: Grosset & Dunlap, 1925.

Zolotow, Maurice, *Marilyn Monroe.* Updated and expanded ed. New York: Perennial Library, 1990.

Articles and Chapters

Angle Paul M. "The Minor Collection: A Criticism." *Atlantic Monthly* 143, no. 4 (April 1929). https://www.theatlantic.com/magazine/archive/1929/04/the-minor-collection-a-criticism/304448.

Ask Me Anything. "The Blond in the Film." https://theblondeatthefilm.tumblr.com/post/142183992172/february-12-1950-actress-grace-kelly-as-ann.

Bartelt, William E. "The Making of *The Better Angels.*" *Journal of the Abraham Lincoln Association* 36, no. 2 (2015). https://quod.lib.umich.edu/j/jala/2629860.0036.205/—roundtable-the-better-angels?rgn=main;view=fulltext.

Bastien, Angelica Jade. "The Feminine Grotesque: On the Warped Image of Joan Crawford." May 14, 2006. https://www.rogerebert.com/features/the-feminine-grotesque-on-the-warped-legacy-of-joan-crawford.

Bathrick, Serafina. "The Mary Tyler Moore Show: Women at Home and at Work."
In *MTM: Quality Television,* edited by Jane Feuer, Paul Kerr, and Tise Vahimagi,
99–131. London: British Film Institute, 1984.

Bennett, Alanna. "Shirley and Marilyn Were Very Similar." *Bustle,* February 11, 2014.
https://www.bustle.com/articles/15317-shirley-temple-marilyn-monroe-had
-something-very-interesting-in-common.

Berg, Gordon. Review of *Abraham Lincoln* (1930). https://www.historynet.com/acw
-review-abraham-lincoln-1930.

Block, Ruth H. "Feminine Ideals in Transition: The Rise of the Moral Mother, 1785–
1815." *Feminist Studies* 4, no. 2 (June 1978): 100–126.

Bunker, Gary L. "The Comic News, Lincoln, and the Civil War." *Journal of the Abraham
Lincoln Association* 17, no. 1 (1996). https://quod.lib.umich.edu/j/jala/2629860.0017
.107/—comic-news-lincoln-and-the-civil-war?rgn=main;view=fulltext.

Burlingame, Michael. "Author Interview: Abraham Lincoln: A Life." 2009. Abraham Lincoln Online. http://www.abrahamlincolnonline.org/lincoln/books
/burlingame.htm.

———. "The Mary Lincoln Enigma: Historians on America's Most Controversial
First Lady." *Civil War Book Review* 15, no. 2 (2013): 1–5.

Business Standard. "Don Murray Opens up about Marilyn Monroe's Anxiety on
Bus Stop Set." April 26, 2019. https://www.business-standard.com/article/news
-ani/don-murray-opens-up-about-marilyn-monroe-s-anxiety-on-bus-stop
-set-119042601378_1.html.

Celebrity Net Worth. "Shirley Temple." https://www.celebritynetworth.com/richest
-celebrities/actors/shirley-temple-net-worth.

Christensen, William I. "Milk Sickness: A Review of the Literature. *Economic Botany*
19, no. 3 (July-September 1965): 293–300.

Clark, Champ. "Merry Christmas, Shirley Temple." December 21, 2018. https://www
.rogerebert.com/features/merry-christmas-shirley-temple.

Clinton, Catherine. "Abraham Lincoln: The Family That Made Him, the Family He
Made." In *Our Lincoln: New Perspectives on Lincoln and His World,* edited by Eric
Foner, 249–69. New York: Norton, 2008.

Couchman, Jeffery, "James Agee's Experimentally Traditional Mr. Lincoln." In *Agee
at 100: Centennial Essays of the Works of James Agee,* edited by Michael A. Lofaro,
167–200. Knoxville: University of Tennessee Press, 2012.

Crawford, Sean. "A Bombshell Dropped (in Bement) 60 Years Ago." Illinois Public
Radio. August 7, 2015. https://will.illinois.edu/news/story/a-bombshell-dropped
-in-bement-60-years-ago.

Daly, Walter J. "'The Slows': The Torment of Milk Sickness on the Midwest Frontier." *Indiana Magazine of History* 102, no. 1 (March 2006): 29–40.

Dean, John, "The Social and Cultural Construction of Abraham Lincoln in U.S. Movies
and on U.S. Television." *American Studies Journal* 53 (2009). http://www.asjournal

.org/53-2009/social-and-cultural-construction-of-lincoln-in-movies-and
-on-tv/.

Donald, David. "Getting Right with Lincoln," *Harper's,* April 1, 1951, 74–80.

Dubruge, Peter. Review of *The Better Angels. Variety.com.* November 7, 2014. https://
variety.com/2014/film/reviews/film-review-the-better-angels-1201350349.

DuCille, Ann. "The Shirley Temple of My Familiar." *Transition,* no. 73 (1997): 10–32.

Dye, Nancy Schrom. "History of Childbirth in America." "Women: Sex and Sexuality, Part 2." Special issue, *Signs* 6, no. 1 (Autumn 1980): 97–108.

Eckert, Charles. "Shirley Temple and the House of Rockefeller." *Jump Cut: A Review
of Contemporary Media* 2 (1974). https://www.ejumpcut.org/archive/onlinessays
/JC02folder/shirleytemple.html.

Fehrenbacher, Don E. "Lincoln's Lost Love Letters," *American Heritage* 32, no. 2
(February/March 1981). https://www.americanheritage.com/lincolns-lost-love
-letters.

Feinberg, Scott, and Scott Johnson. "Catherine Burns: The Vanishing of an Oscar
Nominated Actress." *Hollywood Reporter,* February 3, 2020. https://www.holly
woodreporter.com/movies/movie-features/catherine-burns-inside-50-year
-disappearance-an-oscar-nominee-1275646.

Fleming Mark. "Mike Fleming's Q&A with Steven Spielberg: Why It Took 12 Years
to Find 'Lincoln." Deadline, December 6, 2012. https://deadline.com/2012/12
/steven-spielberg-lincoln-making-of-interview-exclusive-383861.

Foroughi, Andrea. "'Your Household Accounts Have Always Been So Interesting':
Family, Relations and Gender Politics in Lincoln's Two Houses." *Rethinking History* 19, no. 3 (2013): 512–24.

Gannett, Lewis. "The Ann Rutledge Story: Case Closed?" *Journal of the Abraham
Lincoln Association* 31, no. 2 (2011). https://quod.lib.umich.edu/j/jala/2629860
.0011.104/—abraham-lincoln-and-ann-rutledge?rgn=main;view=fulltext.

Gopnik, Adam. "Why We Keep Inventing Abraham Lincoln," *New Yorker,* September 28, 2020.

Grossman, Maryrose Lane. "Happy Birthday, Mr. President," The JFK Library Archives: A Inside Look (May 21, 2022). https://jfk.blogs.archives.gov/2020/05/21
/happy-birthday-mr-president/.

Harbin, John. "A Closer Look at the Carl Sandburg Home." *Burlington (NC) Times-
News,* April 19, 2011.

Hill, Frederick Trevor. "Lincoln's Legacy to America: The Surroundings of Lincoln's
Birth and Childhood." *New York Times,* February 1, 1909.

Hischak, Thomas S. *100 Greatest American Plays.* New York: Rowman & Littlefield, 2017.

Hogan, Jackie. "Searching for the 'Better Angels' of Historical Context." *Journal of the
Abraham Lincoln Association* 36, no. 2 (2015). https://quod.lib.umich.edu/j/jala
/2629860.0036.205/—roundtable-the-better-angels?rgn=main;view=fulltext.

Holroyd, Michael. "History and Biography." *Salmagundi* 46 (1979): 13–26.

Holzer, Harold. "History through a Poet's Eyes." *Wall Street Journal,* February 14, 2020.

Internet Movie Data Base (IMDb). "Brit Marling. Biography." https://www.imdb .com/name/nm1779870/bio?ref_=nm_ov_bio_sm#quotes.

Johnson, Laurie. "Julie Harris Styles Mrs. Lincoln from the Heart Out." *New York Times* December 22, 1972.

Kenny, Glenn. Review of *The Better Angels.* November 7, 2014. https://www.roger ebert.com/reviews/the-better-angels-2014.

Know, David. "Vale: Sada Thompson," Obituary.TVTonight. https://tvtonight.com .au/2011/05/vale-sada-thompson.html.

Leavitt, Judith Waltzer. "Under the Shadow of Maternity: American Women's Responses to Death and Debility Fears in Nineteenth-Century Childbirth." *Feminist Studies* 12, no. 1 (1986): 129–54.

Lehrman Institute. Abraham Lincoln's Classroom. "Lincoln and Women." https://www .abrahamlincolnsclassroom.org/abraham-lincolns-contemporaries/abraham -lincoln-and-women/.

Long, Ray. "Lincoln Foundation Puts Marilyn Monroe Dress on the Block to Save Presidential Memorabilia from Same Fate." *Chicago Tribune,* June 25, 2018. https://www.chicagotribune.com/politics/ct-met-illinois-lincoln-foundation -marilyn-monroe-auction-20180511-story.html.

Malcom, Derek. "John Ford: Young Mr. Lincoln." *Guardian,* June 24, 1999.

McCarthy, Todd. "*The Better Angels:* Sundance Review." *Hollywood Reporter,* January 25, 2014. https://www.hollywoodreporter.com/news/general-news/better -angels-sundance-review-674057.

McDermott, Stacy Pratt. "A Tale of Two Marys": Review of Spielberg's *Lincoln.*" *Civil War Pop.* November 16, 2012. https://civilwarpop.com/category/women.

McGregor, Thomas. "Some New Facts about Abraham Lincoln's Parents." *National Republican,* October 15, 1921; and *Register of Kentucky State Historical Society* 2, no. 59 (May 1922). https://ur.booksc.eu/book/26132901/bd212c.

Minor, Wilma Frances. "Lincoln the Lover. Part I: The Setting-New Salem." *Atlantic Monthly,* December 1928. https://www.theatlantic.com/magazine/archive/1928 /12/lincoln-the-lover/304444/.

———. "Lincoln the Lover. Part II: The Courtship." *Atlantic Monthly,* January 1929. https://ollie.cms-dev.theatlantic.com/magazine/archive/1929/01/lincoln-the -lover/304445/.

———. "Lincoln the Lover. Part III: The Tragedy." *Atlantic Monthly,* February 1929. https://www.theatlantic.com/magazine/archive/1929/02/lincoln-the-lover /304442/.

Mitchell, Stewart. "Worthington Chauncey Ford." *Proceedings of the Massachusetts Historical Society* 69 (1947): 407–11.

Monaghan, Jay. "Was Abraham Lincoln a Spiritualist?" *Journal of the Illinois State Historical Society 34, no. 2* (June 1941): 209–32.

Mooney, Barbara Burlison. "Lincoln's New Salem: Or, the Trigonometric Theorem of Vernacular Restoration." *Perspective in Vernacular Architecture* 2 (2004): 19–39.

Moss, Walter. "Carl Sandburg, Hollywood, Media, and Marilyn Monroe." *Hollywood Progressive,* January 13, 2012. https://www.academia.edu/4209423/carl _sandburg_hollywood_media_and_marylin_monroe.

Movshovitz, Howard. "The Still Point: Women in the Westerns of John Ford." *Frontiers, A Journal of Women Studies* 7, no. 3 (1984): 68–72.

Naremore, James. "The Cinema According to James Agee." *New England Review* 35, no. 2 (2014): 100–115.

National Museum of American History. *The Railsplitter. Abraham Lincoln: An Extraordinary Life.* Exhibition. National Museum of American History. https://americanhistory.si.edu/lincoln/railsplitter.

Nelson, Megan Kate. "Lincoln's Boyhood and Black and White." *Journal of the Abraham Lincoln Association* 36, no. 2 (2015). https://quod.lib.umich.edu/j/jala/2629860 .0036.205/—roundtable-the-better-angels?rgn=main;view=fulltext.

Noah, Timothy. "Kushner Replies about Sources." *New Republic,* January 13, 2013. https://newrepublic.com/article/111833/kushner-replies-about-sources.

———. "Tony Kushner's Real Source for Lincoln." *New Republic,* January 9, 2013. https://newrepublic.com/article/111810/tony-kushners-real-source-lincoln.

O'Brien, Geffrey "Young Mr. Lincoln: Hero in Waiting." *Current: An Online Magazine Covering Film Culture Past and Present.* The Criterion Collection. February 13, 2006. https://www.criterion.com/current/posts/413-young-mr-lincoln-hero-in-waiting.

Osterwell, Ara. "Reconstructing Shirley: Pedophilia and Interracial *Romance* in Hollywood's Age of Innocence." *Camera Obscura* 24, no. 3 (2009): 1–39.

Paquet-Deyris, Anne-Marie. "From 'Plain Abe' to Mythical Mr. Lincoln: Constructing Various Representational Modes of a Screen Idol." *Idées d'Amériques* 7 (Spring 2016): 1–13.

Perkins-Valdez, Dolen. Introduction to *Behind the Scenes or Thirty Years a Slave, and Four Years in the White House,* by Elizabeth Keckley. Originally published by G. W. Carleton & Co., 1868. Eno Publishers, 2016. Kindle.

Peterson, Audrey C. "Brain Fever in Nineteenth-Century Literature Fact and Fiction." *Victorian Studies* 19, no. 4 (June 1976): 445–64.

Pollard, Mark B. "Harriet Monroe's Abraham Lincoln." *Journal of the Abraham Lincoln Association* 37, no. 2 (Summer 2016): 16–41.

Rice, Judith A. "Ida M Tarbell: A Progressive Look at Lincoln." *Journal of the Abraham Lincoln Association* 19, no. 1 (Winter 1998): 57–72.

Rosenberg, Corey. "Spielberg's Lincoln: An Ambitious Pastiche." *Pennsylvania History: A Journal of Mid-Atlantic Studies* 80, no. 2 (Spring 2013): 329–32.

Sandage, Scott A. Review of *Abraham and Mary Lincoln: A House Divided. Journal of American History* 88, no. 3 (December 2001): 1184–86.

Schultz, Robert. "When Men Look at Women: Sex in an Age of Theory." *Hudson Review* 48, no. 3 (1995): 365–87.

Schwartz, Thomas F. "'Not Even Wrong': Herndon and His Informants." *Journal of the Abraham Lincoln Association* 35, no. 2 (2014): 37–54.

Sherrill, Martha. "Simply the Best: Shirley Temple Charmed a Depressed Nation and It Wasn't Just Another Song and Dance." *Washington Post,* July 16, 1995.

Silber, Nina. "Abraham Lincoln and the Political Culture of New Deal America." *Journal of the Civil War Era* 5, no. 3 (2015): 348–71.

Simon, John Y. "Abraham Lincoln and Ann Rutledge." *Journal of the Abraham Lincoln Association* 11 (1990): 13–33.

Smith, Daniel Scott. "Differential Morality in the United States before 1900." *Journal of Interdisciplinary History* 13, no. 4 (Spring 1983): 735–36.

Stauffer, John. "The Christ-Haunted Lincoln." Roundtable: *The Better Angels. Journal of the Abraham Lincoln Association* 26, no. 2 (2015): 57–66.

Stokes, Melvyn. "Abraham Lincoln and the Movies." *American Nineteenth Century History* 12, no. 2 (June 2011): 203–31.

Thompson, Lauren MacIvor. "'I Wish I Could Forget Myself . . .': Mary Todd Lincoln and the Pursuit of True Womanhood." *Annual Journal,* Corcoran Department of History, University of Virginia, 44 (2011): 1–30. https://essaysinhistory.com /articles/abstract/271.

Thomson, David. "Spielberg's *Lincoln* Is a Film for Our Political Moment." *New Republic,* November 12, 2012. https://newrepublic.com/article/110113/spielbergs -lincoln-film-our-political-moment.

Trunick, Austin. "Filmmaker A. J. Edwards Discusses *The Better Angels.*" *Under the Radar,* November 7, 2014. https://www.undertheradarmag.com/interviews /filmmaker_a.j._edwards_discusses_the_better_angels.

Variety Staff. Review of *The Littlest Rebel. Variety,* December 31, 1934. https://variety .com/1934/film/reviews/the-littlest-rebel-1200410951.

Walsh, Margaret. "Women's Place on the American Frontier." *Journal of American History* 29, no. 2 (August 1995): 241–55.

Webb, Derek A. "The Natural Rights Liberalism of Franklin Delano Roosevelt: Economic Rights and the American Constitutional Tradition." *American Journal of Legal History,* 55, no. 3 (2015): 313–46.

Welter, Barbara. "The Cult of True Womanhood: 1820–1860." *American Quarterly* 18, no. 2 (1966): 151–74.

Theses and Dissertations

Duhon, Madelyn Kay. "Journalist and Hoaxer: William Francis Mannix and the Long History of Faked News." Master's thesis (no. 4415), LSU, 2017. https://digital commons.lsu.edu/cgi/viewcontent.cgi?article=5416&context=gradschool_theses.

Rosa, Rafael. "Abraham Lincoln and Women: A Psychohistorical Analysis." PhD diss., Drew University, May 2017.

Published Lecture

Jean H. Baker. "The Lincoln Marriage: Beyond the Battle of Quotations." Paper presented at the 38th Annual Robert Fortenbaugh Memorial Lecture. Gettysburg College, Civil War Institute, 1999.

Websites and Other Online Sources

Abraham Lincoln to Mary S. Owens. December 13, 1836. Sotheby's Auctions. https://www.sothebys.com/en/auctions/ecatalogue/2015/fine-books-manuscripts-americana-n09435/lot.71.html?locale=en.

Abraham Lincoln to Mrs. Orville H. Browning, April 1, 1838, In *The Collected Works of Abraham Lincoln,* vol. 1, edited by Roy P. Basler, Marion Dolores Pratt, and Lloyd A. Dunlap. New Brunswick, NJ: Rutgers University Press, 1953. https://quod.lib.umich.edu/l/lincoln/lincoln1/1:134?rgn=div1;view=fulltext.

AFI (American Film Institute) Catalog. https://aficatalog.afi.com.

APA (American Psychological Association) Dictionary of Psychology, s.v. "False Memory." https://dictionary.apa.org/false-memory.

Internet Movie Database (IMDb). https://www.imdb.com.

Library of Congress. "The Light of Other Days." Music for the Nation: American Sheet Music, ca. 1820–1839. 1830–1839. https://www.loc.gov/collections/american-sheet-music-1870-to-1885/about-this-collection.

Papers of the Abraham Lincoln Digital Library. https://papersofabrahamlincoln.org/persons/OW47299.

Petition 20784112. "To the Hon. The Judge of Fayette Court of Chancery." Filing Date, July 6, 1841. Ending Date, March 1843. Race and Slavery Petition Project. University of North Carolina, Greensboro. http://library.uncg.edu/slavery/petitons/details.aspx?=6313.

Roosevelt, Theodore, "Address of President Roosevelt on the Occasion of the Celebration of the Hundredth Anniversary of the Birth of Abraham Lincoln." Hodgenville, Kentucky, February 12, 1909. New York State Library. http://www.nysl.nysed.gov/mssc/tr/address.htm.

———. "The Heirs of Abraham Lincoln." February 12, 1913. Document. Teaching American History, Ashbrook Center at Ashland University. https://teachingamericanhistory.org/library/document/the-heirs-of-abraham-lincoln.

Winstead, Mary Elizabeth. Interview with Ezequiel Gutierrez, HeyUGuys (June 19, 2012). https://www.youtube.com/watch?v=15VEFbkTziQ.

Film Scripts

Burke, Edwin. *The Littlest Rebel.* N.p., September 12, 1935.

Hodges, Adrian. *My Week with Marilyn.* Internet Movie Script Database. https://imsdb.com/scripts/My-Week-with-Marilyn.html.

Trotti, Lamar. *Young Mr. Lincoln: Original Story and Screenplay.* Revised final script. N.p., February 27, 1939.

Reference Works

Neely, Mark E., Jr. *The Abraham Lincoln Encyclopedia.* New York: McGraw Hill, 1982.

Riese, Randall, and Neal Hitchens. *The Unabridged Marilyn: Her Life from A to Z.* New York: Bonanza, 1987.

Robbins, Peter, ed. *The Columbia Companion to American History on Film: How the Movies Have Portrayed the American Past.* New York: Columbia University Press, 2003.

Thomson, David. *The New Biographical Dictionary of Film.* New York: Knopf, 2002.

Victor, Adam. *The Marilyn Encyclopedia.* Woodstock, NY: Overlook, 1999.

FILMOGRAPHY

Selected Feature Films and
Television Productions by Date of Release

The Birth of a Nation

Format: DVD

Date of original release: February 8, 1915 (feature film)

Producers: D. W. Griffith, Harry Aitken

Production company: David W. Griffith Corp.

Distributed by: Epoch Producing Company

Director: D. W. Griffith

Writers: Thomas Dixon Jr., D. W. Griffith, Frank E. Woods

Cast: Joseph Henabery, Lillian Gish, Mae Marsh, Henry Walthall, Miriam Cooper, Mary Alden, Ralph Lewis, George Siegmann, Walter Long, Robert Harron

Abraham Lincoln

Format: DVD

Date of original release: August 25, 1930 (feature film)

Producers: Joseph M. Schenck, D. W. Griffith

Production company: Feature Films, Inc.

Distributed by: United Artists

Director: D. W. Griffith

Writers: D. W. Griffith, Stephen Vincent Benét, John W. Considine, Gerrit W. Lloyd

Cast: Walter Huston, Una Merkel, Kay Hammond, E. Alyn Warren, Hobart Bosworth, Fred Warren, Henry B. Walthall, Frank Campeau, Francis Ford, W. L. Thorne, Helen Freeman, Lucille La Verne

The Littlest Rebel

Format: DVD

Date of original release: December 19, 1935 (feature film)

Producers: Darryl F. Zanuck, B. G. DeSylva

Production company: Twentieth Century–Fox Film Corp.

Distributed by: Twentieth Century–Fox Film Corp.

Director: David Butler

Writers: Edwin J. Burke, Harry Tugend (uncredited). Based on the novel *The Littlest Rebel* by Edward Peple.

Cast: Shirley Temple, Bill Robinson, Frank McGlynn Sr., John Boles, Jack Holt, Karen Morley, Guinn "Big Boy" Williams, Willie Best, Bessie Lyle

Young Mr. Lincoln

Format: DVD

Date of original release: June 9, 1939 (feature film)

Producer: Kenneth Macgowan

Production company: Twentieth Century–Fox Corp.

Distributed by: Twentieth Century–Fox Corp.

Director: John Ford

Writer: Lamar Trotti

Cast: Henry Fonda, Alice Brady, Marjorie Weaver, Arleen Whelan, Eddie Collins, Pauline Moore, Richard Cromwell, Ward Bond, Donald Meek, Spencer Charters, Milburn Stone

Abe Lincoln in Illinois

Format: DVD

Date of original release: April 19, 1940 (feature film)

Producer: Max Gordon

Production company: Max Gordon Plays and Pictures Corp and RKO Radio Pictures, Inc.

Distributed by: RKO Radio Pictures

Director: John Cromwell

Writer: Robert Sherwood. Based on the play *Abe Lincoln in Illinois* by Sherwood, 1938.

Cast: Raymond Massey, Ruth Gordon, Gene Lockhart, Mary Howard, Dorothy Tree, Harry Stephens, Minor Watson, Alan Baxter, Howard da Silva, Louis Jean Heydt, Charles Middleton, Elizabeth Risdon, Maurice Murphy

Mr. Lincoln

Format: DVD
Date of original release: November 16, 1952 (television miniseries)
Producer: Richard de Rochemont
Production company: Vavin, Inc.
Originally aired: CBS
Director: Norman Lloyd
Writer: James Agee
Cast: Royal Dano, Joanne Woodward, Blanche Cholet, Marian Seldes, Joanna
    Roos, James Agee, Crahan Denton, Marian Seldes, Doris Rich, Martin Gable

Bus Stop

Format: DVD
Date of original release: August 31, 1956 (feature film)
Producer: Buddy Adler
Production company: Twentieth Century–Fox Film Corp.
Distributed by: Twentieth Century–Fox Film Corp.
Director: Joshua Logan
Writers: George Axelrod. Based on the play *Bus Stop* by William Inge.
Cast: Marilyn Monroe, Don Murray, Arthur O'Connell, Hope Lange, Helen Mayon

Sandburg's Lincoln

Format: DVD
Date of original release: September 6, 1974 (television miniseries)
Executive Producer: David L. Wolper
Production company: David Wolper Productions
Distributed by: NBC
Director: George Schaefer
Writers: James Prideaux (1 episode, 1974); Irene Kamp (1 episode, 1975); Louis
    Kamp (1 episode, 1975); Emmet Lavery (1 episode, 1975); Jerome Lawrence, (1
    episode, 1975); Robert E. Lee (1 episode, 1975); Jerry McNeely (1 episode, 1975);
    Loring Mandel (1 episode, 1976); Philip H. Reisman Jr. (1 episode, 1976); Carl
    Sandburg (*The Prairie Years* and *The War Years*)
Cast: Hal Holbrook, Sada Thompson, Elizabeth Ashley, Beulah Bondi, Catherine
    Burns, Richard A. Dysart, John Randolph, Whit Bissell, Michael Ivor Cristofer,
    James Carroll Jordan, Lee Bergere

The Last of Mrs. Lincoln

Format: DVD or Amazon Prime
Date of original release: September 16, 1976 (filmed play/Broadway theater film)
Producer: George Schaefer
Production company: PBS, WNET (New York)
Director: George Schaefer
Writer: James Prideaux
Cast: Julie Harris, Robby Benson, Michael Cristofer, Patrick Duffy, John Furlong, Linda Kelsey, Kurtis Lee, Macon McCalman, Priscilla Morrill, Denver Pyle

Gore Vidal's Lincoln (also titled Lincoln)

Format: DVD
Date of original release: March 27, 1988 (television miniseries)
Producers: Bob Christiansen, Rick Rosenberg
Production company: NBC
Director: Lamont Johnson
Writers: Earnest Kinory. Based on Gore Vidal's *Lincoln: A Novel.*
Cast: Sam Waterston, Mary Tyler Moore, Richard Mulligan, Deborah Adair, Gregory Cooke, Stephen Culp, Ruby Dee, Jerome Dempsey, James Gammon, Thomas Gibson, Fay Greenbaum

My Week with Marilyn

Format: DVD
Date of original release: November 11, 2011 (feature film)
Producers: David Parfitt, Harvey Weinstein
Production company: Weinstein Company, BBC Films, and Trademark Films
Distributed by: Weinstein Company
Director: Simon Curtis
Writer: Adrian Hodges. Based on the memoir *The Prince, The Showgirl, and Me* by Colin Clark.
Cast: Michelle Williams, Kenneth Branagh, Eddie Redmayne, Dominic Cooper, Julia Ormond, Zoé Wanamaker, Emma Wilson, Judi Dench

Abraham Lincoln: Vampire Hunter

Format: DVD
Date of original release: June 18, 2012 (feature film)
Producer: Tim Burton, Timur Bekmambetov, Jim Lemley

Production company: Bazeleus Productions, Dune Entertainment, and Tim Burton Productions
Distributed by: 20th Century Fox
Director: Timur Bekmambetov
Writer: Seth Grahame-Smith
Cast: Benjamin Walker, Rufus Sewell, Dominic Cooper, Anthony Mackie, Mary Elizabeth Winstead, Marton Csokas, Jimmi Simpson Joseph Mawle, Robin McLeavy

Lincoln

Format: DVD
Date of original release: November 9, 2012 (feature film)
Producers: Steven Spielberg, Kathleen Kennedy
Production company: 20th Century Fox, DreamWorks Pictures, and Participant Media
Distributed by: Walt Disney Studios Motion Pictures
Director: Steven Spielberg
Writer: Tony Kushner
Cast: Daniel Day-Lewis, Sally Field, David Strathairn, Joseph Gordon-Levitt, James Spader, Hal Holbrook, Tommy Lee Jones, John Hawkes, Jackie Earle Hailey, Gloria Reuben, David Costabile, Wayne Duvall, John Hutton

The Better Angels

Format: Amazon Prime video/streaming
Date of original release: 2014 (feature film)
Producers: Terrence Malick, Nicolas Gonda, Jake DeVito, Charley Beil
Production company: Brothers K Productions
Distributed by: Amplify
Director: A. J. Edwards
Writer: A. J. Edwards
Cast: Jason Clarke, Diane Kruger, Brit Marling, Wes Bentley, Braydon Denney, Cameron Mitchell Williams, McKenzie Blankenship, Ryan McFall, Madison Stiltner

INDEX

Abe Lincoln in Illinois (1938 play), 2; and liberal themes in, 102
Abe Lincoln in Illinois (1940 film), 1, 19, 20, 46, 77, 83, 87, 89, 90, 97, 102, 124, 134
Abell, Bennett, 60
Abraham Lincoln (1930 film), 9, 11, 35, 78, 95–96
Abraham Lincoln Presidential Library Association, 170
Abraham Lincoln: Vampire Hunter (2012 film), 7, 10, 17, 125–26
Actor's Studio, 173
Adam's Rib (1949 film), 77
Adams, Charles Francis, 106
Adventures of Sherlock Holmes, The (1939 film), 81
Affair to Remember, An (1957 film), 81–82
Age of Obama, 127
Agee, James (critic, writer, screenwriter), 16, 19, 46; and depiction of birth of AL, 9–11; romantic view of frontier life, 12; romantic depiction of relationship between AL and Nancy Hanks Lincoln, 12; influenced by Carl Sandburg, 12, 13; and early interest in AL, 53–54; and debate with Alan Nevins, 55, 190n96; on influence of D. W. Griffith in filmmaking, 73; and creation of popular image of AL, 177
All About Eve (1950 film), 161

Allgood, Sara, 83
Ameche, Don, 81
American Marriage: The Untold Story of Abraham Lincoln and Mary Todd, An (Burlingame), 71. *See also* Burlingame, Michael
American Spelling Book or "The Blue-Backed Speller" (Webster), 15
American Standard and Mirror Films, 28
Ames, Mary Clemmer, 107
Ancker, Julian, 162
Angel at My Table, An (1991 film), 136
Angle, Paul M., 30
"Ann Rutledge" (theme music), 82
Another Thin Man (1939 film), 81
Armstrong, Duff, 48, 82
Armstrong, Jack, 54
Arthur, Jean, 161
Ashley, Elizabeth, 112
Ashley, James, 131, 132
Astaire, Fred, 81
Astor, Mary, 75
At the Circus (1939 film), 81
Atlantic Monthly, 28
Awful Truth (1937 film), 75

Baby Burlesks (1932–33 film shorts), 144, 148
Babyface (1934 film), 74
Baker, David, 140

Baker, Jean: reply to Michael Burlingame and other Mary Todd Lincoln critics, 71

Baker, Norma Jeane (birth name of Marilyn Monroe), 158, 159, 161, 175, 202n45

Bancroft, Ann, 83

Banner, Lois, 158

Barbee, David Rankin, 118

Barrett, Oliver R., 30

Barron, Robert, 11

Bartelt, William F., 26

Barton, William Eleazar, 29

Basler, Roy P., 108

"Battle Hymn of the Republic, The" (song), 174

Baty, S. Paige, 171

Baxter, Alan, 90

Beau Geste (1939 film), 81

Bedell, Grace, 42

Behind the Scenes or Thirty Years a Slave, and Four Years in the White House, 113

Belafonte, Harry, 171

Bell, Alexander Graham, 81

Belle of Amherst, The (1976 play), 138

Bement, Illinois, 164

Ben Hur (1959 film), 27

Benét, Rosemary Carr (poet), 46, 188n79

Bénet, Stephen Vincent (writer, poet, novelist, screenwriter), 44, 177

Bennett, Alanna, 174

Benny, Jack, 171

Berle, Milton, 170

Better Angel, The (2014 film), 20, 22–27, 178, 181n16

Beveridge, Albert J., 29

Billings, George, 42

Bingham, Dennis, 136

Biopics (biographical films), 4, 81, 136, 180n12

Birth of a Nation, The (1915 film), 73, 147, 150

Black, Shirley Temple (née Temple), 8, 144, 148, 157, 174

Blitz, The, 148

Blockbuster Video, 149

Blonde: A Novel (Oates), 158

Blondell, Joan, 74

Blue Bird, The (1940 film), 7–8, 9, 143

Blue Bird, The (1976 film), 9

Body Heat (1981 film), 76

Boles, John, 151

Bond, Ward, 47

Bondi, Beulah, 21

Bow, Clara, 160

Brady, Alice, 48, 50

Bright Eyes (1934 film), 148

Brontë, Emily, 31

Brothers' War, The, 43, 151

Brush Creek Academy, 60

Bryant Cottage, 164

Bryant, Francis, 164

Bunce, Alan, 114

Bunyan, John, 26

Burke, Edwin (screenwriter), 177

Burlingame, Michael: and historiography of Mary Todd Lincoln, 11, 15, 34, 70–71

Burns, Catherine, 60, 190n7

Burton, Tim (film director), 10

Bus Stop (1956 film), 165

Callas, Maria, 171

Cameron, Ben, 150

Captain January (1936 film), 146, 147

Carey, Olive, 83

Carl Sandburg Home National Historic Site, 162

Carpenter, Francis: and *First Reading of the Emancipation Proclamation of President Lincoln* (portrait of AL and his cabinet), 125; recalls Mary Todd Lincoln's fighting spirit, 125

Carrington, Dora, 138

Carson, Kit, 81

Cary, Henry, 151

Cary, Virginia (Virgie), 150

Chaplin, Charlie, 160

Chase, Kate (Katherine Jane Chase Sprague): as rival to Mary Todd Lincoln, 110, 111–12, 196n45

Chase, Salmon P., 111, 112, 196n41

Chérie (Marilyn Monroe's character in *Bus Stop*), 165

Chicago Daily News, 41

Child, Maria Lydia, 105

Christian Science Monitor, 114
Christian Science, 159
Cimarron (1939 film), 81
Clark, Champ, 149
Clark, Colin, 166
Clary's Grove, 53
Clay Abigail (character in *Young Mr. Lincoln*),
   49–50
Clay, Henry, 77
Clifford, Ruth, 31
Clifford, Ruth, 42
Clinton, Catharine, 15, 18, 71, 130
Cloud Cuckoo Land, 150
Code, The (1934 Motion Picture Production
   Code or "Hayes Code"), 73–75
Cogdal, Isaac, 52–53
Colbert, Claudette, 146
Colburn, Nettie, 119
Coles County, Illinois, 21
Columbus, Christopher, 159
Comic News, 107
Commercial spirit in moviemaking, 180n13
Conkling, Roscoe, 112
Considine, John W., Jr. (screenwriter), 44
Contraband Relief Association, 114
Cooke, Alistair, 55
Cooper, Gary, 148
Costabile, Davis, 131
Cox, Bill, 159–60
Crane, Hart, 23
Crawford, Joan, 77, 160
Cristofer, Michael, 141
Cromwell, John (film director), 83, 90
Crowell, Josephine, 150
Cult of domesticity, 26, 72, 124, 174. *See also*
   Welter, Barbara
Cult of true womanhood, 72, 73, 75, 122, 174.
   See also Welter, Barbara

Dall, Caroline Healy, 35
Dana, Richard Henry, 105
Dano, Royal, 54
Darin, Bobby, 171
Dark Victory (1939 film), 81
Darwell, Jane, 83

Davis, David, 35
Davis, Jefferson (Jeff), 9, 115
Davis, Mrs. Varina Howell, 113, 114, 115
Day-Lewis, Daniel, 127, 128, 129, 130, 178,
   186n54
Days of Heaven (1978 film), 23
Dean, John, 71
Death on the frontier, 17
DeBoyer, Cora, 30
Debruge, Peter, 26
Decker, Beauregard (Bo), 165
Dee, Ruby, 115
Del Río, Dolores, 144
DeMille, Cecil B., 73
Denton Crahan, 10
Destry Rides Again (1939 film), 81
"Dew upon the Blossom, The" (song), 48
Dickinson, Emily, 20, 138
Dietrich, Marlene, 81, 147, 171
Dimples (1936 film), 150
Dinesen, Isak, 138
Disneyland, 54
Dix, Richard, 81
Dodge City (1939 film), 81
"Dog, Man's Best Friend" (Baker), 158
Doheny Drive (Beverly Hills, California), 163
Donald, David, 15
Double Indemnity (1944 film), 75–76
Dougherty, James, 163
Douglas, Stephen A., 78, 98, 128, 152, 164
Downs, Cathy, 87
Dramatic Life of Abraham Lincoln, The
   (Wright), 41–42
Dru, Joanne, 83
Drums Along the Mohawk (1939 film), 42, 82, 83
Dubois, Blanche, 139
Duhon, Madelyn Kay, 31
Durante, Jimmy, 171
Dusenbury, Winifred, 105
Duvall, Wayne, 131

Earp, Wyatt, 87
Ebert, Roger (critic), 23, 81, 182n49
Eddy, Mary Baker, 159
Edison, Thomas, 7, 81

Educational Films (studio), 144

Edward, A. J. (film director, screenwriter), 14, 22, 26–27, 177, 182n46

Edwards, Elizabeth, 91

Edwards, Ninian, 91

Eisenstein, Sergei, 50

Election of 1860, 53, 107, 141

Elkin David, 19

Emerson Junior High School, 158

Esmond, Mr. (character in *Gentlemen Prefer Blonds*), 173

Factor, Max, 90

Fairbanks, Douglas, 160

False memory, 185n32

Family (1976–80 television series), 122. *See also* Thompson, Sada

Faulkner, William, 44

Federal Bureau of Investigation (FBI), 173

Female gaze, the, 25

Feminism, 76, 109, 123, 196n38

Field, Sally, 127, 129–30, 131, 132, 134, 178, 186n54

Fields, W. C., 81, 160

Film Guide to the 20th Century—Fox Picture, A Cosmopolitan Production, Young Mr. Lincoln: A Study Plan Prepared in Hollywood (Turney), 47

Final Freedom: The Civil War, the Abolition of Slavery, and the Thirteenth Amendment (Vorenburg), 129

Fitzgerald F. Scott, 44, 74

Fitzgerald, Ella, 171

Fonda, Henry, 27, 42, 50, 108, 171, 187n61

Ford, Chauncey Worthington, 29

Ford, John (film director), 45, 27, 50, 160; depiction of role of men and women on the western frontier, 47; depiction of Rutledge-Lincoln affair in *Young Mr. Lincoln*, 47–48; and image of women in Ford films, 82–83; on making *Young Mr. Lincoln* (1939), 82

Ford, William Chauncey, 29

Foroughi, Andrea, 127

Foster, Stephen, 81

"Fountain Filled with Blood, A" (song), 19

Fox Film Corporation, 147, 148

Frame, Janet, 136

Fraser, George McDonald, 176, 205n1

Freeman, Helen, 10

"Frog-Went a-Courtin" (song) 63, 66

Gable, Martin, 10

Garbo, Greta, 82

Gardner, Ava, 83

Gentlemen Prefer Blondes (1953 film), 173

Gentryville, Indiana, 22

Gerhart, Michael J., 96, 97

Gettysburg (1993 film), 127

Gettysburg Address, The, 157, 163, 165–66, 169

Gibbon, Edward, 176

Gish, Lillian, 150

"Great Moments with Mister Lincoln," 54

"Great Moments with Mr. Lincoln," 54

Gods and Generals (2005 film), 127

Gone with the Wind (1939 film), 80, 81

Goodbye, Mr. Chips (1939 film), 81

Goodwin, Doris Kearns, 128, 129

Gopnik, Adam, 4, 106

Gordon Ruth, 90–91

Gordon, Berg, 43–44, 97, 99, 124

Gore Vidal's Lincoln (1984 television mini-series), 107, 118–19, 126. *See also* Vidal, Gore

Graham, Mentor, 1

Grapes of Wrath, The (1940 film), 75, 83, 89

Grauman's Chinese Theater, 149

Gray, Nancy, 120

Great Depression, The, 143, 149, 153

Greatest Story Ever Told, The (1961 film), 162. *See also* Sandburg, Carl

Green County (Kentucky), 59

Green, Bowling, 55

Green, Michael S.: on AL's political ambition, skill, and election of 1860, 102

Greenbaum, Fay, 126

Greene, Graham: on Lincoln-Rutledge affair in *Young Mr. Lincoln*, 48; on sexuality of Shirley Temple; 146–48; on *Wee Willie Winkie* (film), 200n10

Greene, Milton, 163, 167

Greene, William "Slickly Bill," 32
Griffith, D. W. (film director, screenwriter), 9, 19, 35, 36, 78, 82, 96, 104, 107, 150, 160, 177; and AL's image and association with Progressive themes, 38; alcoholism and decline of career, 43; and the Lost Cause theme, 43–44; and Victorian sentimentality, 37; contributions to filmmaking, 73; Victorian sentimentality and cult of true womanhood, 73
Griffith, Raymond, 157
Gunga Din (1939 film), 81

Hall of Presidents (Disney World), 54
Halleck, Henry W. (Old Brains), 110, 124–25
Hammond, Kay, 178; film career, 193n31
Hanks, Denis, 11
Hanks, Lucy: reputation of, 15
Hannond, Kay, 97
Haring, Sidney, 159
Harris, Julie, 138, 139–40
Hart, William S., 160
Havoc, June, 138
Hawthorne, Nathaniel, 171
Hay, John, 71, 111
Hefner, Hugh, 113
Helena Drive (Brentwood, California), 163
"Hello, Susie Brown" (song), 87
Helm, Emilie, 138
Helm, Katherine: on failed Lincoln-Todd engagement, 94
Henabery, Joseph, 150, 177–78
Henderson, Paris, 42
Hepburn, Katherine, 77
Herndon, William (Billy), 2, 3, 52, 56, 58, 69, 101, 104, 105, 108, 177, 181n23; and role in creating popular image of AL, 2; on death of Nancy Hanks, 17; 1866 lecture on Lincoln-Rutledge affair, 34; on AL's view of Nancy Hanks Lincoln, 15; on failed Lincoln-Todd engagement, 94–95
Herndon's Lincoln (1889), 102
Heydt, Louis Jean, 1
Hill, Frederick Trevor, 22
Hischak, Thomas S., 101

Hogan, Jackie, 25
Holbrook, Hal, 178, 122
Holliday, Judy, 77
Hollywood, 32, 37, 151, 152, 153, 160, 161, 163, 164, 171, 177, 178; and popular images of AL, 2–3, 4, 175, 178; and filmmaker's narrative truth v. historical truth, 4; and patriarchal nature of AL films, 5; treatment of the Lincoln-Rutledge affair by, 39–41, 87; and cult of true womanhood, 75 (*see also* cult of domesticity); and films of 1939, 80–82; criticism of the influence of film on modern culture, 146; and interpretation of history, 176; and cult of domesticity, 174 (see also cult of true womanhood); and history of AL's relationship with women, 176
Hollywood's Television Theater, 139
Holmes, Taylor, 173
Holroyd, Michael, 135
Holst, Erika, 69
Holt, Jack, 151
Holzer, Harold, 59
Houston, Sam, 81
How Green Was My Valley (1941 film), 83
Howard, Mary, 31, 50, 178; film career, 189n88
Hughes, William, 12
Hurt, William, 76
Huston, John (film director), 54
Huston, Walter, 178; film career, 188n77
Hutton, John, 131

"I See and Am Satisfied" (Miller), 4
Inge, William, 165
It Happened One Night (1934 film), 75

Jefferson, Thomas, 171
Jesse James (1939 film), 81
John Brown's Body (Benét), 144, 87n72
Johnson, Nunnally, 151
Johnston, Elizabeth, 11
Johnston, Joanna, 131
Johnston, John D., 11
Johnston, Matilda, 11

Jones, James, 23
Jones, Tommy Lee, 131

Kael, Pauline, 82
Kasson, John F., 152
"Kate Chase Wedding Song," 110
Kay, Danny, 171
Keaton, Buster, 160
Keckley, Elizabeth (Lizzie), 5, 110, 113, 114,
    118, 120; as a mother of the nation, 121;
    and conversation with AL in Spielberg's
    Lincoln, 120–21; and relationship with
    Mary Todd Lincoln, 113; and alternate
    spelling of last name, 196n47
Kelly, Grace, 31, 83
Kennedy, Jackie, 139
Kennedy, John F. (JFK or Jack), 170, 172, 173,
    175; and Camelot motif in Kennedy legacy,
    170; and alleged affair with Marilyn
    Monroe, 172; and the "male gaze," 204n80
Kennedy, Kathleen, 130
Kennedy, Robert (Bobby), 171
Kennedy, Rose, 171
Kenny, Glenn, 26
Kentucky, 9, 158
Kentucky Historical Society, 14
Kinoy, Earnest, 109
Kirkland, George, 114
Knox, William, 35
Kruger, Diane, 25
Ku Klux Klan, 150
Kushner, Tony (playwriter, screenwriter),
    127, 128, 198n71; on sources for Lincoln
    (2012 film) script, 129

La Verne, Lucille, 10
Lamon, Ward: on AL's ambition, 102
Lamont, Charles, 148
Last of Mrs. Lincoln, The (1976 television
    miniseries), 137, 139
Laurie, Ann Margaret, 119
Laurie, Cranston, 119
Lawford, 170, 172
Lawrence, Kate, 122
Lee, Lorelei, 173

Lee, Peggy, 171
Let Us Now Phrase Famous Men, 180n14
Let Us Now Praise Famous Men (Agee and
    Evans), 13
Let's Make Love (1960 film), 169
"Light of Other Days, The" (poem), 36–37
Lincoln (1984 novel), 108, 137
Lincoln (2012 film), 107, 120; race and politics
    in, 127
Lincoln Beard Contest, 164
Lincoln Boyhood Memorial, 11
Lincoln Memorial (Washington, D.C.), 160
Lincoln the Lover (1914 film), 41
Lincoln-Rutledge affair, 30, 31, 33, 34, 58;
    popular appeal of, 40; decline in popular
    interest in 1960s, 40–41; and Hollywood
    image of, 35–57
Lincoln, Abraham: depicted in Abe Lincoln
    in Illinois, 1; as " lover," 2; conflicting
    images of, 3; as the Great Heart, 3, 127,
    140, 150, 151, 152, 153; as hero of the
    common man, 3, 40, 90, 102, 160; image
    as man of sorrow(s), 3, 4, 20, 36, 37, 54,
    90, 99, 104, 105, 109, 112, 141, 177; as the
    Great Humanitarian, 3, 38, 144, 152, 160;
    as the Great Emancipator, 3, 40, 127, 152,
    160, 171, 186; melancholy of, 3; sadness,
    of 3, 6, 37, 104, 105, 109, 112; as Savior
    of the Union, 3, 5, 9, 26, 40, 53, 160, 171,
    174; apotheosis of, 4; and destiny, 5, 6,
    7, 37, 39, 40, 41, 48, 49, 53, 91, 100, 102,
    103, 109, 128, 178; as the Studious Boy, 7,
    9, 25, 27, 37, 53, 54, 143; Hollywood and
    popular image of, 6; depicted in The Blue
    Bird (1940 film), 7–8; boyhood home
    depicted in Mr. Lincoln, 11; and childhood
    on frontier farm, 12; embarrassed by
    ancestry of Nancy Hanks Lincoln, 14;
    relationship with father, 14; relationship
    with Nancy Hanks Lincoln, 14; meaning
    of reference to his "angel mother," 15; and
    writing style, 15; and distain for farming
    life, 16; as Rail-Splitter, 16; negative view
    of father, 19; negative view of stepbrother
    John Johnston, 19; dialogue with Sarah

Bush Johnston Lincoln in *Abe Lincoln in Illinois,* 20; relationship with Sarah Bush Johnston Lincoln, 20; last meeting with Sarah Bush Johnston Lincoln in *Sandburg's Lincoln,* 21–22; Lincoln-Hanks-Sparrow household, 25; and romance with Ann Rutledge depicted in Minor hoax, 28; and alleged reply to Ann Rutledge letter, 29–30; reaction to death of Ann Rutledge, 32–34; depicted in *The Dramatic Life of Abraham Lincoln,* 43; and "moonlight" murder case, 48; letters to Mary S. Owens, 58; on racism and justice in *Sandburg's Lincoln,* 62; and courtship of Mary S. Owens, 58–66; courtship of Mary S. Owens depicted in *Sandburg's Lincoln,* 60–64; letter to Mrs. Orville Browning on courtship of Mary S. Owens, 64–65, 190–91n12; background, education, appearance compared to Mary Todd Lincoln, 78; depicted in *Abraham Lincoln* (1930 film), 78; and memory of Ann Rutledge in porch scene in *Young Mr. Lincoln,* 88; talks of mother Nancy in porch scene in *Abe Lincoln in Illinois,* 93–94; and failed engagement with Mary Todd, 94–95; and disputed evidence of venereal disease, 96n36; strained courtship with Mary Todd, 97; and tension with Mary Todd Lincoln over visit of Republican nomination committee in *Abe Lincoln in Illinois,* 99–100; contemporary criticism of, 106; attends Kate Chase Sprague wedding, 110; tensions in marriage, 113; and 1864 assassination attempt in Vidal's *Lincoln,* 118, 197n57; and spiritualism, 119; and spiritualism, 120; and conversation with Elizabeth Keckley in Spielberg's *Lincoln,* 120–22; "Rock Creek" conversation with Mary Todd Lincoln in *Sandburg's Lincoln,* 123; in Mary Todd Lincoln's memory, 141–42; depicted in *The Blue Bird* (1940 film), 143; "seduction" by Shirley Temple in *The Littlest Rebel,* 148; in popular memory

of 1930s and 1940s, 149; depicted in *The Littlest Rebel,* 150, 152–57; and theme of North-South reconciliation in *The Littlest Rebel,* 157–58; in the mind of Marilyn Monroe, 159, 160, 161, 163, 168, 170, 171, 175; 1858 photograph of, 162, 203n62; 1858 portrait of, 162; and Belmont, Illinois, Lincoln-Douglas debate anniversary celebration, 164; and Lincoln-Douglas Debates, 164; mentioned in *My Week with Marilyn* (1999 film), 166, 168; 1858 photograph and bust of owned by Marilyn Monroe, 169; memorabilia of, 170; John F. Kennedy compared to, 171; Gore Vidal on, 174; melancholy of, 181n28; visit to grave of Ann Rutledge in *Sandburg's Lincoln,* 185n38; phases in Hollywood's treatment of, 186n54; law partners, 194n49; actors who played AL in film, 201n34

Lincoln, Hanks Nancy, 5, 7, 12, 14, 15, 22, 24, 25, 26, 30, 32, 33, 46, 47, 50, 49, 53, 56, 94, 97, 126, 153, 177, 178; and death of children of, 9; depicted in *Mr. Lincoln,* 10; as mother of the nation's redeemer, 11, 14, 17; support for AL's education, 13; as AL's "angel mother," 14; AL's view of intelligence and background of Hanks family, 15; description of, 16; melancholy of, 16; death and burial of, 17–19; depicted in *The Dramatic Life of Abraham Lincoln,* 43; mentioned in *Young Mr. Lincoln,* 49–50; mentioned in porch scene in *Abe Lincoln in Illinois* (film), 93–94

Lincoln, Mary Todd: as supporting character in AL films, 5; depicted in Spielberg's *Lincoln,* 6; reaction to 1866 Herndon lecture on Lincoln- Rutledge affair, 35; and Ann Rutledge in popular memory, 37–38; reputation of the "Bad Mary," 67–68; reputation of the "Good Mary," 68–69; feminist interpretations of, 71–73; possible alternative film interpretations of, 76–77; early political interests of, 77; depicted in *Abraham Lincoln* (1930 film), 78; depicted in D. W. Griffith's *Abraham*

Lincoln, Mary Todd (*continued*)
Lincoln, 45; deleted scene with Stephen Douglas in *Young Mr. Lincoln,* 83; meets AL in *Young Mr. Lincoln,* 84–86; dances with AL in deleted scene in *Young Mr. Lincoln,* 87; image in *Abe Lincoln in Illinois* (1940 film), 90; dialogue with Stephen Douglas and AL in *Abe Lincoln in Illinois* (1940 film), 91–92; political ambitions of, 91; and ritual of courtship, 91; and "left-at-the-alter" myth, 96; reaction to failed engagement with AL, 96; as *co-redemptrix,* 97; ambitions of becoming First Lady, 98; despair over AL's lack of ambition in *Abe Lincoln in Illinois* (1938 play), 100–101; as AL's political companion, 102; contemporary criticism of, 105–6; phrase for, 106–7; and Ord affair in *Gore Vidal's Lincoln* novel (1984), 108, 109; and "parlor politics," 109; and rivalry with Kate Chase Sprague, 110–12; rivalry with Kate Chase Sprague, 112; first meeting with Elizabeth Keckley, 114–17; dialogue about slavery with Elizabeth Keckley (Lizzie) in *Gore Vidal's Lincoln,* 116–17; and spiritualism, 118–20; depicted in *Sandburg's Lincoln,* 122–23, 128; and Ord affair, 123; and Ord affair in *Sandburg's Lincoln,* 123, 126; on military strategy in *Gore Vidal's Lincoln,* 124–25; showing her fighting spirit in *Gore Vidal's Lincoln,* 125; and Ord affair in *Gore Vidal's Lincoln,* 126; and family relations and gender politics in *Lincoln* (2012), 127; argument with AL about Robert's enlistment in the army in *Lincoln* (2012 film), 129; and the Grand Reception scene in *Lincoln* (2012 film), 131–33; the Lincolns' last conversation in Spielberg's *Lincoln,* 133; AL's deathbed in *Lincoln* (2012 film), 134; depicted in film, 134; depicted by film actors, 134, 178; family tragedies, and emotional, physical, and mental problems, 135–36; mental, emotional, and physical problems of, 135–37; depicted in *The Last of Mrs. Lincoln,* 137–42; influence

on AL, 153; compared to image of Ann Rutledge, 56; and insecurity, ambition, and love for AL, 169; Good and Bad Mary character compared to Marilyn Monroe 173; relationship with AL, 177; historiography of, 193n12; health, death, and medical history, 199n5; post-war life depicted in Broadway plays, 199n16

Lincoln, Robert Todd: depicted in *Sandburg's Lincoln,* 21, 122; depicted in *Abe Lincoln in Illinois* (film), 98–99; depicted in *Gore Vidal's Lincoln,* 109; and censorship of Keckley's White House memoir, 114; MTL's opposition to enlistment, 129; at Grand Reception in Spielberg's *Lincoln,* 132–33; alienation from MTL, 136; depicted in *The Last of Mrs. Lincoln,* 139, 141–42

Lincoln, Sarah (AL's sister), 9, 11

Lincoln, Sarah Bush Johnston, 5, 27, 56, 153, 177; living condition of, 11; in AL's memory, 15; character and reputation of, 15; relationship and impact on AL, 16, 19; and courtship and marriage to Thomas Lincoln, 18–19; affection for AL, 20; final visit with AL in *Sandburg's Lincoln,* 20–21; as character in *Sandburg's Lincoln,* 20–22; depicted in *The Dramatic Life of Abraham Lincoln,* 43

Lincoln, Thomas, 10, 11, 12; depicted in *Mr. Lincoln,* 9, 10, 16; attitude toward AL's education, 13–14; as gifted story teller, 15; and gossip about premarital relationship with Nancy Hanks, 15; and courtship of Sarah Bush Johnston, 18–19; depicted in *Abe Lincoln in Illinois* (1940 film), 20; depicted in *The Better Angels,* 26; reputation of 193n30

Lincoln, Thomas (Tad, Taddy, or Taddie), 71, 110, 119, 129, 139, 141, 142

Lincoln, Thomas, Jr. (AL's brother), 9

Lincoln, William Wallace (Willie), 98, 110, 113

Lincoln: A Picture Story of His Life (1952), 164

Little Colonel, The (1935 film), 150

Little Engine, The, 172

Little Pigeon Creek, Indiana, 20
Little Princess, The (1939 film), 143
Littlest Rebel, The (Peple) theme of North-South reconciliation in, 152; and differences between film and novel, 201n35
Littlest Rebel, The (1935 film), 108, 147, 150, 157, 158; and theme of North-South reconciliation in, 150, 153; and Lost Cause trope, 153
Lloyd, Harold, 160
Lloyd, Matthew J., 23
Lockhart, Gene, 91
Logan, Joshua, 165
Lorant, Stefan, 164
Louis, John, 171
Love Affair (1939 film), 81
Lovejoy, Elijah, 62
Lucille Las Verne, 10
Lyons, Richard (1st Viscount), 106, 110, 111

Macaulay, Thomas Babington, 176
Mackie, Bob, 171
MacLaine, Shirley, 171
Madison Square Garden, 170
Maeterlinck, Maurice Bernard, 7
Mailer, Norman, 163
Makeba, Miriam, 171
Malcolm, Derek, 48
Malick, Terrance (film director), 23
Man Who Shot Liberty Valance, The (1966 film), 82, 83
Mannix, William Francis, 30
Manseau, Peter, 137
Marling, Brit, 24
Martyred Presidents, The (1901 film), 2
Marx Brother, The, 81
Maryologists, 70
Massante, Rev. Silvio, 146
Massey, Raymond, 1, 99, 104, 108, 178, 19, 90, 99; physical affinity with Lincoln, 50; on ideological issues in *Abe Lincoln in Illinois* (1938 play), 102; film career, 189n87
Master and His Servant, The, 3
May, Elaine, 171

McCarthy, Todd, 25
McDermott, Stacy Pratt, 72
McGlynn, Frank, Sr., 152, 178, 201n29
McGregor, Thomas, 14
McIntosh, Francis, 62
McLaglen, Victor, 47
McMurtry, Gerald, 59
McNamar (or McNeil), John, 32; as character in *Abe Lincoln in Illinois* (1949 film), 51–52
Mellon, James, 162
Melville, Herman, 23
Memoirs of Li-Hung Chang, The, 30. *See also* Mannix, William Francis
Merkel, Una, 31, 45; film career, 188n78
Meuel, David, 82–83. *See also* Ford, John
MGM (Metro-Goldwyn-Mayer), 4, 7
Middleton, Charles, 20
Midnight (1939 film), 81
Miles, Vera, 83
Milk sickness, 17
Miller, Arthur, 161
Miller, Belle, 119
Miller, Kelly, 4
Minor, Wilma Frances, 28, 30
Miracle, Bernice Baker, 169
Mix, Tom, 160
Mogambo (1953 film), 83
Monroe, Harriett, 203n60
Monroe, Marilyn, 6, 113, 162, 164, 170; identifies with AL, 158–59, 163, 169, 171, 175; mental, emotional, and physical problems of, 161, 174, 175, 203n71; as sexual icon, 164; bust of Sandburg owned by, 170; and JFK, 170–71, 173; birth and baptismal names of, 202n45; depicted in *Norma Jean's Wishes in Time: A Four-Part Adventure,* 203n73
Moore, Mary Tyler, 114, 115, 134, 178; as feminist figure in *The Mary Tyler Moore Show* (1970–77 television series), 123–24; as Mary Lincoln in *Gore Vidal's Lincoln,* 114–15, 123–25, 126
Moore, Pauline, 31
Moore, Phil, 173

Morgenthau, Henry, 158

Morley, Karen, 151

Morrill, Patricia, 141

Morrill, Robert, 171

Morrison, Colonel, 151

"Mortality"(Knox), 35–36

Movshovitz, Howard, 47

Mr. Deeds Goes to Town (1936 film), 161

Mr. Lincoln (1952 television miniseries), 13, 14, 16, 17, 27, 46, 47, 48, 50, 53, 55, 57; courtship of Thomas Lincoln and Sarah Bush Johnston depicted in, 18–19; depiction of the Lincoln-Rutledge affair in, 53–56; influence of, 189n95

Mr. Smith Goes to Washington (1939 film), 162

Mumler, William H., 137

Murry, Don: recites the Gettysburg Address to Marilyn Monroe character in *Bus Stop*, 165–66; interview with, 203n71

"My Childhood Home I See Again" (Lincoln), 20–21

My Darling Clementine (1946 film): dance scene from *Young Mr. Lincoln* reimagined in, 87. *See also* "Hello, Susie Brown"

"My Heart Belongs to Daddy" (song), 169–70

My Week with Marilyn (1999 film), 166

Myra Breckinridge (1968 novel), 108

Myron (1974 novel), 108

Mytyl (character in *The Blue Bird* story and films), 7

"Nancy Hanks" (Agee), 46–47

National Arts foundation, 164

Natwick, Mildred, 83

Nazareth Academy, 60

Neely, Mark E.: on Lincoln-Rutledge affair, 58; on Lincoln's ambition, 101–2

Nesmith, James, 105

Nevins, Alan, 55–56. *See also* Agee, James

New Deal, 13, 38, 40, 102, 145, 152, 157

New Salem, Illinois, 1, 11, 28, 29, 31, 32, 33, 34, 37, 41, 42, 47, 48, 49, 51, 52, 54, 56, 59, 60, 64, 88, 89, 90, 97, 104, 140, 176, 178; and historic restoration, 39

New World, The (2005 film), 23

New York Evening Post, 107

New York Times, 7, 113, 139, 143, 146; and reparatory obituaries, 112; review of *Behind the Scenes or Thirty Years a Slave, and Four Years in the White House,* 114; and Mary Todd Lincoln obituary, 135

New York World's Fair (1964–65), 54

New York's Birthday Salute to the President, Inc., 170

Nichols, Mike, 171

Nicolay, John, 71

Night and Day, 146

Ninotchka (1939 film), 81

Nixon, Richard, 171

Noah, Timothy, 128–29

Normand, Mable, 160

Nugent, Frank, 50, 99, 143; review of *Young Mr. Lincoln,* 89; review of *Abe Lincoln in Illinois* (1940 film), 89–90; on character of Mary Todd Lincoln in *Abe Lincoln in Illinois* (1940 film), 104

O'Brian, Geoffrey, 48

O'Brian, Pat, 81

O'Connor, John, 139–40

O'Hara, Maureen, 83

O'Hara, Scarlett, 81

Oates, Joyce Carol, 158

Of Mice and Men (1939 film), 81

Offutt, Denton, 1; description of 179n1

Oliver, Edna Mae, 83

Olivier, Laurence, 113, 166, 173\

"On the Good Ship Lollipop" (song), 148

Omnibus, 180n7

Onassis, Aristotle, 139

Only Angels Have Wings (1939 film), 81

Ordeal of the Union, The (Nevins), 55

Orne, Sally, 127

Osbourne, Fanny, 138

Osservtore Romano, 146

Other Men's Women (1931 film), 74

Our American Cousin (1858 play), 42

Our Dancing Daughters (1928 film), 74

Owens, Mary S., 177; AL courtship of, 58–66; letter to William Herndon on Lincoln

Owens courtship and Ann Rutledge, 58–59; description of, 59; family and education, 60; defies cult of domesticity (cult of true womanhood), 60; grave of, 65–66, 191n14

Owens, Nathaniel, 60

Padnami, Amisha, 113

Palm Beach Story, The (1942 film), 75

Palmer, R. Barton, 127

Pearson, P. T., 162

Peple, Edward, 157

Peterson, Merrill D., 40

Phoenix (Arizona), 165

Pickford, Mary, 160

Pigeon Creek Farm, 11

Pilgrim's Progress, 26

Pitt, Brad, 25

Pleasant Ridge Baptist Church, 65

Polly Tix in Washington, 144 (1931 film short), 145

"Polly Wolly Doodle" (song), 151, 152

Popular memory v. historical reconstruction, 4

Power, Tyrone, 81

Prairie Years, The: 1948 edition of Sandburg's AL biography, 2 vol., 53

Pre-Code Hollywood, 37, 73

Price, Leontyne, 171

Prideaux, James (playwriter, screenwriter), 137–38, 139

Primitive Baptists sect, 24

Prince and the Showgirl, The (1957 film), 166

Public Broadcasting System, 139

Pyle, Denver, 138

Quiet Man, The (1951 film), 83

Randall, James G., 34

Randall, Ruth Painter, 71

Rat Pack, The, 170

Red Badge of Courage, The (1951 film), 54

Redmayne, Eddie, 166

Reid, Alex D., 5

Reinhart, Mark S., 42, 124

Reuben, Gloria, 197n60

Reynolds, David S., 36

Reynolds, Gene, 7

Rich, Doris, 10

Richard (enslaved man/carriage driver), 117–18

Rio Grande (1950 film), 83

Ripley's Believe It or Not (Ripley's Entertainment, Inc.), 170

Risdon, Elizabeth, 20

Roaring Twenties, The (1939 film), 81

Robinson, Bill: as "Uncle Billy" in *The Littlest Rebel* (film), 151–57; and image of African Americans in film, 201n128; and appeal to FDR, 152

Rockett, Al, 41

Rockett, Ray, 41

Rockne, Knute, 81

Rogers, Will, 160

Rooney, Mickey, 81

Roosevelt coalition, 157–58

Roosevelt, Franklin (FDR), 8, 38, 144, 149, 152, 159, 171, 174; as hero of the common man, 102; image in American civil faith in 1930s and 1940s; awkward meeting with Shirley Temple, 158

Roosevelt, Theodore (Teddy): "The Heirs of Abraham Lincoln" address, 38; Lincoln Centennial Address and Progressive principles, 38

Rosenberg, Cory, 122, 131

Rozsa, Miklos, 27

Ruben, Gloria, 120; on interpreting the character of Elizabeth Keckley in Spielberg's *Lincoln*, 121–22

Rutledge, Ann, 1, 2, 3, 5, 11, 28, 29, 31, 34, 35, 39, 40, 41, 42, 45, 46, 47, 48, 49, 50, 51, 53, 54, 55, 56, 57, 58, 59, 70, 77, 82, 88, 90, 93, 96, 97, 101, 108, 139, 140, 153, 177, 178: as cause of AL's sadness, 3; letters to AL in Minor hoax, 28, 29; physical description of, 31–32; compared to Victorian literary heroines, 32–33; death of, 32–33, 36; in popular memory, 37–38; historiographical issues and, 183n3. *See also* Sandburg, Carl

Rutledge, James, 31
Rutledge, Mary Ann, 31
Rutledge, Nancy, 30

Safe in Hell (1931 film), 74
Sandburg, Carl, 25, 50, 56, 128, 160, 162, 164, 169, 177, 202n53; role in creating popular image of Lincoln, 2; on Lincoln's sadness, 4; on AL's relation with Nancy Hanks Lincoln, 12, 25–26; romantic view of the Lincoln-Rutledge affair, 12, 34–35, 39, 50, 56; on Sarah Bush Johnston Lincoln, 26; opinion on Minor hoax letters, 29; and AL biography and Progressive principles, 38; and phrase for William Herndon, 41; review of *The Dramatic Life of Abraham Lincoln,* 41–42; approached to write script for Griffith's *Abraham Lincoln,* 44; description of Mary S. Owens, 59; description of Mary Todd Lincoln, 77–78, 87; as film critic, 160–61; and physical likeness to AL, 162; popularity and influence of biography of AL, 202n52
Sandburg's Lincoln (1974/1976 television miniseries), 21, 58, 60, 107, 109, 112, 122, 123, 139
Sanders, George, 161
Sarris, Andrew, 173
Schenck, Joseph, 43–44, 69, 187
Schwartz, Barry, 153
Scotland Yard, 148
Searchers, The (1956 film), 83
Sedgwick, Ellery, 28, 30
Seldes, Marian, 10
Sennwald, Andre, 157
7 Women (1966 film), 83
She Wore a Yellow Ribbon (1949 film), 48, 83
Shenk, Joshua Wolf, 4, 37, 38
Sherrill, Martha, 149
Sherwood, Robert (playwriter, screenwriter), 1, 19, 20, 98, 100, 102, 104, 177; on tension between Mary and Abe on election night, 1860, 102–4
Silber, Nina, 160
Sinatra, Frank, 170, 171

Sinking Springs Farm, 11
"Sky Boat Song, The," 13, 181n15
Sleepless in Seattle (1993 film), 82
Smith, Carleton, 164
Smith, Cecil (critic), 122
Smyth, J. E., 102
So Proudly, We Hail! (1943 film), 75
Some Like it Hot (1959 film), 174
Sotheby's auctions, 58
Soup to Nuts (1930 film), 41
Spanish-American War, 159–60
Spectator, 147
Speed, Joshua, 92, 99, 95
Spider-Man: Far from Home (2019 film), 23
Spielberg, Stephen (film director), 6, 107, 126, 127, 128, 129, 133, 134; and liberal themes in *Lincoln* (2012), 126–27; on character of Mary Todd Lincoln in *Lincoln* (2012 film), 128
Spottiswoode, Aitken, 150
Sprague, William, IV, 110, 112
Springfield, Illinois, 20, 37, 39, 42, 52, 54, 55, 60, 62, 63, 69, 78, 79, 80, 84, 89, 91, 94, 104, 117, 123, 140, 141, 176
Stagecoach (1939 film), 82, 83, 89
Stand Up and Cheer (1934 film), 148
Stanton, Edwin M., 125
Stanwyck, Barbara, 74–75, 77
Steckler, Len, 162
Steinem, Gloria, 163
Stephens, Harvey, 91
Stephenson, Nathaniel Wright, 53
Stevens, Thaddeus, 131, 132
Stevenson, Adlai, 170
Stewart, James, 81
Stone, Milburn, 83
Stoneman, Elsie, 150
Story of Vernon and Irene Castle, The (1939 film), 81
Stozier, Charles B., 34
Strasberg, Lee, 174
Streetcar Names Desire, A (1947 play), 139
Strong, Charles E., 105
Summer of Love of 1967, 25
Sumner, Charles, 131, 132

Sundance Film Festival, 23
Supporting or secondary characters as film tropes, 5
Swanson, Gloria, 160

Tacitus, 176
Tackach, James, 21
Taper, Louise, 170
Tarbell Ida: on validity of Minor letters; 29; and influence on Julie Harris interpretation of Lincoln marriage, 139: and influence on Carl Sandburg, 179n2
Tarzan, 144
Team of Rivals: The Political Genius of Abraham Lincoln (Goodwin): disputed as inspiration for Spielberg's Lincoln, 128
Temple, George, 8
Temple, Gertrude, 146
Temple, Shirley, 6, 143, 144–45, 146, 148–49, 150–51, 152, 153, 158, 174, 175; as Mytyl meets pubescent AL in The Blue Bird, 7–8; Shirley Temple Development Team, 149; and AL's lap, 156, 158, 159, 174, 175; and sexual images of, 200n18
Texas, 159, 160
Texas Panhandle, 23\
"Thanks for the Memory" (song), 172
They Knew Lincoln (Washington), 118
Thin Red Line, The (1998 film), 23
Thinking Body, The (Todd), 163
Thomas, Benjamin: on AL's sadness, 37
Thompson, Sada: as Mary Todd Lincoln in Sandburg's Lincoln, 112, 122, 123, 134, 178
Thomson, David, 59, 144, 149
Thorne, William, 9
Todd, Mable Ellsworth, 163
Tom Thumb (stage name of Charles Sherwood Stratton), 122
Townsend, Alfred George, 111
Tracy, Spencer, 81
Tree of Life (2008 film), 23
Trevor, Claire, 83
Trotti, Lamar (screenwriter), 50, 83, 177; and inspiration for Young Mr. Lincoln (1939 screenplay), 82

Troy (2004 film), 25
Truman, Helen, 42
Turner, Caroline (Mrs. C. A. Turner), 116, 117, 118, 197n54
Turner, Kathleen, 76
Twentieth Century-Fox, 4, 7
Tyltyl (character in The Blue Bird story and films), 7

Uncle Tom's Cabin (Stowe), 150–51
Union Pacific (1939 film), 81
United Artists, 162
United Artists/Art Cinema, 43

Valdes, Zelda Wynn, 113
Valentino, Rudolph, 160
Vallee, Rudy, 75
Van Nuys (California), 163
Variety, 157
Victoria, Queen, 138
Vidal, Gore, 107, 111, 123, 133–34, 137, 174, 177; and allegations of syphilis in Lincoln marriage, 108
Village Voice, 173
Vineyard, Jesse, 65
Virgie, 152, 153, 157
"Voice of God": as film narrative trope, 11
Vorenberg, Michael, 129

Wade, Franklin Benjamin (Bluff), 131, 132
Wagonmaster (1950 film), 83
Waldorf-Astoria, 163
Wall Street Journal, 11
Walmart, Inc., 149
Walsh, Margaret, 12
Walthall, Henry, 150
War Babies (1932 film short), 144
Warner Brothers, 4
Washington Post, 149
Washington, George, 171
Washington, John E., 118
Waterson, Sam, 115, 178
Wayne, John, 47
Weaver, Marjorie, 97
Webster, Noah, 15

Wee Willie Winkie (1937 film), 147, 146, 148

Welter, Barbara: and cult of domesticity (or cult of true womanhood), 72

Weston (Missouri), 65

What Price Gloria? (1933 film short), 144

What Price Glory? (1926 film), 144

Whitman, Walt, 23

Whole Town Is Talking, The (1935 film), 83

Williams, Cameron Mitchel, 123

Williams, Michelle, 166

Williams, Tennessee, 139

Wilson, Edmund: critical of Sandburg's description of Lincoln-Rutledge affair, 39

Wilson, Minor, 92

Winstead, Mary Elizabeth: on instability of Mary Todd Lincoln, 198n82

Wizard of Oz, The (1939 film), 7, 81

Women in the Films of John Ford, 82

Women, 18, 23, 24, 26, 130, 138, 152, 176, 177, 178; at intersection of biography and film, 4; in AL myth, 5; as secondary characters in AL films, 5; and dangers of pregnancy and childbirth in nineteenth century, 9; and rituals of home life, 12; and resistance to prescribed roles, 12; in Hollywood AL biopics, 40, 43; in John Ford films, 47, 50, 82–83; and James Agee, 53; in formation of AL; 56; in *Sandburg's Lincoln,* 59

Women, The (1939 film), 81

Woodrow, Margaret Stuart, 136–37

Woodward, Joanne, 31, 54, 178; film career, 189n94

Wright, A. M. R., 42

You Can't Cheat an Honest Man (1939 film), 81

Young Men's Lyceum (Springfield, Ill.), 62

Young Mr. Lincoln (1939 film), 27, 45, 46, 48, 49, 50, 55, 57, 82, 83, 87, 89, 93, 97; AL's grave-side reflection on death of Ann Rutledge in, 48–49; voice-of God scene deleted in, 88–89

Young, Brigham, 81

Zanuck, Darryl F., 8, 82, 143

Zolotow, Maurice, 163–64

Printed in the USA
CPSIA information can be obtained
at www.ICGtesting.com
CBHW031014270324
5933CB00002B/18

9 780807 16